Social Democracy without Illusions

RENEWAL OF THE CANADIAN LEFT

edited by
JOHN RICHARDS
ROBERT CAIRNS
LARRY PRATT

M&S

To Anna, Gabe, and Heidi
To Lynn, Malcolm, and Meredith
To Tricia

Canadian Cataloguing in Publication Data
Main entry under title:
Social democracy without illusions

Includes bibliographical references.
ISBN 0-7710-7450-6

1. Socialism.   2. Right and left (political science).
I. Richards, John, 1944– .   II. Cairns, Robert D., 1947– .
III. Pratt, Larry, 1944– .

HX73.S62 1991   335.5   C90-095742-5

McClelland & Stewart Inc.
The Canadian Publishers
481 University Avenue
Toronto, Ontario
M5G 2E9

Printed and bound in Canada by John Deyell Company

Contents

Preface

THIS BOOK OF ESSAYS HAS GROWN OUT OF OUR SHARED FRUSTRATION
with the parochial thinking and practice of the Canadian left. We are
living through a period of remarkable historical change and crisis. It is
characterized by shifting ideological alignments and conflicting
nationalisms – in Quebec, the rest of Canada, and world-wide. It is also
characterized by the growth of an ecological and economic interdependence that demands broader consensus than can be obtained by limiting
political vision to the nation-state. As social democrats we are mindful of
the Brundtland Commission's warning:

> Policies formerly considered to be exclusively matters of 'national
> concern' now have an impact on the ecological bases of other
> nations' development and survival. Conversely, the growing reach
> of some nations' policies – economic, trade, monetary, and most
> sectoral policies – into the 'sovereign' territory of other nations
> limits the affected nations' options in devising national solutions to
> their 'own' problems. (World Commission on Environment and
> Development, 1987, p. 312)

In the European Economic Community interdependence has been
recognized in the move toward a single integrated market by the end
of 1992. Notwithstanding the prominent role of the largest blocs of
European capital in leading this integration, European parties of the
left have, by and large, supported it as a progressive response to
changing technological economic – and ecological – conditions.

In view of the all-too-obvious limits to Canada's national autonomy, it might be expected that Canadian social democrats would have
a sophisticated understanding of the problems of interdependence
and a realistic strategy for advancing social democratic ideas in a
world of decreasing sovereignty. Instead, they appear to be mired in

policy positions that are frequently *dépassé* in the context of interdependent economic and political realities.

Canadian social democrats are at their most eloquent in defending the Canadian welfare state. Aspects of this welfare state – such as Canada's system of high-quality universal health insurance – are worthy of eloquent defence. And the goals of the welfare state – social insurance policies, full employment, rights for organized labour – remain valid. But we have too often slipped from a defence of the goals into a defence of interest groups committed to particular means. As a result, social democrats, on many matters of Canadian public debate, have taken up the conservative pole, defending the status quo. Too often we oppose market innovations without exploring how social democrats elsewhere have harnessed the market to social ends; too often we oppose changes to labour law without exploring the practice of social democrats elsewhere.

The authors in this collection all share the conclusion that capitalist society is seriously flawed and needs a social democratic alternative. The goal of these essays, however, is not to restate that conclusion; it is the more challenging one of facing the painful truths about the inadequacies of our own analyses and prescriptions. We want social democracy – but without illusions.

This book was conceived at a conference, "The Economics of Social Democracy," held at McGill University in March, 1988. The conference, at which many of these essays were presented in earlier versions, was jointly sponsored by the Douglas-Coldwell Foundation and McGill's Department of Economics. We are especially grateful to Tommy McLeod, treasurer of the Douglas-Coldwell Foundation, and to John McCallum, Chairman of the Economics Department at McGill, for their enthusiastic support for the conference and the publication of this book. Kari Levitt also helped in organizing the conference, and we thank her. We gratefully acknowledge the assistance of Marianne Morse, Richard Schwindt, Tricia Smith, and Aidan Vining in reading parts of the manuscript. Finally, we thank Michael Harrison of McClelland & Stewart, our publisher, for his patience, his support, and his good-humoured reminders that to make a book you must first write it!

John Richards, Vancouver
Bob Cairns, Montreal
Larry Pratt, Edmonton

February, 1990

REFERENCE
World Commission on Environment and Development (1987). *Our Common Future*: G.H. Brundtland, Chairperson, Oxford. Oxford University Press.

JOHN RICHARDS

I   Painful Truths

The form of association, however, which if mankind continue to improve, must be expected in the end to predominate, is not that which can exist between a capitalist as chief, and work-people without a voice in the management, but the association of the labourers themselves on terms of equality, collectively owning the capital with which they carry on their operations, and working under managers elected and removable by themselves. . . .

But while I agree and sympathize with Socialists in this practical portion of their aims, I utterly dissent from the most conspicuous and vehement part of their teaching, their declamations against competition. With moral conceptions in many respects far ahead of the existing arrangements of society, they have in general very confused and erroneous notions of its actual working; and one of their greatest errors, as I conceive, is to charge upon competition all the economical evils which at present exist. They forget that wherever competition is not, monopoly is; and that monopoly, in all its forms, is the taxation of the industrious for the support of indolence, if not of plunder.

– John Stuart Mill, *Principles of Political Economy*

There is no talk and there will be no talk of a market economy, which always and everywhere brings with it social injustice and social inequality. We need as much socialism as possible, a maximum of socialism.

– Yegor Ligachev, *Pravda*

I WAS AT HOME EDITING MANUSCRIPTS FOR THIS BOOK. RAIN HAD BEEN falling in a slow, relentless manner all day. The sky, the ground, the surrounding houses and trees: all had taken on sombre shades of green, brown, and grey – as if Vancouver were an intertidal zone. The tide was out, revealing dripping roofs and leaves, and rivulets of running water. In a few hours the sea would rise to submerge it all. A typical day in the Pacific Northwest.

I was interrupted by a knock on the door. My visitor was Tom. Delighted by the excuse to stop working, I invited him in. He accepted a beer and I added a log to the fire.

"On a day like today, I long for the bright sun in a prairie sky," I began.

"If you want the prairie sun," he replied, "you must pay for it – dust storms, mosquitoes, blizzards, numbing winds, and cold snaps of minus 40°." I must warn the reader that Tom is an economist by both training and conviction. He instinctively mistrusts idle wishes – whether they be for sun and blue sky, or for socialist utopias.

In due course our conversation turned to this book. Tom was sceptical: "Doubtless one more collection of essays by earnest social-ists parading their concern for the workers, the poor, the environ-ment, and other worthy causes! Why don't you socialists ever pose tough questions about political reality? I have one to start you off. What is the difference between East and West? It made the rounds in Eastern Europe as the Soviet Empire disintegrated in 1989."

I shrugged and gave up.

"The answer is that in the West they still have socialists and com-munists." Tom chuckled. "I realize that, as it applies to the left in Canada, the joke rings false. Apart from the two spikes of support in public opinion polls – the first during World War Two and the second during the last Parliament – you socialists have languished in third place in national politics.

"Here's another from Eastern Europe. What's the socialist road to development?"

Again I shrugged and gave up.

"The long way round to capitalism!" Tom smiled with self-satisfaction. He stared into the fire for a while until a new thought captured him. "As recently as our youth in the 1960s socialism was alive. It was still reasonable to believe that centrally planned econo-mies could be more productive than market economies, and that they could generate a more egalitarian income distribution. Now we know they are less productive and, the more we learn of the privileges enjoyed by communist elites, the more dubious are the claims for equality. Socialism is dead!"

The warm fire and a beer were doing nothing to mellow my friend.

He was in an argumentative mood. If I was to prolong his visit and avoid the task of editing manuscripts, I would have to invite him to continue. I did so. Czechoslovakia having been much in the news, Tom used it as springboard into his eulogy on the death of socialism.

"Do you remember Alexander Dubcek presiding over the Prague Spring of 1968 and promising 'socialism with a human face'? It was a slogan that symbolized confident aspirations of many that socialism could still combine personal liberty, economic productivity, equality, and community. Do you recall Ota Sik? He was Dubcek's Minister of Finance, a respected economist. He could credibly talk of an expanded role for markets in a socialist economy where the state continued to own the means of production. That year I vicariously went into the streets with Parisian students revolting against Gaullist paternalism and, full of self-righteous rage, I marched here in Canada with fellow students against America's invasion of Vietnam. I thought that Mao's 'cultural revolution' was freeing the Chinese from stifling bureaucracy. Compared to all this, social democrats were somewhat boring. Nonetheless, I was pleased that a Labour government had replaced Tory rule in Britain. When the NDP won its first provincial election – Ed Schreyer led the NDP to victory in Manitoba in 1969 – that, too, pleased me.

"That was the sixties. I am embarrassed as I recall the naiveté of youth. As Lenin says somewhere, facts are stubborn things and I have learned since about the limits of politics as a means to produce a moral order in the world. As the old maxim says, if you are not a socialist before forty you have no heart. If you are still a socialist after forty, you have no brains."

Tom returned the conversation to Czechoslovakia.

"After a generation of communist hypocrisy, they have recaptured their civic life and once again the world is paying attention to Prague's magic lantern theatre. Dubcek came out of retirement to speak in support of the 1989 revolution. Both Czechs and Slovaks revere him as a symbol of their historic resistance to foreign-imposed communism, but few identify any longer with his vision of socialism. Vaclav Havel, the new president and symbolic leader of contemporary Czech liberation, has no such interest. Let me remind you of Havel's own conclusion. The word 'socialism,' he insists, has lost all meaning in the Czech context. And unlike Ota Sik's timid embrace of the market, the new Czech Minister of Finance, Klaus Havel, believes passionately in competitive markets composed of privately owned competing firms.

"At this moment of fundamental intellectual re-evaluation in Eastern Europe, who is being read? Certainly not classic Marxists, not writers of the French Enlightenment such as Rousseau, not moderate communists such as Bukharin, not social democrats such as the Fabians, not even liberals with socialist tendencies such as John Stuart Mill. They are devouring Von Hayek, Milton Friedman, and writers in the conservative public choice tradition! To the extent they are interested in political theories, the new Czech leaders are interested in classic liberal questions. How do you guarantee a judiciary and police force free from political interference? How do you create checks and balances against pathological leaders like Stalin or Ceausescu? How do you eliminate the power of a cancerous political party whose 'cells' have multiplied throughout the body politic? What can we learn from *The Federalist Papers* about the management of ethnic tensions between Czechs and Slovaks? How do you dismantle central planning and promote competitive markets?"

"There are socialists in this East European dialogue," I insisted. "They have experienced first hand the perverse effects of endless political lobbying over all dimensions of economic life by state-owned firms under central planning. Accordingly, they are sympathetic to the positive role of private property and markets. But, unlike you, Tom, these 'market socialists' have not abandoned the ideal of economic democracy."

I rummaged in my files for an appropriate quote, and forced Tom to listen to an excerpt from a recent speech by Gorbachev to the Soviet Parliament:

> The market democratizes economic relations, and socialism is unthinkable without democracy. In reforming ownership relations we are creating realistic and healthy grounds for true collectivism, not the nationalization of everything, but the creation of free associations of producers, shareholding societies, producers' and consumers' co-operatives, associations of leaseholders and entrepreneurs. . . . (Gorbachev, *New York Times*, 18 September 1990)

" 'Market socialism' sounds like an oxymoron to me! Such socialists are preserving a tattered faith. Gorbachev's hope that worker-run enterprises and consumer co-operatives can compete efficiently against capitalist firms is a naive illusion. The most efficient form of industrial organization will doubtless prove – in Eastern Europe as elsewhere – to be the capitalist firm managed and owned by those who finance it."

"Perhaps, Tom, you are right. But perhaps the undemocratic nature of the capitalist corporation will ultimately doom it – in the West as in the East. Undeniably, experience has forced socialists to accept the productive potential of the market. The socialist challenge nonetheless remains. One aspect is to promote fair competition between alternate forms of private ownership. Your dogmatic assertions on behalf of the capitalist corporate form are no more convincing than those of aging Bolsheviks on behalf of state ownership and central planning.

"Furthermore, there are cycles – in public affairs as in the seasons. Communists grotesquely overemphasized the social at the expense of the individual. In reaction, many East European intellectuals have embraced classic liberal doctrines. Poland is an even better example than Czechoslovakia. The Solidarity government has aggressively promoted the market – by freeing prices, reducing subsidies to state firms, making the zloty convertible, and privatizing state-owned firms. But, in a year, when Polish unemployment has risen and the newly privatized firms continue to pollute the rivers and the air, there will be renewed public appeals for government action to correct the excesses and failures of 'free markets.'"

"Maybe the revulsion against socialist illusions and central planning will wane over time," Tom admitted, "but after forty years of communism East Europeans are well immunized against the socialist virus. If you hope to persuade the working class that competitive markets always yield to monopoly, that private capital is the source of all evil, and that militant collective bargaining, tight regulation, and nationalization of corporations are the answer, then you had better stick to the prosperous West. Here, capitalism has generated enough wealth that we can indulge socialism – at least in its milder variants – while still maintaining reasonable living standards.

"You think I am scoring easy points by reference to communists in Eastern Europe. Well, let us consider the left in the West. Why," Tom posed the paradox with mock innocence, "does popular support for socialism rest so completely on conservative grounds? In the West, socialists have become romantic conservatives defending nineteenth-century industry and social arrangements against progress. Look at Canada. You in the NDP defend open-ended public subsidies for passenger trains that nobody rides. In order to preserve the status quo in old textile towns in the Eastern Townships you support quotas against foreign-made clothing. You argue for ever-higher subsidies to Newfoundland fishermen, subsidies that keep them in their cold, fog-bound, and poverty-ridden villages decimating the available stocks of cod.

"During the debate over free trade with the United States you and your nationalist allies in the Liberal Party claimed to favour *multilateral* free trade under GATT; you opposed *bilateral* free trade with the United States. What hypocritical nonsense! Every protectionist lobby in the country, fearful that free trade might erode its profits or force it to change its ways and increase efficiency, got your unqualified support.

One test came when GATT made two rulings against Canada – objecting to our protection of lousy domestic wines and our regulations preventing British Columbia fishermen from selling to foreign processors. I don't recall a single NDP politician offering a defence of the GATT rulings.

"A second test is to draw the analogy of the Common Market expanding to include Iberia, Greece, and – in the future – Turkey. Do opponents of the Canada–U.S. free trade agreement prefer its extension to include Mexico? The immediate response is 'no.' The prospect of increased competition from 'slave wage' Mexican labour flushes out the underlying protectionist sentiments."

I protested. "You are obsessed by free trade. Do you see no circumstances under which a country may legitimately resist international market trends? For several years world cereal prices have been artificially low because the Common Market and the United States are engaged in a subsidy war. Should the Canadian government keep its wallet closed, salute free trade, and let prairie agriculture collapse until the subsidy war ends? If a multinational company can realize a saving by reallocating production from one corner of the globe to another, do you expect government to do nothing? The costs of reallocating industry cannot be measured solely by the balance sheets of the companies involved. Workers cannot costlessly shift from making clothes in Trois-Rivières to building houses in Vancouver. It is a healthy instinct of a community – and a nation is a community – to protect its members against essentially random misfortune. Whether we choose to protect workers by some restrictions on trade or, alternatively, by generous public support for displaced workers, the collective instinct to protect is valuable. The world will not be a better place by allowing free rein to corporate executives tirelessly hunting the world for cheaper labour."

Tom snorted. "You socialists defend protection with romantic appeals to community. You forgot the line about wanting no part of the fruits of Third World labour 'exploited' by multinational companies. Rather than let Canadians buy cheaper shirts from 'exploited' workers in Manila, you would have these workers earn even less in the paddy fields where their parents laboured. You socialists refuse to allow that there can be a conflict between the public good and the short-run interests of the interest groups allied to your party. Canadian socialists have become intellectual hacks, echoing in Ottawa the self-serving rhetoric of any self-proclaimed 'progressive' interest group that might support your party. Take the case of dairy farmers and their marketing boards. Defending agricultural marketing boards has become part of your socialist creed."

Tom warmed to his subject. Like the reformed alcoholic testifying to the destructive seduction of booze, my ex-socialist friend reveled in exposing the sins of marketing boards. "Do you know how much milk costs per litre in Vancouver?"

"For homogenized milk it's over a dollar."

"That's right. And do you know what it costs in Seattle?"

"No," I admitted.

"It costs sixty-five cents per litre." He assured me he had taken account of the exchange rate and was quoting the price in Canadian dollars. "Same quality milk costs over 50 per cent more in Canada. American farmers have price supports and subsidies, too, but at least in the 'land of the free' there are some checks and balances on farmers' greed. Not in Canada. Goddamn Canadian government lets farmers monopolize milk supply. If you produce milk without a quota, you pay fines and lose your cows. We're not talking about some luxury item bought by the plutocracy. We're talking about a basic food that our government is forcing Canadian mothers to buy at a price 50 per cent higher than in the U.S.

"And who benefits from this scheme to gouge Canadian mothers? I'll tell you. Old established farmers – those who were lucky enough to be producing when the quota scheme came into effect. When they decide to get out of the dairy business, they don't give their quota to some young deserving farmer. Oh, no. They're brighter than you socialists. They *sell* it to the highest bidder. Young farmers wanting into the dairy business have bid up the price of these quotas so that, once they pay for their quota, their net incomes are probably no higher than they would have been without the marketing board.

"These agricultural marketing boards illustrate a lot of what's wrong with socialism. Trudeau's policy planners – they were all closet socialists – looked at dairy farmers and said to themselves, here's a group with unstable low incomes. How can we use the government to help them? Socialists dogmatically oppose markets and so the planners looked around for some government intervention to regulate dairy markets. They commissioned studies by overpaid consultants on a 'reasonable' milk price to allow a 'fair return' to the farmer. Then they set up marketing boards to restrict milk supply in order to force the market price up to this 'reasonable' level. They let their bleeding hearts run away with their bloody heads. As Adam Smith said 200 years ago, 'the propensity to truck and trade' is a universal aspect of human nature. You suppress the competitive market in milk and, instead, farmers create a competitive market in quotas – which in effect are shares in your government-created milk monopoly.

"What's more, once they introduced milk marketing boards they created a narrow interest group with a large stake in preserving it. The nature of politics is to grease the wheel that squeaks the loudest and pluck the goose that squawks the least. How loud you squeak or squawk depends on how much pain you feel. Each mother paying 50 per cent too much for her milk feels a little pain. If we eliminated the quota system and allowed competition, each farmer who paid good money for his milk quota would feel a lot of pain. If you added up the pain inflicted by milk marketing boards on millions of mothers across the country, it would far exceed the pain inflicted on a few thousand dairy farmers by eliminating the boards. But who's going to squeak and squawk the loudest in government corridors – the mothers or the dairy farmers? To pose the question is to know the answer.

"I want to make a final point," Tom insisted with smug self-satisfaction. "You mentioned earlier the cereal subsidy war between the Common Market and Americans. Who is responsible for it? You on the left released the evil genie of government regulation of agricultural markets. Now it has turned, and is devouring the very farmers who conceived it. For decades the planners in Brussels sought to increase the incomes of farmers – primarily in France and Italy – by imposing food prices far above international levels. They produced, as any first-year economics student could predict, massive excess supplies – of cereals among other commodities. The Common Market has exported its cereal surplus and driven down international prices. The Americans retaliated with their own export subsidies and further depressed cereal prices. Canadian prairie wheat farmers, who undeniably are among the most efficient in the world, can no longer earn a decent living from export markets and they, in their turn, have become dependent on government handouts to live."

"Enough," I interjected. I contemplated lecturing on the instability of agricultural markets and the positive role of marketing boards – such as the Wheat Board – in eliminating speculative transactions, in communicating reliable market information to farmers, and in stabilizing incomes. I thought better of it. I told Tom to read Bob Cairns's essay on the symbiotic relationship between markets and the state and turned to another matter.

"Adam Smith and Karl Marx may both agree that businessmen seldom gather together but their conversation turns to schemes whereby politicians can be persuaded to suppress competition. But," I admonished, "you cannot use milk marketing boards as a parable to explain politics. If it is fundamental to men and women to haggle in markets for gain, it is equally fundamental for people to act collectively in democratic institutions – legislative assemblies, political parties, unions, or co-operatives.

"Socialism means faith in the ability of people, acting collectively in democratic institutions, to undertake more ambitious tasks than capitalist society – even liberal capitalist society – allows. Such a definition is not utopian. It has none of the millenarian conviction of those who have envisioned socialism as a radical break with the present. I perceive socialism as relative; it refers to more as opposed to less. It says nothing about the classic criteria that historically have demarcated socialists: opposition toward markets and private property, or support for state planning. I subscribe to the revisionist tradition of Eduard Bernstein, the German socialist who annoyed his more orthodox contemporaries at the beginning of the twentieth century by insisting that movement was everything, the goal was nothing."

Tom was not impressed. "However chastened your definition, you are still giving an inspirational speech about the potential of men and women to act creatively together. You make two errors. First, you blur the distinction between voluntary collective activity and state intervention. If socialism means merely support for voluntary collective activity and does not impinge on the civil rights of others, I, too, am a socialist. The essence of the state, however, is its legal monopoly on the use of force and you socialists, however moderate, have paternalist instincts. You always seek rationales to invoke the force of the state on behalf of your projects. Ordinary Canadians understand this simple distinction far better than you.

"Let me give an example – unions. The majority of Canadians unambiguously favour the right of workers to bargain collectively with their employer over wages and terms of work if that is the wish of the majority of workers involved. But Canadians are dubious about government legislating sanctions that pressure workers to join a union, that give wide scope to secondary strikes and make it difficult to get rid of an unwanted union.

"The second error is that you socialists never come clean and define clearly the limit where state intervention ends and the domain preserved for civic society begins. Like any pressure group, unions constantly press for legislation making their members and leaders better off. I never hear an NDP politician discussing the limits of collective bargaining – this far and no further.

"One of civilization's accomplishments in the last millennium is to have developed legal institutions that give the citizen some protection from arbitrary acts by others – including both the state and other individuals. To mention the obvious, you socialists have an erratic record on civil liberties. I am not accusing earnest social democrats and union leaders of wanting tyranny, but they, too, can be adept psychological manipulators who flout the spirit if not the letter of the liberal tradition of civil liberties."

"You betray, Tom, a simplistic view of civil rights based solely on assuring individual freedom from others. Voltaire, the sceptic, should appeal to you, and yet it is Voltaire who attacked the romantic naiveté implicit in Rousseau's 'noble savage' living free from society's artifice. Man lives in imperfect communities, and he strives to improve them.

"If you read Pierre Fortin's and John McCallum's contributions, you will see that they discuss at some length the unemployment and inflation policies of countries such as Sweden and Japan, whose experience has been far better than ours in Canada. They both bluntly admit that any successful policy to reconcile full employment and low inflation requires some limits on collective bargaining. But they also attack the romantic naiveté implicit in your view of civil rights. Presumably you – like the federal Conservatives and the Bank of Canada – advocate tight money as the preferred policy against inflation because it entails minimum interference in the rights of individuals to 'truck and trade' in the market. Controlling inflation by means of monetary constraint admittedly works. But it works by throwing many out of work and making factories idle, so that firms and unions can no longer sustain wage-price spirals. You want to impose ideological blinkers on Canadians, to prevent them from pursuing alternative policies that violate civil liberties in the market. Better a million Canadians unemployed than any alternative that violates, however tangentially, your civil liberties!

"I have more to say about full employment, but since you began to talk of unions, let us continue with them. From the beginning of the industrial revolution in Britain, workers have formed associations to defend their collective interests. It is as natural for workers to unionize as it is for Adam Smith's merchants to 'truck and trade.'

"Throughout the nineteenth century and up to the present, capitalists and their political allies – using exactly your arguments – have considered unions an unwarranted constraint on the common law rights of individuals to make voluntary contracts in markets for mutual advantage. But the majority of workers in all industrial countries have adamantly refused to accept that the same legal principles should govern the sale of a sack of potatoes and the employment of men and women. The potential for employers to collude and engage in arbitrary acts against their employees is nearly always greater than the reverse. The result in democratic society has been legislation to enable workers to unionize. When well organized, unions can not only improve overall equality of incomes – lower wage differentials and redistribute monopoly-level profits to wages – they can also serve to increase the efficiency of a firm by serving as an efficient means of giving voice to workers' interests. I grant you this much. Adversarial collective bargaining in North America and Britain does concentrate too much on the narrow short-term wage interests of union members and enjoys only limited support among the general public. The solution, however, is not legislation to weaken unions."

18

"Before, you accused me of naiveté. If any of our arguments deserves the label, it is your defence of unions," Tom objected.

I offered him a second beer and he consented to hear me out.

"I accept that competitive markets are the most efficient institution in general to allocate capital and labour. But that proposition does not imply that we accept Anglo-Saxon corporate law, with its deification of the shareholder-owned corporation. There are alternatives. The Scandinavians – and, increasingly, governments in the Common Market – have extended workers' rights in the market far beyond collective bargaining. Significantly, labour legislation is one area where most of the post-communist East European leaders want to avoid Anglo-Saxon traditions. They are far more attracted to the social democratic traditions of continental Europe.

"Capitalists may supply some portion of a firm's financial requirements in the form of debt, receiving a fixed rate of interest and no voice in management. But the larger the share of finance supplied by a given capitalist, the more likely he or she is to want a share of management – in other words, to want equity, not debt. There is a parallel between capitalists who supply finance and workers who supply their labour – economists even describe skilled workers as 'human capital.' There is also a parallel between debt capital and collective bargaining. One fixes an interest rate for financial investors, the other a wage rate for workers; neither provides any share in the right to manage. Why, I ask you, should workers – any more than capitalists – operate under legislation that precludes their exercise of authority in corporate management? Canadians need to experiment with extension of workers' rights beyond collective bargaining to include a serious role in the management of firms in the marketplace."

"So," Tom noted, "you have snuck in a pitch for your essay on worker participation in management. I see you also found a sympathetic quotation from John Stuart Mill. That surprises me. I thought Mill more sensible. Even great economists, after conducting their rigorous analysis, unfortunately indulge sentimental fantasies."

Tom was quiet for a minute. He then pursued a quite different line of argument.

"Perhaps unions *can* under some ideal circumstances contribute to economic efficiency, but Scandinavian-style social democracy is not what we know. Canada suffers many of the symptoms of the 'British disease.' Our unions pursue little more than adversarial wage bargaining. In the 1970s and 1980s Canada's strike rate was above Britain's and put us in serious contention with Italy for worst strike record among major industrial countries. Our economy is shackled with strongly entrenched, narrow, regionally based interest groups that demand high subsidies and resist furiously adaptation to changed markets whenever that means reallocation of labour and capital. On the other hand, Canadians are not prepared to pay for all these unnecessary public handouts and consequently we have a deficit, measured as a percentage of GNP, far higher than in the United States. We have parties of the centre-left – Liberals and the NDP – captured by special interest groups and unable to advocate independent policy. Even the Conservatives, the only vaguely coherent politicians in the country, are led by compromised moderates, what Margaret Thatcher dismissively labelled 'wets.'"

Once Tom mentioned Margaret Thatcher, I knew what was coming. I was not disappointed.

"At the end of World War Two Britons had the highest per capita incomes of any European country; by 1979, when Thatcher took over from a dispirited Labour government, per capita incomes were a third lower than in either Germany or France. Under Labour and the Tory 'wets,' Britain suffered from a cancerous political illness that was slowly paralysing the country. Powerful vested interest groups in inefficient state-owned companies had a seemingly unshakable claim to public subsidy. Oxbridge-trained mandarins in Whitehall, having lost an empire, smothered the public life of the country with their elaborate centralized administration. Adversarial militant unions infused with quasi-Marxist rhetoric opposed all market-induced reallocation of resources. They dominated the Labour Party and intimidated the Tory 'wets.' British inflation rates were chronically worse than those in other industrial countries. It all came to a climax in the wave of self-indulgent public-sector strikes of 1978-79. Ordinary Britons – a phrase you NDPers should understand – had had enough. They elected a genuine right-wing populist who promised to reduce inflation, constrain militant unions, reduce the size of the public sector, and make Britain 'great' again. Perhaps her methods were rough, but Margaret Thatcher accomplished much of what she set out to do. Now that her Tory colleagues have lost their will to support her reforming zeal, we should invite her to Canada. We need more than Mulroney's tentative reforms – free trade with the U.S., the GST, and tinkering with the deficit. We need a Canadian Margaret Thatcher."

"You pass rather lightly over the cost of Thatcherism – high unemployment throughout most of the 1980s, the glorification of paper entrepreneurship in the City of London, increased inequality of incomes, and erosion of social services. You worship Margaret Thatcher because she shares your excessive faith in private enterprise. You assume the impossibility of success from government interventions, and bring to government attitudes that are self-fulfilling. You insult unions in general, and public-sector unions in particular; you insult the senior civil service. Your ideal is to reduce government to simple-minded rules such as monetarist nostrums on the optimum rate of monetary growth.

"And, as we speak, Margaret Thatcher's Britain is enduring the bitter harvest from her divisive dogmas. Motivated by an ideological mistrust of all political activity, she forced municipal governments to switch their revenue base from property taxes to a poll tax. The poll tax – in principle an equal levy on all adults – is supposed to make citizens aware of the cost of local services and vote out spendthrift local politicians. The poll tax may have the virtue of revealing costs, but it is a flagrant assault on community standards of equity. The majority, both rich and poor, believe that a just tax is one that, within limits, varies according to the taxpayer's wealth. Hence the new poll tax is replacing a potentially just tax with an unjust one. The massive public demonstrations against the poll tax illustrate dramatically that equity matters."

Having hit one of Thatcher's Achilles' heels, I managed to keep Tom temporarily silent. I pursued my advantage. "There is a lesson here for Canadians. One reason that the Conservatives cannot persuade ordinary Canadians to accept the tax increases required to balance our budget is the Conservatives' ideological inability to understand the importance of fairness. Why should ordinary Canadians accept the goods and service tax when they see flagrant exemptions on capital gains for the rich?"

Tom recovered his composure by resort to an ad hominem diversion. "If you believe you on the left can govern better, why do your NDP Members of Parliament not behave more maturely in opposition? All I hear are monotonous pleas for subsidies to Via Rail, subsidies to Atlantic fishermen, subsidies to prairie farmers, subsidies to single mothers. Tell Canadians how you would resolve the painful trade-offs of governing. Tell Canadians how you would balance the budget and pay for even more largesse. You socialists never get beyond vague appeals for 'fairness' in taxation, implying that you could satisfy every interest group and pay for it painlessly by taxing the rich."

Not wanting to be accused of parochialism, I had so far resisted reference to Saskatchewan's left-wing heritage, but I could do so no longer. "Since 1944 we socialists governed Saskatchewan – through booms and busts. Perhaps we should have assumed a greater responsibility for maintaining aggregate demand during the busts and run deficits – as Clarence Barber would have wished – but we didn't. We balanced the budget throughout our years of office. We faced conflicts with special interest groups – such as public-sector unions wanting excessive wage increases – but we managed to respect popular conceptions of equity and in general Saskatchewan citizens agreed to pay for our ambitious agenda of social programs. Ironically, our Conservative opponents defeated us in 1982 by fomenting a classic tax revolt, promising to eliminate major provincial taxes. Their fiscal management since 1982 has been abysmal and led to consistent red ink.

"If you read Allan Blakeney's contribution, you will see that we on the left accept the need to balance budgets. Good democratic government is a demanding skill, Tom, but not, as you maintain, an impossible one. That, in summary, is the message of Gregory Baum's survey of recent Catholic social theory. The prerequisite is to choose politicians who – unlike you – have faith that people can manage democratically their collective affairs."

I attended to the fire, which had died down. Tom took the opportunity to return the conversation to more compatible territory. "Do you realize," he asked as I sat down, "that, as we speak (in December, 1990), Britain's unemployment rate is 6.5 per cent and Canada's is 9.3 per cent?"

"I do," I allowed. "But do you realize that Sweden's unemployment rate is 1.8 per cent? A social democratic agenda of full employment, generous social programs, equity in taxation, and high per capita incomes is feasible. The crucial first principle, as Henry Milner argues in his essay, is that all major interest groups – political parties, labour, and business federations – accept that genuine full employment is a policy priority. Swedes do not engage in the intellectual charade of defining full employment as 'the natural rate of unemployment' required to stabilize inflation under existing institutional arrangements. If the 'natural rate' is too high, they are prepared to change institutions."

"Before you take too much delight in Sweden's performance, let me emphasize its fragility. Operating an economy with such a low unemployment rate poses the constant risk of inflationary wage-price spirals – and Sweden currently has inflation above 10 per cent. And even the Social Democrats have now realized the need to constrain the public sector and reduce the disincentive effects on work of high income taxes."

"But, Tom, you are merely stating the obvious. Certainly, Scandinavian social democracy has created a set of political tensions, but it has survived more-or-less in its present form for nearly three decades, long enough to deserve serious consideration as an alternative to Mrs. Thatcher's 'handbagging' of British institutions into accepting market discipline."

"So you want to import the Swedish 'model' into Canada. To do so would require a left-wing equivalent of Margaret Thatcher prepared for much 'handbagging' of your traditional allies. It would require that brothers and sisters in the NDP and the unions abandon their quasi-Marxist dogmas. Look at some of the ingredients of the Swedish model. First, the Swedes practise free trade with the Common Market and have been prepared to shut down large sectors when they could no longer remain internationally competitive. Second, while unions play a significant role in firm management, virtually all firms are privately owned; Swedes do not tolerate permanently subsidized inefficient state-owned firms. They understand that industrial productivity can only be achieved over the long run in privately owned firms buying and selling in competitive markets. Third, both Canada and Sweden spend between 2 and 3 per cent of GNP on programs to aid unemployed workers. The Swedes are generous in spending to retrain the unemployed and relocate them, but they are as hostile as any small businessman Tory about untied transfers to the unemployed. Fourth, unions, employer associations, and the government jointly administer Swedish labour market programs. It would require an ideological earthquake before Canadian union leaders would engage in 'tripartism' and administer unemployment insurance programs in as financially prudent a manner as the Swedes."

The rain stopped as night descended. I invited Tom to supper. As the chicken stew simmered, Tom perused a jumble of fading NDP pamphlets piled in a corner of the kitchen counter. They were left over from the door-to-door canvass in the 1988 federal election campaign. "Let us look more closely at your New Democratic Party. I admit that the NDP victory in Ontario surprised me. When people become sufficiently disgusted with their politicians, they are willing to do anything, even elect the NDP. But in national politics the NDP remains forever hopeful, forever mired in third place. I have a few words of advice to you muddle-headed NDPers.

"During the last Parliament the NDP ranked first or second in national opinion polls between late 1986 and mid-1988. For once NDP leaders actually believed their predictions that, after the next election, they would become the official opposition in Ottawa. Some of you even dreamed of government. NDP hopes survived until the last half of the election campaign when the electorate polarized over the issue of free trade with the United States. At that point your wine turned – if not to vinegar – once more to *vin ordinaire*. Opposition to the Conservative government coalesced around the Liberals' anti-free trade 'crusade'; NDP support fell by election day back to the traditional range of 15 to 20 per cent, a range in which it has stagnated ever since the general election of 1965. The NDP elected no members in Atlantic Canada. The expected breakthrough in Quebec proved to be a mirage; no Quebec NDP candidate was elected. The party lost seats in

Ontario and Manitoba. The only gains occurred in the three western-most provinces and the northern territories."

"Don't ignore the corporate-funded publicity blitz on behalf of the Canada-U.S. free trade agreement during the last half of the campaign."

"I don't ignore it," Tom insisted. "Politics is a complicated social process and doubtless the business lobby explains some of your losses. But it is always easier to blame *external* foes than to deal with your *internal* contradictions. Relative to your expectations, your 1988 *vin ordinaire* tasted so sour that NDP leaders indulged bitter internal critiques. But these critiques were so personally vindictive and intellectually superficial! I understand why Ed Broadbent resigned the party leadership; he wanted to escape the hothouse of muddled internal recriminations."

"The NDP is a 'hothouse of muddled internal recriminations'? Explain yourself."

"With pleasure! Let me start with the nationalists within your ranks. Within a week of the 1988 election, Bob White was on record with a leaked critique of the NDP's election campaign for having permitted moral leadership of the 'crusade' against the Canada-U.S. free trade agreement to pass to the Liberals. And throughout 1989, the candidates who ran to replace Broadbent as leader all, with varying explicitness, accused the NDP of having been soft on the issue. Nationalists within your ranks extol the beauty of Canadians without admitting that we, like every other people, also have warts. They are engaged in an internal critique of a sort but, more fundamentally, they, too, are avoiding the painful truths of self-examination. To what extent does Bob White's nationalism go beyond a self-interested desire of autoworkers to limit foreign competition from Japanese carmakers? Is Bob White's nationalism fundamentally different from that of Adam Zimmerman, who, as head of British Columbia's major forest company, wrapped himself in the Canadian flag to oppose higher provincial royalties at the time of the softwood lumber dispute with Washington?"

I assured Tom that both Larry Pratt's and Tom Keating's essays dealt at length with the seductive dangers of nationalism on the left.

"Maybe they understand the need to resist nationalist excess. Your new Quebec Member of Parliament, Phil Edmonston, also valiantly tried to reconcile Quebec and Anglo-Canadian nationalism within your ranks, but the Quebec wing of the NDP has little impact on your party's thinking. Elsewhere in the country your party leaders have been two-dimensional roosters perched atop weathervanes flapping in the wind of Anglo-Canadian nationalism that is sweeping the land. To be fair, I admit that is not true of all; there are a minority of notable exceptions, including Ed Broadbent himself. The message carried on these winds is, like nationalism everywhere, a crude one: we should all be proud Canadians without qualifications and, in particular, the Quebec National Assembly should enjoy no special powers to coerce non-Francophone Québécois into using French. Yet you know as well as I that the social compact underlying Confederation implies that the National Assembly exercise jurisdiction over language and culture within Quebec and that, if the compact is broken, Francophone Québécois will ultimately opt for sovereignty."

I invited Tom to leave the constitutional wrangle to political scientists. He obliged, and turned once more to his critique of nationalists within the NDP.

"The principal target for the nationalists within your ranks was the core of professional party officials and pollsters who devised electoral tactics that allowed you in the NDP to evade your fundamental weakness as a political party. That weakness, and the underlying explanation for your electoral frustrations, is the accurate perception by most Canadians that you cannot distinguish between what it means for a political party to *govern*, as opposed to *advocate*. In particular, Canadians do not trust you to promote a productive full-employment economy. Your 'backroom boys' understood this. They understood that the free trade debate raised public anxieties about the competence of the NDP to manage the economy, and that it was in your tactical interest to stress other, non-economic issues. It is unfair to scapegoat your tacticians who, knowing the public mistrusts your ability to manage a corner grocery store, crafted a campaign that emphasized non-economic themes.

"Governing concerns the allocation of scarce public resources to realize collective goals. It entails painful decisions to limit the claims of interest groups – including the claims of interest groups with which you on the left sympathize. To adapt Abraham Lincoln's famous maxim, while all Canadians vote for their narrow interests some of the time, and some do so all of the time, most Canadians begrudgingly vote most of the time for a political party willing to recognize political limits.

"Let me give one concrete example where – much to my surprise – you actually undertook an act of responsible government. During the recession of the early 1980s the Manitoba NDP cabinet found itself grappling with a budget deficit. Cabinet decided on the level of borrowing and tax increases it could tolerate. It further decided it could not meet the wage expectations of the provincial public service union. Ultimately, government and union negotiated an agreement that guaranteed job security, but the union was obliged to accept a decline in wages. Union leaders were not pleased with wage restraint, but they continued to support your party and you won the subsequent provincial election. The moral is that, with the exception of those few having experience in one of the provincial NDP governments in western Canada, no leaders of the federal party understand from personal experience that governing *inevitably* entails frustrating some expectations. Perhaps now some in Ontario will also learn the art of governing.

"Given your perennial third-party status it is easy to understand why you have been a party of advocacy and why allied interest groups – the most important of which are the unions – have expected your federal leaders to behave as their advocates. Ultimately, however, the success of any political party lies in the creativity with which it handles the tension between governing and advocacy, not in denying that such a tension exists.

"What evidence exists, you may well ask, that Canadians perceive the NDP as a party of advocacy, unable to manage the economy? I want to discuss a particular poll." Tom set about hunting through my files until he found what he wanted, a crumpled newspaper report of a poll conducted by Environics for *The Globe and Mail* in October, 1988. He showed it to me, a sly grin creasing his face.

In your view, which of the three federal political parties is best able to ...

	Con.	Lib.	NDP	other responses
1. manage the economy	40%	21%	17%	22%
2. encourage economic development in your region	39	22	19	20
3. create jobs	36	18	21	25
4. defend Canada's sovereignty and independence	29	28	19	24
5. handle foreign policy and international relations	42	25	11	22
6. maintain health care and social services	23	23	34	20
7. protect the environment	22	18	33	27
8. create a fair tax policy	25	20	26	29

"You socialists disparage polls as a tool of the corporate devil seeking ways to sell detergent. You call yourselves democrats but you don't like evidence – such as good political polls – that shows the extent of popular distrust of your policies. At least within the inner circle of party professionals, however, you have overcome your moral objections. You relied on polling during the 1980s as much as any other party.

"What is significant about this poll is its timing. It was conducted at the beginning of the election campaign when the NDP still ranked second among the three parties in overall support. From the first three questions the only reasonable conclusion is that twice as many Canadians had confidence in the Conservatives as in you to manage the economy. An analogous conclusion is implied by the fourth and fifth questions dealing with the conduct of foreign policy. The pre-eminent current issues of advocacy are probably environmental protection, defence of social services, and equity in taxation. Only on these issues do Canadians rank you highly.

"As an aside, you talk in the NDP of an environmental crisis, but your solutions reflect your anti-market dogmas. Those responsible are always some corporation; the solution is stiffer fines and jail sentences for corporate executives. But, Walt Kelly's cartoon character, Pogo, put it well: 'The enemy is us.' We all pollute in a million small ways. Why not use the market to tackle the problem? A major tax increase to double, say, hydrocarbon fuel prices would eliminate the federal deficit and would have a dramatic effect on persuading people to burn less oil and gas. People would insulate their houses, stores, and factories better, drive less, and buy smaller cars."

"You've made your point," I retorted. "Lynn McDonald, in the book I'm working on here, makes it better. Get back to your thesis."

"Agreed, agreed. The next question," Tom continued unperturbed by my irritation, "is, do issues determine how people vote? Other factors, such as 'image' of the leader, obviously matter. Indeed, for all your earnest distaste in the NDP for political hype, you exploited to the full the public perception that Ed Broadbent was a more trustworthy, caring leader than either John Turner or Brian Mulroney. But, the two years following the onset of the 1982 recession illustrate the ability of people to base their political choices on a rational assessment of their self-interest.

"Between 1982 and 1984 support for the federal NDP collapsed from approximately 25 per cent to 10 per cent. Faced with the prospect of electoral disaster, the federal NDP engaged a new – incidentally American – polling firm to find out what was wrong. Surveys showed that economic recession had raised the importance of economic management as an issue for the electorate and, however unpleasant to admit, Canadians had little confidence in your ability to do anything about the economy. You were not credible economic managers; you were credible only as advocates for the issues illustrated above.

"From such results emerged the 1984 NDP election campaign. You stopped talking economics – no more speeches on 'industrial strategy' – and instead portrayed yourselves as the defenders of social programs for 'ordinary Canadians.' You recovered and captured 18 per cent of the vote. To be fair, you should give some of the credit for your recovery to John Turner and the incompetence of the Liberal campaign.

"Having feared disaster, your expectations in 1984 were low. You were delighted to have maintained your traditional post-1965 level of support. There was no criticism then that 'backroom' tacticians had corrupted your principles. Quite the contrary. And your continued success in the polls during the last Parliament suggested that this tactic, born out of desperation in 1984, might be a winning strategy for 1988.

"Older and wiser after the 1988 election, you now know the limits of such a strategy. What's to be done? To be blunt, you need consistent economic policy that is credible not only to the interest groups with which you are aligned, but also to 'ordinary Canadians.' You want to stick your quotation from Mill at the head of your introduction; I challenge you to accompany it with mine from Comrade Yegor Ligachev, leader of the anti-Gorbachev orthodox Communists in Moscow. I do not want to 'red-bait.' You NDPers are earnest defenders of civil liberties, but I suspect that most within the NDP feel closer to the sentiments expressed in my quotation than in yours. Your problem is that on economic issues your ideas are on a par with those of Comrade Ligachev."

Supper had been eaten; the fire had subsided to a few glowing coals; the hour was late. Before my argumentative friend finally took his leave, I invited him to read the book.

I.
MARKETS AND THE STATE

R O B E R T   D.   C A I R N S

2

On a Necessary Tension
of a Democratic Society

NEO-CONSERVATIVE "PUBLIC CHOICE" THEORY HOLDS THAT POLITICAL action, or government intervention, is a coercive interference with voluntary transactions in the market. The public demand on the state for redistributional policies is also viewed as a retarding force on social well-being. A conflict between market and state is the underlying premise. Ideally, the neo-conservative "minimal state" would limit itself to contract enforcement and national defence.

On the contrary, historically the state and market have developed in parallel. This essay emphasizes that the market is itself a political instrument, with attendant advantages and disadvantages. An active state is warranted not only for reasons of distributive justice, but for the efficient operation of a complex industrial economy. Evidence suggests that some – certainly not all – state intervention and regulations lead to efficiency as well as distributional gains in an industrial society. Furthermore, the role of the state is founded on shared collective values, including compassion and moral sense, the expression of which is precluded in the individualistic market.

To view the market as a political institution, rather than an abstract, external "invisible hand" in social relations, has implications beyond the day-to-day formulation of economic policy; it helps give substance to the concept of democracy and individual participation in industrial society.

Markets are important and valuable institutions within Canadian society. Many times, when I hear an attack on markets in general, I sense that the underlying purpose of the critics is to afford their particular group a market advantage by political means. By the same token, when I hear extravagant praise of the virtues of the market, what I am really hearing is a demand that some interest groups relinquish their political means of advancement. Neither of these positions promotes the admittedly vague goals that policy ought to promote, namely, the benefit of society as a whole and the dignity of the individual.

I have come to the following proposition: from an analytic and historic standpoint, if a line is to be drawn, it is more reasonably drawn *around* the market and the state, not *between* them. This has important implications for the way that social democrats ought to approach the setting of policy.

MARKETS AND POLITICS

When economists speak of a market, what they refer to is a more-or-less idealized mechanism by which interactions between or among *individuals* are facilitated. The interactions are held to be for mutual benefit; otherwise, if an individual did not benefit, he or she would refuse to take part. The fact that a market exchange takes place is *prima facie* evidence of mutual benefit. Economists allow that the relative bargaining strengths and wealth of the individuals, i.e., their "endowments," may be unequal and hence one individual may be more able to hold out for a better deal than another; but however unequal are endowments, markets are of mutual benefit to all involved. Most economists accept uncritically the existence of unequal endowments – and, thereby, inequality of opportunity. This is a weak spot in the argument, only partially answered by appeals to realism or "positivism," or by arguments about the extent of social mobility.

The state, on the other hand, is the predominant *collective* mechanism. Through it individuals can be induced or coerced (sometimes economists do not distinguish) to do things they otherwise would not do. Ideally, the state promotes some measure of collective benefit, but historical experience unfortunately illustrates an inherent tendency for the state to deviate from any reasonable interpretation of collective benefit.

It is a truism that the role of government has grown rapidly in this century in all Western industrialized countries. This growth troubles certain economists. When introducing a symposium on the subject, Myrhman (1985, p. 276) observed that conservatives would limit government to the "minimal state consist[ing] of defence, police and the legal system, all the necessary institutions to define, protect and enforce property rights and to solve conflicts between subjects." For such economists growth of the state beyond these limits is a coercive infringement of individual prerogatives – and hence of the market. A conflict between market and state is the underlying premise.

In the last generation economists have invaded the domain of political scientists, applying theories of individual "rent-seeking" to political outcomes. For such "public choice" economists the political process is very different from the democratic ideal. Based on the analogy of individuals seeking to maximize their well-being by exchange in ordinary economic markets, they view politics as another form of market in which self-seeking interest groups attempt to promote their own advantage, irrespective of the effect produced on the rest of society. Implicit in much of this analysis is the idea that the economic marketplace, working ideally, can provide an efficient distribution of income, promote participation by all citizens, and promote the "collective benefit." Interventions by government are viewed typically as the result of undesirable rent-seeking by interest groups.

To be fair to this approach, it is undeniably true that special interest groups promote government policies in their members' interest while wrapping them in the rhetoric of the public good. Consider milk marketing boards, which control supply by requiring dairy farmers to produce no more than their individual quotas. At the time of the system's introduction, the quota system reduced supply, raised milk prices, and clearly benefited existing farmers. But the next generation of dairy farmers has had to buy quotas from retiring farmers before producing milk. Farmers have bid milk quota prices up to substantial levels, and the net income remaining to them after paying the interest cost on the quota may be close to what it would have been in an unregulated market. It is a wasteful system that does not benefit farmers beyond the first generation and worsens income distribution by increasing the price of an essential food. Social democrats who criticize proposals for imposing sales taxes on food would do well to recognize the tax implicit in the operation of agricultural marketing boards, a tax that does not augment government revenues.

Other examples of rent-seeking abound, and are convincing evidence that government policies can work against the broad public interest. On the other hand, the critique cannot be true in general. Our social safety nets arose as a result of government policies. Moreover, if interest groups pressuring for government intervention are rent-seeking, it also must be true that those who advocate a greater role for the market are so motivated. There is no reason to suppose that the Business Council on National Issues or other supporters of the Canada-U.S. trade agreement have acquired an enlightened concern for the well-being of all Canadians, any more than has the textile workers' union, which advocates protection against foreign competition.

Our view of government, then, must be realistic. It must admit the role of a multitude of special interest groups working against the public interest and seeking special advantage. Social democrats ought to be honest enough – and if they hope to have credibility among the majority of voters, will have to be honest enough – to concede that some of their own policies, promoting the interests of their supporters, are not in the interest of the general public. Yet our view must also retain idealism, insisting that society, through institutions that promote both collective and individual interaction, has the potential to improve its future. Neither capitalism nor socialism can be looked upon as the ideal culmination.

Social democrats must admit the need for balance between social and personal, between collective and individual aspirations. Put differently, there must be an ongoing tension between the political and market domains.

Even though there is *tension*, it is not historically accurate to view the market and the political system as having developed in *conflict*. Rather, they developed hand-in-hand. We measure the beginnings of civilization from the point at which codified laws governing social relations began to be promulgated. It is part of the tradition of the English-speaking world that legislative and public concepts of democracy grew in parallel with the growth of commerce. Closer to the present, North (1985, pp. 388ff) outlines reasons for government growth in the United States in the nineteenth century, reasons likely applicable to other countries. Change in technology led to change in economic organization, increased trade, and increased division of labour in production. All this increased the number of special interest groups that turned to government to fulfil various needs, including enforcement of the complex contracts that emerged from the new technology. North (1985, p. 390) gives the particular example of farmers' political agitation in the midwestern states: "The best predictor of farm political activity, i.e. the variability of income, is a direct function of growing dependence on the world market." In summary, the growth of interest group politics paralleled, and was a result of, the extension of markets.

North implies that extension of the market (as measured in increased division of labour and extension of trade) is inextricable from extension of politics. To North a central factor in the pace of change, and presumably the extent of change, is the institutional environment. Institutions, then, matter. Like a gas in a bottle, one might say, the market takes the shape of its institutional container. The market is really a political institution. It is *defined by*, not simply *limited by*, the regulations that govern economic transactions.

Nor are the institutions of society purely technologically determined. Armstrong and Nelles (1986) give the example of telecommunications, a timely one for the contemporary debates on deregulation. Canadian jurisdictions were the first to regulate telecommunications, before the turn of the twentieth century; the Americans followed shortly thereafter. Armstrong and Nelles's thesis is that the monopoly accorded to Bell Canada was "made" by the political and market processes, not "born" by the technology. If the technology is such that unit costs fall as firm size increases, then unit cost is lowest when one producer supplies the entire market and optimal policy may be that government permits a "natural monopoly" and regulates its price. While some aspects of telecommunications technology are natural monopolies, other aspects are not. For example, there never was any reason to accord a monopoly through regulation of entry in the production of telephones themselves. Recent changes in "terminal equipment" technology make this point obvious now. For generations an aspect of regulation served no ostensible public policy purpose; on the other hand, the protected market gave Northern Telecom an opportunity to develop into a technological leader in terminal equipment. Changing telecommunication technology has changed the social costs of continuing the protected market and has led to a rethinking of the appropriate form of regulation. But if the debate is properly understood, new technology has not justified an abstract intellectual attack on the desirability, in appropriate circumstances, of regulation as an instrument to realize policy goals.

A simultaneous concern for the social good and for the dignity of the individual requires a tension between collective and individual interests, between politics and markets, and not the suppression of one to the advantage of the other. The existence of exchange and a market implies more than one person, which in turn implies a social and moral context; we cannot imagine a market without political interaction. Nineteenth-century classical economists recognized the political nature of markets and accepted the functioning of greed only to the extent that individualistic competition constrained or eliminated its evil effects. They were explicit that only when competition harnessed human greed to advance collective goals could it be given free rein.

The market is not the natural touchstone by which social progress may be judged. On the contrary, regulation and the market are natural complements. The market depends on political regulation for its definition and adequate functioning and is thus a political institution. As such it is to be judged on the basis of its performance relative to other possible political institutions. Having established this much, we should consider the benefits of markets.

To an economist the greatest benefit of a market is efficiency. Given an initial distribution of wealth as morally acceptable, competitive markets produce optimal quantities of all goods and services, optimal in the sense that no slack exists and one individual or group can be made better off only at the expense of some others. If scarcity of goods and services is an important constraint, then this property of markets is important. Presumably, as social wealth increases – as scarcity diminishes – the appeal of efficiency diminishes somewhat.

A second benefit, related to the idea of efficiency but not identical to it, is that competitive markets have a ring of natural justice to them. An alternative way of stating the efficiency property is that the competitive price of any good exactly equals the cost (more precisely the marginal cost) of its production. One must pay into the system (in the price paid for a good or service) exactly the sacrifice imposed on society (the marginal cost) to produce what one takes out of the system. This argument gains moral appeal as individuals are removed from the margin of subsistence, so that material demands are less pressing. The moral claim of markets to justness is not absolute, but it is sufficiently compelling to have attracted those socialists, such as Oskar Lange, who a half-century ago interested themselves in optimal pricing for a socialist economy.

A third benefit of markets is their contribution to individual dignity; markets accord independence. With a well-functioning market a productive individual can be assured of the ability to exchange his or her labour, or the fruits thereof, for the material needs he or she cannot produce. The satisfaction of one's own material needs and those of one's dependants, which are among the most coercive aspects of life, does not depend on conformity to a particular bureaucratic imperative. The anonymity of market exchange encourages employers to hire the most productive, consumers to seek the least expensive, regardless of the personal characteristics of the other party to the exchange. Hence markets can provide incentives to break down discrimination and established sources of power. Yet it must also be recognized that exploitation and discrimination of individuals by those with power is often exercised in markets.

All of these benefits require the existence of competition among individual consumers and firms. Whether industrial society conforms more or less to competitive theory is a continuing debate. Some insist that it does. Winn (1985), for example, finds evidence of considerable economic mobility among minority groups in Canada. On the other hand, the modern corporation has a hierarchical neo-feudalistic organization and executives espouse an ethos of "knowing your place"; it is clearly not atomistically competitive. Consider Newman's (1975, p. 144) statement of the "theology of free enterprise":

Adherents of the creed genuinely believe that virtue can be certified by worldly accomplishment, that success is tangible evidence of

34

holy favour. Power is no judge of values, but it acts instinctively to create order, because no order can exist without power and no power exists without order. That's why businessmen place so much emphasis on institutions and hierarchies in which people know and keep their place. It is this deeply felt faith in institutions that is at the heart of the capitalist ethic.

The economic view of markets is that competition by atomistic individuals leads to social benefit, through a continual shaking up of entrenched interest. But the "creed" emphasizes hierarchy, order, and power. Newman (1975, p. 185) characterizes "the corporate order [as] a system of private governments lacking the restraints of public accountability." In another passage a bank director notes that "no individual in Canada, to my mind, can do much without the support of the chartered banks" (Newman, 1975, p. 110). The idea of corporation as quasi-government returns us to the idea that markets develop in step with government.

What political structures will evolve, including what market structures? That is the question central to the protection of the social good and individual dignity, not whether the market of economic models will dominate, or whether the economy will be "market-oriented." None of this denies that in many circumstances the advancement of social good and individual dignity will be aided by a greater reliance on individual market transactions.

GAINS TO COLLECTIVE ACTION

I have argued that market and non-market forces can be harnessed into a creative tension, that they are not in a simple position of conflict. They place constraints on one another and define each other's range of operation. It is schizophrenic to hold that egoistic behaviour in the economic realm is invariably salutary while egoism in a political setting is invariably contrary to social welfare or individual freedom. Especially in a complicated society that respects the rule of law, the economic measure of social welfare in terms of aggregate willingness-to-pay for commodities traded by all consumers cannot provide a means to evaluate the appropriate role of governments or of markets.

Buchanan (1987, pp. 245-46), one of the founders of the public choice school of economics, notes that "the differences in the predicted results stemming from market and political interaction stem from differences in the structures of these two institutional settings rather than from any switch in the motives of persons as they move between institutional roles." Clearly the *motives* of individuals do not change; they are, after all, the same persons in both settings. But one may argue that their *choices* are expanded or restricted by the political structure within which they operate. In competitive markets it is possible to pursue nothing but one's selfish advantage. By "political interaction," to use Buchanan's expression, it is possible to change laws and institutions that can help raise society from a non-optimizing ("Cournot-Nash" in the jargon) equilibrium to a superior solution for all concerned. Improved legal sanctions, for example, may prevent or limit the emergence of non-co-operative behaviour, in the same way as the economic theory of oligopoly stresses that political sanction on behalf of a cartel's decisions aids cartel cohesion.

A mundane example is city traffic laws. Political decisions about driving on one side of the road, speed limits, traffic lights, parking, etc. increase the efficiency of the "market" of urban transportation relative to the alternative of unregulated "free competition." Admittedly, flexible, creative, non-traditional approaches might be even more useful. To continue with the traffic example, society would likely be better off without urban automobile traffic.

This implies that the legitimate role of the state is much greater than protection of the status quo through defence, police, and contract enforcement. The state is justified not solely or even mainly by efficiency. Man is the only moral, as well as the only rational, animal. Man is not only egotistical but compassionate. A minimal extension of the role of the state beyond protection of the status quo is to protect those to whom the notion of the optimality of freely negotiated contracts cannot conceivably apply because they cannot participate in a market. The government must protect children, the aged, the handicapped, and others who might die or live in misery if left to their own devices in an anarchistic market. Compassion for such individuals is where the modern welfare state begins; the capacity for collective compassion is a fundamental measure of a civilized society. Children, for example, are citizens, not "consumption goods." They enter in their own right into the "social welfare function," not just as arguments in the "utility functions" of some adults. One would not take a doll away from someone who regularly beat it; one would a child.

Once the need for collective compassion is admitted, debate over the welfare state becomes a matter of degree. It cannot be reduced to the outcome of interest group calculations – even if welfare lobbies, nurses' unions, and doctors' associations do vie for political influence at the margin. A society must collectively decide – whether explicitly or implicitly – what to do about the economic well-being of single-parent families, of those who might be ruined financially by medical expenses, of those whose market productivity collapses because technological change renders their skills obsolete, of those who suffer psychological and social debilitation from unemployment, or – to cite a controversial group – of the employable who refuse work.

Choices must be made. A totally collectivist society in which welfare state transfer payments approached 100 per cent of gross national product (GNP) would be socially stagnant, not progressive. (A professor of mine, Robert Bishop, once observed that brotherly love is a scarce resource, which must be economized in policy-making.) This is the thrust of McCallum and Blais's (1987) work. In comparison of national rates of growth of GNP among industrialized countries, they find a negative effect when transfer payments become very high. However, they find a range of attractive choice: at intermediate levels (of transfer payments relative to GNP) an increased share of transfer payments increases rates of economic growth. McCallum and Blais (1987, pp. 14ff) offer two reasons for the positive contribution, to a point.* First, the welfare state may help foster co-operation among groups by creating a climate of social consensus. Second, the guarantee of at least partial compensation may overcome the drag on economic growth exercised by politically organized groups that lose from technological and social change. While adoption of any such change may have positive net social benefits, it will almost certainly create identifiable groups of losers as well as winners. In a pluralist democracy, it is to be expected that the losers mobilize to block changes from which they stand to lose.

There is a further rationalization of these results, one that is in keeping with the historical fact that increased growth and expansion of the market have gone hand-in-hand with the development of the state. This argument has to do with the high level of risk in any market economy – the inherent uncertainty surrounding the rewards to be realized in the future from investment today. Contrary to the emphasis of much economic work, the greatest risks in our economy are borne, not by shareholders, who are in the final analysis basically "rentiers," people who receive income from property, but by *workers*. Workers' potential losses from unfavourable market events – plant closure, economic depression, rising interest rates, etc. – involve their basic livelihood, not just an accountant's assessment of their financial net worth. Unemployment to a family living primarily on the wages of its working members means not only an immediate decline in living standards, but increased family problems, psychological stresses, and lost prestige for its members in the community. The welfare

---

*The estimated optimum ratio of transfer payments to GNP is about one-sixth. This result is of some curiosity value, because it is close to the current median of the seventeen countries examined. But one hesitates to quote the particular value with too great faith: confidence limits are fairly wide.

state – especially unemployment insurance, but also other programs such as universal health care insurance – has shifted some of the economic risk facing the individual worker to the entire community. To this extent the welfare state, far from being an inefficient redistribution of income from the productive to the "lazy," actually contributes to economic efficiency.

The rhetoric of the right is to shift risk back to the individual worker: redundant workers should be fired; unemployment insurance and welfare benefits should be reduced. This is all in the name of individual responsibility and market competitiveness. But human skills are an investment; they are even called "human capital" in economists' jargon. The returns to these skills can be eliminated by events beyond the control or predictive capacity of the individual. Increasing the strength of the safety net lowers the risk of investing in "human capital" and increases the willingness of people to do so.

During the period of high unemployment in the 1980s – when the private and social opportunity costs of training were low – there developed an acute shortage of skilled workers in many sectors across the country, including my own city of Montreal. This means that either the expected return (difference between skilled and unskilled wage level) is too low or the risk in acquiring skills is too high. Human skills are fast becoming the driving element of the economy. The risk of acquiring these skills should be lowered, and the welfare state is an important means of doing so.

One further observation is that, while workers assume a good deal of market risk, they have very little role in economic decision-making. As "human capital" becomes ever more important, one can expect workers to seek an increasingly active role in economic decision-making (cf. Richards, Mauser, and Holmes, 1988). If this is achieved, and some measure of it seems inescapable, then managers – within both corporations and government – must yield a measure of their traditional managerial autonomy. Such a change would affect the nature of political institutions and, hence, the market. The desirability of such change, from the perspective of democratizing society, will be discussed below. A strong labour movement tends to strengthen a country's social programs. An increased role for labour in economic decision-making may also be desirable for reasons of efficiency. Another of McCallum and Blais's (1987) findings was that increasing unionization tends to reduce rates of economic growth, but centralizing wage bargaining damps this effect and can overcome it. In countries with centralized bargaining, policy is more apt to be formulated with meaningful input from organized labour, which in turn assumes some responsibility for policy decisions.

Here in Canada collective bargaining obviously needs an overhaul.

As measured by percentage of working time lost to strikes and lock-outs, Canada's strike rate has worsened relative to major OECD countries in the last two decades. We have exceeded Britain's rate and rank second only to Italy. Strikes are valuable and legitimate as organized labour's ultimate weapon, but they cannot serve as the basis for industrial relations. Strike action in industries serving the public harm, not employers and employees who would then have an incentive to bargain seriously, but third parties. Even in the private sector, where collective bargaining is an important institution, labour can only fight for a bigger share of an existing pie.

With proper safety nets growth may be aided by an increase in social consensus and also by institutional reforms that serve to internalize the effects of interest group actions (McCallum and Blais, 1987, p. 15). In particular, if labour has a greater role in decisions, it will internalize more the effects of its actions – both within firms and in politics. Increased labour power will have the further beneficial effect of increasing the share of employment in secure, well-paying jobs. Such institutional changes in organized labour's role may release unions from their excessive focus on decentralized collective bargaining and encourage them to be a critical force for collective advance.

Policies that increase growth of national income tend to be accepted in a secular society (Waterman, 1983, p. 380). If they also serve to redistribute income more equally, they acquire a moral force as well. How, then, do we explain the vigour of the contemporary attack on the welfare state? In the 1960s and 1970s there was admittedly naiveté on the left about the capacity of collective processes to solve all social problems. The welfare state is one of the great accomplishments of post-war industrial society, but it cannot solve all problems, such as environmental degradation, or even eliminate all poverty. From exaggerated expectations in the welfare state many have succumbed to exaggerated scepticism. Government is an easy target for frustrated hopes, and some have now developed excessive faith in the market as an institution to solve all problems.

A PERSPECTIVE ON ECONOMIC ANALYSIS

As we social democrats confront changed circumstances, we must become psychologically more accepting of the constructive role of markets in our society and not seek solely to accentuate their destructive potential. I am not suggesting we forsake scepticism of markets or abandon our commitment to collective solutions to social problems. Civilization advances by refining its institutions, including the market. Refinement of the market may be accomplished through better combinations of both regulation *and* deregulation. As circumstances change, the appropriate scope of market transactions also changes.

Many theories of mainstream economists, though sometimes presented in an ideologically biased way, are really fairly neutral. For example, social democrats have to date rejected the theory of political "markets," according to which political outcomes depend on competition among special interest groups for favourable government policy. At best, social democrats interpret the model to mean no more than a vulgarization of the traditional socialist thesis that under capitalism property-owning interest groups (or classes) exercise overwhelming political power, that political conflict can largely be reduced to conflicts between those who do and do not own property, and that appropriate strategy is to support the current claims of the latter. While I have insisted that selfish pursuit of self-interest by special interest groups does not explain all political action, it can hardly be disputed that such self-interested activity occurs – or that special interest groups allied to social democratic parties are themselves actively engaged in such behaviour.

The criticism I make of my profession is not of the theory of political markets, but of its selective application. To the extent economists saw the 1988 trade debate in interest group terms, for example, they criticized the opponents as a collection of special interest groups seeking to preserve tariffs and other market impediments that redistribute income from the Canadian consumer to themselves. If economists had truly digested the interest group theory of politics, they would be equally sceptical of proponents of the trade agreement with the United States. The managed trade arising from the "free trade" agreement simultaneously requires continual interpretation by binational regulatory agencies and limits the scope for Parliament to govern. Such a change is in the interest of major business lobbies desirous of lessening popular constraints on their actions.

I use this example to urge upon social democrats a tolerance of mainstream economics; its new developments are not ideological sophistry. This does not mean we accept the uses made of the market by particular powerful interests. But it does mean we accept the market as a legitimate constraint on the scope of politics and the size of the public sector relative to GNP.

SOME VIEWS ON POLICY

If we accept the market as a legitimate, potentially useful political institution in our society, that has implications. For example, just as uncritical advocacy of market (individual contracting) solutions to all social issues will be rejected, so, too, will uncritical reliance on political (collective) solutions. Acceptance of an inevitable individual-collective tension implies abandonment of ideological positions; we must justify any particular public policy through careful thought and argument.

What does this mean in practical terms? There can be no progress if defence of the welfare state is the only *raison d'être* of a social democratic party. It becomes quite literally a conservative force in a period of great technological and social change. It does our society little service for social democrats to stand in the way of all technological change. To the extent we succeed in blocking change, the change will simply occur in other countries, leaving Canadians with obsolete high-cost production processes and lower living standards that can only be preserved by recourse to ever-increasing protection. Social democrats have the obligation to propose policy to manage change.

A first principle for any social democratic government is that the costs of innovation not be borne by particular groups of workers whose skills are rendered obsolete by technological change and who are thrown out of work. It must be widely accepted that such costs are to be borne by society as a whole, in other words, by those who gain the benefits through better goods and services at lower prices or through new jobs elsewhere in the economy. Were this principle fully accepted – and among most economists it is a subject for the appendix to the treatise on gains from free trade – unions would not automatically resist technological change as equivalent to job loss. It is a principle that enhances both the efficiency of the economy and the dignity of workers.

Such a principle may ultimately be endorsed even by the present governing party. The sharp and broadly based dislocations that the Canada-U.S. trade agreement will bring, to some sectors at least, may force even the Conservatives to come to grips with this problem. Social democrats must go further than this first principle. A second principle is a greater degree of worker involvement in the decision-making of their own firms. We cannot foresee the future, but this surely is the most obvious way in which individuals can attain a greater degree of control over their lives. It promotes democracy in the broadest sense of popular participation in the making of decisions. Richards et al. (1988) found that the majority of workers wanted greater control over their own working environments, especially over decisions affecting them directly, such as scheduling of work and holidays. These findings, as the authors point out, are not definitive, but they are in agreement with any social democrat's intuition. The idea of worker input will advance slowly – in the thinking of social democrats as well as that of conservatives – and at this personal level the process may make its most significant start.

In the promotion of democracy at the workplace, a social democratic government could aim for 25-30 per cent worker representation on "mundane" decision-making bodies; the percentage and scope of worker-influenced decisions could then possibly increase over time. Nonetheless, a quarter is a sufficiently significant minority position for collective worker actions to place limits on the vagaries of marketplace forces; it would be consonant with promoting the dignity of the individual and the benefit of society as a whole. Presumably worker representatives on such bodies would remain part of the work force; worker participation in management should not become a paternalistic method of individual career advancement.

While collective bargaining is a valuable institution that has in the past advanced democracy at work, further advances require that unions go beyond it. Union leaders must show an enlightened concern for broad social issues, which, I suspect, occupy them less now than in the beginnings of industrial unionism. For union leaders to interest themselves in broad issues of policy requires no great theoretical leaps; it would be a worthwhile, achievable goal.

Technological change is one field needing practical social democratic policy; another is government regulation of business. What should be our response to the deregulation debate? Consider four industries: telecommunications, airlines, electrical utilities, and trucking.

It is simply not acceptable that deregulation and recourse to market forces raise the price of basic telephone service to the point of a significant reduction in the percentage of telephone subscribers in any community. Telephone service has strong implications for social cohesiveness and individual ability to interact with others in the society. By the same token, uncritical defence of regulatory imposition of "flat rates" for local service is not defensible. Such a policy amounts to subsidy by those who need a telephone of those who, for example, use local telecommunication facilities for data transmission or telephone solicitation. Social goals may best be protected in this case by rates that approximate social costs.

Airline fare deregulation also has been very controversial on the left. There are now many people with very price-sensitive demand for airline services, whereas there were not in the early days of air travel when financial viability of commercial airlines was uncertain in the face of thin demand. As the industry matured, over-regulation led to higher-than-necessary average fares and underutilization of capacity. There is little public policy justification to support regulation that limits the travel options of a price-sensitive public in order to provide empty seats on which businessmen may spread their newspapers. None of this eliminates the justification for regulation of safety standards.

Uniform pricing of electricity at all hours of the day leads to substantial inefficiencies. Particularly in hydroelectric systems, the fixed capital costs (dams, generators, distribution grids) far exceed the operating costs that vary with electrical consumption. The cost of providing for growing peak demand includes both the capacity and operating costs; the cost of off-peak demand is operating costs only. Uniform pricing encourages wasteful peak demand, discourages use at off-peak hours, and requires investment by provincial utilities in capital-intensive capacity that need not be installed. Canadian electrical utilities are typically Crown corporations and hence public investment is being diverted from more socially constructive uses such as health and education toward hydroelectric dams. Yet, proposals for regulatory reform to adopt marginal cost time-of-day pricing are met with distrust on the part of social democrats.

On the other hand, some industries could be rendered more efficient by more regulation. Abouchar (1987) argues that heavy trucks cause far more damage to highways than their fuel and other taxes cover, not to mention their contribution to such externalities as congestion, air pollution, and traffic accidents. In this case, increased regulation and taxation could induce some transport to be diverted from truck to train and could contribute to an improved transportation system. The issues are complex: other regulations, such as those preventing back-hauling by trucks, clearly do not contribute to an efficient system.

In summary, as technological and social conditions change, so, too, must regulation. This conclusion follows from the public policy purpose of regulation – which is to protect the social good and individual dignity. A refusal to allow for reform, like a refusal to allow for regulation, must eventually be inimical to these goals.

A third institution needing attention by social democrats is the Crown corporation. I do not automatically advocate the establishment of new Crown corporations, or the maintenance of existing Crown corporations, or the privatization of them, except on reasoned public policy grounds. There are many reasons for establishing Crown corporations, but they do not imply the abandonment of markets. In Canada we have a tradition of Crown corporations competing in markets with private enterprises. Each form of organization has advantages and disadvantages, and competition between forms has had generally beneficial results. There is no reason not to extend this competition further. Competing Crown corporations could be set up in the same industry but report to different ministers or even to different levels of government. The discipline of market forces could be an important means to make these corporations more accountable to government.

Beyond this, I think it worth re-emphasizing that institutions should be developed so that labour has a role in decision-making. Decisions cannot be left to management and shareholders whose risk is frequently minimal. We cannot tolerate markets in which workers can be made "redundant" by technological change and simply jettisoned – as Canada Post has repeatedly tried to do. This means more than social safety nets, even though these must remain strong and safe from political attack. On the other hand, work incentives also need to be retained. And there must be a greater acceptance of change – with democratic participation in business decisions.

All this requires flexibility. And flexibility means a scepticism toward bureaucratic modes of thought. Regulation and publicly owned firms have many virtues, but they should be recognized as being most useful in periods of stability. In periods of rapid techno-logical and social change, looser forms of social control must be accepted. This looser control, however, should include internal worker participation in management decisions. Indeed, if such partic-ipation can be achieved, then such currently popular regulations (in social democratic circles) as laws restricting plant closures may be counter-productive. If labour participates effectively in major corpo-rate decisions regarding the opening of new plants and the closing of old ones, then such decisions will only be made where workers losing jobs are adequately compensated. The economy will be able to divest redundant inefficient industries with less (and internalized) disloca-tion. Supporting redundant industry ceases to be a drain on funds destined to finance social safety nets and ceases to impair the growth of other industry. For example, Canada Post, an arm of government, and its unions have an opportunity to formulate new approaches to worker displacement arising from technological change. It is a failure of the government *and* of the institution of collective bargaining that Crown corporations are not generating experiments in dealing with this problem.

Canadian society needs flexibility, economic agility, security of "human capital," and imaginative government. Although the market provides a constraint to our advancing collective ties, we need to find ways to help make markets work better. Maturity of social demo-cratic thought requires that we learn to live with the tension between market and state, not seek to eliminate it.

REFERENCES

Abouchar, A. (1987). Presentation to Canadian Economic Theory Confer-ence, Montreal (June).

Armstrong, C., and V. Nelles (1986). *Monopoly's Moment*. Philadelphia: Tem-ple University Press.

Buchanan, J. (1987). "The Constitution of Economic Policy," *American Economic Review*, LXXVII, 3 (June), pp. 243-50.

McCallum, J., and A. Blais (1987). "Government, Special Interest Groups and Economic Growth," *Public Choice*, 54, pp. 3-18.

Myrhman, J. (1985). "Introduction: Reflections on the Growth of Government," *Journal of Public Economics*, 28, pp. 275-85.

Newman, P.C. (1975). *The Canadian Establishment*, Vol. I. Toronto: McClelland and Stewart.

North, D.C. (1985). "The Growth of Government in the United States: An Economic Historian's Perspective," *Journal of Public Economics*, 28, pp. 383-99.

Richards, J.G., G. Mauser, and R. Holmes (1988). "What do Workers Want? Attitudes Toward Collective Bargaining and Participation in Management," *Relations Industrielles*, XLIV, 1, pp. 133-52.

Waterman, A.C. (1983). "The Catholic Bishops and Canadian Public Policy," *Canadian Public Policy*, IX, 3 (September), pp. 374-82.

Winn, C. (1985). "Affirmative Action and Visible Minorities: Eight Premises in Quest of Evidence," *Canadian Public Policy*, XI, 4 (December), pp. 684-700.

3 The Social Democratic Challenge: To Manage Both Distribution and Production

IN THIS ESSAY I SHALL ATTEMPT TO PUT INTO ORDER SOME OF MY EXPERI-ences as a practising politician and give my sense of what should be our aims as a political movement in the next ten to twenty years. But it is not helpful to pose grand questions about our aims in a utopian vacuum. Let me begin with a brief summary of what I conclude to be our accomplishments as social democrats in Canada.

In the last fifty years we have concentrated primarily on distributive justice. It is true that the Regina Manifesto in 1933, the Winnipeg Declaration of Principles in 1956, and the statements prepared prior to the founding of the New Democratic Party in 1961 all spoke of the need for change in the structure of the economy. They addressed the need for planning, a role for public ownership, and much more. We have these ideas on paper. But when we look at the actual policies of NDP governments, or the themes publicly stressed by NDP politicians in opposition, the emphasis has consistently been on how wealth and power are *distributed* rather than on how they are *produced*.

"From each according to his ability, to each according to his need" is a slogan I have used; "humanity first" and "fair shares for all in a free society" are two others. These are rallying calls that primarily address distributive justice. Not all is clear cut. For example, in Saskatchewan we limited potash investment during the boom years of the late 1970s in an attempt to dampen the inefficient boom-bust cycles that have been the curse of potash and many other resource industries in western Canada. But, overall, the basic tendency has undeniably been to emphasize equity of distribution over efficiency of production.

By "fair shares for all" I have meant not only fair shares of income and wealth but also, I want to emphasize, fair shares of power – a fair distribution of the power to make decisions that affect our lives. Nineteenth-century liberal economic theory called for free markets: one dollar/one vote, with every dollar having the same weight. The majority, with only a few dollars,were never as enthusiastic about this theory as the minority with many dollars. And the majority demanded change. Out of this fundamental and radical demand have grown multiple variations on the social democratic theme whereby governments, chosen on the principle of one person/one vote, significantly modify the operation of a market economy. The economy has, however, continued to be largely market-directed in the sense that private market agents have dictated most production decisions. Government has used taxation and social welfare policies primarily to redistribute income.

There has been some recourse to government ownership in Canada, which I want to recall in order to give historical perspective. It has occurred mainly in the field of utilities, transportation, and social services. Nationally, we have publicly owned railroads, ferries, and airlines; provincially, we have publicly owned electrical, telephone, and natural gas utilities and hospital and educational facilities. In some provinces, such as Saskatchewan, public ownership has been important in the insurance sector. There has been some limited public ownership in basic industrial activities beyond those already mentioned: for example, Crown production in Saskatchewan of sodium sulphate, bricks and tiles, lumber, oil and gas, potash, hard-rock minerals, and pulp. At the federal level, the government has established an integrated oil and gas company, mined uranium and developed nuclear reactors, and created an investment holding company.

Where we have seen public ownership of commercial assets, the goal of economic efficiency has often been secondary to the goal of redistributing income. The Saskatchewan government acquired 40 per cent of the provincial potash industry, for example, not because we expected to operate the existing mines more efficiently but because we, as a cabinet, concluded in 1975 that we had exhausted the potential of taxation to redistribute revenue from the mining companies to Saskatchewan citizens – the ultimate owners of the Crown-owned potash reserves being exploited.

I mentioned the slogan "fair shares for all in a free society." The public demand for a "free society" has led in Canada to laws to aid union organization and to establish human rights commissions, legal aid for the poor, and ombudsmen to champion the citizen against state bureaucracy. I do not intend to trace the history of these innovations in Canada. I want, however, to emphasize this important historical trend.

In the 1930s, the United States under Roosevelt's "New Deal" was clearly ahead of Canada in social policy. To cite just two examples, the United States introduced social security legislation that was more comprehensive than Canada's, and the 1935 Wagner Act gave American unions a legislative base far stronger than that enjoyed by Canadian unions at the time. The post-war trend in Canadian social policy, however, has enabled Canada not only to catch up but become a more egalitarian society than is the United States. This post-war trend owes much, I would argue, to the work of democratic socialists. Some of the innovations are direct programs of social democratic provincial governments. Saskatchewan's universal hospital and medical care insurance programs are the most obvious examples. Some are pre-emptive policies by "old-line" governments warding off the NDP. Finally, some are the result of senior social democratic planners who have wielded influence within non-NDP governments. An example of such influence is Tom Shoyama, who began his career in the Economic Planning Board in Regina and ended it as deputy minister of finance in Ottawa. He played a major role in the creation of Petro-Canada as a federal Crown corporation in the 1970s.

"Democratic socialist" is too strong a term to describe post-war policy changes in Canada. These changes clearly have not uprooted capitalist market relations. But, however they are described, their cumulative impact has been to transform Canada into a "mixed economy" with a good – if far from perfect – welfare state. What Canadian social democrats have achieved in the past is, thus, far from insignificant.

I turn now to a different set of questions. What must we advocate for the future? What is democratic socialism in the 1990s? And, when given the opportunity to govern, what must be our practical agenda?

First, we need to defend past accomplishments. Even if they are no longer sufficient under changed circumstances, they were real accomplishments in their time. But circumstances have fundamentally changed in the Western industrial economies. The international competitive position of many industries in these economies has been eroded in the last two decades. Rather than "erosion" to describe industries threatened by international competition, it might be more accurate to use the image of a runner who used to be unquestionably the fastest but who has not improved her "personal best" in recent years while her competitors have.

In Western Europe and North America the sustained economic growth during the quarter century following World War Two (1945-70) enabled a social compromise to develop whereby profits, wages, and social spending by government all rose together. Most politicians and businessmen – not only social democrats and union leaders – recognized that sustained growth of industrial output and profits

48

required sustained growth of consumption by the majority of working people. With varying degrees of subtlety and conviction, we were all Keynesians until the end of the 1960s, and we all accepted this social contract.

One changed circumstance since 1970 is apparent at the political level with the resurgence of conservative political ideology. Conservative ideologues from Milton Friedman to Margaret Thatcher have denied the ability of government to sustain full employment at stable prices via economic policy measures, or to better the lot of the poor or average-income citizen. In their passionate critique of the inadequacies of the post-war welfare state – and it does have inadequacies – conservatives forget or minimize the inadequacies of the interwar economy. They believe that you can dispense with unions and so lower wages, that you can impose tight fiscal restraints, and that you can effectively control inflation merely by restricting the money supply – all this with only minor disruptions to aggregate demand and employment.

By the late 1970s the central bankers and political leaders of many of the Western industrial countries, including the United States, Britain, and Canada, had committed themselves to "monetarist" theories of inflation. They succeeded in restricting credit and ultimately did lower inflation, but at a terrible cost in terms of unemployment and lost incomes. The one benefit of the economic depression of the early 1980s has been to discredit the more extreme conservative ideologues.

A second post-1970 change, this one economic, is the emergence of successful new industrial countries. The Japanese are the obvious example of a people who have dramatically improved the relative industrial capacity of their economy. Other examples are South Korea, Hong Kong, Thailand, Taiwan, and Brazil. One consequence is that many millions of lower-skilled manufacturing jobs have already shifted from Western industrial countries to these newly emerging industrial economies – and many more millions of jobs will shift in the near future.

These new industrial economies have created important problems of industrial adjustment for Western economies. If these countries enjoyed social contracts similar to those in the West, their domestic profits, wages, and government social spending could all rise together. The problem posed in the West by their export-led industrial growth would be less acute because they would have created larger domestic markets. By way of example, not enough Koreans are able to buy Korean cars. For a variety of reasons – including the need to export to earn foreign exchange to repay foreign debt – these countries have maintained artificially low-wage economies. Some have used authoritarian political measures to suppress unions. The result is export-oriented industrialization dependent for its success on the ability to displace higher-wage and higher-cost producers in Western industrial countries.

This is one reason – not the only reason but a major one – why Canadian manufacturing faces an uncertain future.

In theory there are three options we can choose politically in response to increased international competition. The three are not mutually exclusive.

One, we can raise tariffs and other trade barriers to protect our mass manufacturing industries, either within Canada alone or as part of a "Fortress North America" trading block. Two, we can gradually phase out our low-skill manufacturing industries in favour of the "knowledge industries" where we can sustain a comparative advantage. Three, we can assist Third World countries to develop internal markets by relieving them of foreign debt, by discouraging their governments from military expenditures, by promoting more equitable income distribution within their countries, etc.

Politics is not a set of simple intellectual choices, and Canada will doubtless pursue some combination of the three options. Deciding the relative weight that should be placed on each is a tough test for social democrats.

We can all agree on the desirability of the third. By all means, let us assist Third World countries to develop internal markets – to create more wealth and consume it.

But, even if we can assure full employment in Canada, deciding the balance between protectionism and phasing out existing low-productivity industries is going to pose a continuing test for us. (What precisely we mean by full employment is an interesting question. We can worry about it when unemployment falls below 4 per cent.)

At this point I want to state a thesis, not merely to analyse options. What do I think social democrats should advocate? I want Canada to minimize reliance on the protectionist option. Social democrats must guard against a mindless defence of all existing manufacturing jobs. Only the switch to new knowledge-based industries can assure in the long run that Canadians enjoy incomes comparable to those in other Western industrial countries, and at the same time allow developing countries a place in the sun. Their place in the sun for the next several decades will be defined by their ability to export manufactured goods embodying relatively low labour skills.

We Canadians need a more positive attitude toward technological change – the getting rid of obsolete technologies – even when it means factory closures. Having said that, I am not content to leave the process of technological change to blind market forces. Although the adoption of new technology may well create *net* social benefits, it inevitably creates losers as well as winners. As socialists concerned with distributional equity, we must create a safety net for the losers. For example, the adjustment costs of displaced employees with obsolete skills cannot be left for them alone to bear. Nor should we expect communities threatened with major job losses to face adjustment unaided.

To let the market determine the losses from technological change is to turn workers into players at a roulette table, unable to predict the long-term benefits and costs of their career choice. Not only is such a system unjust; in the long run it is inefficient. It encourages employers, employees, and whole communities to act as conservative lobbies opposed to the adoption of new technology. A key to any democratic socialist response is to spread the cost of technological innovation, to socialize the costs of making Canada internationally competitive. Only by creating confident expectations among Canadians that the "losers" will be fairly compensated can we have popular support for technical change, and only then can governments reduce the pressure to subsidize and protect the status quo.

Nor is it enough that we cushion the phasing out of non-competitive industries. We will need to promote emerging world-competitive knowledge-based industries, and train and retrain the people who will make them successful. This demands a massive commitment to a broadly based, universally accessible education system, unconstrained by an individual's wealth or position in society.

I refrain from elaborating it in detail, but I subscribe to the "truncated firm" argument about the problems posed to Canada by a branch-plant economy. Basically the argument is as follows. Look around at the major firms engaged in international trade – from Olivetti to Phillips, from Volvo to Toyota, from IBM to Northern Telecom – and you will find that most of the basic research and product development of these firms takes place in their respective home countries. This R&D activity is fundamental to generating high-wage employment in these countries. I spare you any further development of my concerns about Canada's dependence on foreign equity investment, but I want to underline that the fostering of Canadian-owned firms is necessary to the strategy of switching to knowledge-based industries.

As part of a program for promoting technological change, I advocate a multilateral trade strategy of the kind Canada has pursued through GATT with great success for forty years. I believe we can pursue a multilateral trade strategy of relatively free international trade and simultaneously pursue a domestic "industrial strategy" that allows a significant range of freedom for government intervention. Certainly, many of the Western European countries have successfully combined the two.

In summary, I want an industrial strategy that phases out lower-skill manufacturing industries and emphasizes the growth of higher-skill knowledge-based industries. None of this eliminates the need for traditional Keynesian fiscal and monetary policies to deal with unemployment. But the difficulties of France – with a larger, relatively less open economy than that of Canada – in the early 1980s demonstrates the difficulties of "Keynes in one country." The French Socialists, upon coming to power in 1981, nobly attempted to resist international economic depression by fiscal stimulus. France experienced a severe balance-of-payments crisis and large government deficits, and ultimately the Socialists adopted a fiscally more conservative stance. I do not believe, in a relatively free trading environment, that we can achieve full employment using only fiscal and monetary policies. Resort to wholesale protectionism – while it might ease the problem of assuring full employment – comes at too high a price in terms of lower living standards for Canadians.

The trade strategy I am advocating is, I think, straightforward, but I do not underestimate the difficulty of its implementation. Machiavelli tells us: "there is nothing more difficult to take in hand, more perilous to conduct or more uncertain in its success than to take a lead in the introduction of a new order of things." First, the Canada-U.S. trade agreement poses a number of potential constraints on the freedom of action by Canadian governments. Second, I am basically calling for a fundamental change in the relationships among the trade union movement, government, and business.

Difficult or not, the alternatives are even less appealing. The radical right would allow the market to dictate technological transition. This I reject. The social carnage of such laissez-faire can be seen in American steel towns or in cities of the north of England. Mindless traditionalists would protect all, or almost all, present manufacturing jobs. Canadian costs would steadily rise vis-à-vis world costs. The level of Canadian tariffs required would attract retaliation abroad, which in turn would pit workers in export-oriented sectors against those in import-substitution sectors. We would become resource exporters and high-cost manufacturers for our small domestic market. That is not an impossible scenario, but most Canadians will reject it in the long run.

The industrial strategy I suggest obviously has affinities to the so-called "neo-corporatist" policies pursued by Sweden and other European countries. It will require far more comprehensive co-operation among governments, business, and labour than at present, and strong leadership from government. It is clearly imperative that Canadians retain for our governments – federal and provincial – the ability to lead and not render them impotent pawns of the market system, as I fear they may be under the Canada-U.S. trade agreement.

But such an industrial strategy not only requires more of governments. Canadians will have to rid themselves of their fear of trade unions playing a major role in moulding our industrial future, and trade unionists will have to lay aside their fears of assuming responsibilities beyond collective bargaining. Business managers will have to recognize the roles of both governments and labour in charting our industrial course. Public ownership will be one of the tools used, especially by provincial governments, which have fewer alternative regulatory tools available. This industrial strategy also calls for a substantial measure of federal-provincial co-operation.

I realize that some on the left will part company with me at this point. They are convinced that entrenched adversarial relations between unions and management, and between unions and government, are an inevitable feature of a capitalist economy, and that any neo-corporatist industrial strategy is impossible to undertake. Such socialists insist that joint economic planning may be a good idea, but it is just not going to work! And they may be right. Clearly, we cannot replicate the Swedish model or the Austrian model in Canada. As an aside, Canadians are fundamentally committed to the federal nature of our country, and any industrial strategy would have to engage provincial governments far more intimately than do the precedents in small, culturally homogeneous European countries.

But, I submit social democrats have learned there are limits to the ability of government to manage any complex industrial economy. We want to channel, not to eliminate, the market. If we see a major role for private firms as desirable, it is surely legitimate to ask whether we could organize the relationship between unions, business, and government in a more efficient and consultative manner.

I suppose I bring to the problem the approach of the politician addressing the public servant: "Don't tell me what won't work; tell me what will. And if no policy is a sure thing, and rarely does one policy option clearly dominate all others, give me your idea of our best bet." Were I the civil servant answering that request from my political master – in my career I have found myself both answering and giving such requests – I would say: "Well, there's certainly no guarantee of success, but setting out economic goals and strategies jointly is our best bet." And that is what I am suggesting for Canadian socialists. It is a major undertaking in which we will never achieve total success, but a social democratic government in Ottawa, supported by at least some provincial governments, could, I believe, realize substantial success. I emphasize the need in such a venture for trade union support.

Let me speculate on the two political prerequisites for any new social democratic economic policy.

First, the federal government must achieve a better fiscal balance; persistent large deficits over all phases of the business cycle must be ended. No federal government can exercise economic leadership when it is forced to devote an ever greater proportion of its tax revenues, and of the country's national income, to debt servicing. In the 1960s public debt charges were, on average, 2 per cent of gross domestic product. By the 1988-89 fiscal year that ratio had risen to 5.5 per cent, and Ottawa was spending one dollar of every four on interest payments. The servicing of the growing accumulated deficits represents a huge annual transfer of income from wage and salary earners, from whom most taxes are collected, to the owners of government securities. There is some overlap between wage and salary earners and owners of securities, but overall this is a regressive transfer that moves us further from our goal of "fair shares for all." If huge deficits persist, the problem will, perforce, be dealt with by allowing inflation to reduce the debt burden. Such a policy-by-default would transfer wealth from those who own fixed securities – including pensions and life insurance – to those who own real estate and corporate shares. Again, this is a transfer that moves us away from "fair shares for all."

In summary, a policy of fiscal prudence is required for three reasons. The first is to allow the possibility of a more egalitarian tax and expenditure system. The second is to permit some reallocation of government expenditures toward programs that encourage knowledge-based industries and shelter the "losers" during transition. And lastly, fiscal prudence will lower or eliminate the need to use private Canadian savings to finance government. If the government has no deficit to finance, it is not "crowding out" private investors. New investment will, hopefully, increase and thereby improve Canada's international competitiveness and the share of economic assets owned by Canadians.

The second political prerequisite for a social democratic economic policy is commitment to high employment, labour mobility, and labour training and retraining. Without this commitment it will be impossible to enlist management, labour, and provincial governments in the definition and pursuit of economic objectives.

For those who believe effective joint planning too visionary, I point to the tradition within the province of Quebec of joint economic consultation. As a modest example, unions, employer associations, and co-operatives organized in November, 1989, a major "Forum sur l'Emploi." The new entrepreneurial class in Quebec has matured in the context of business-government co-operation, with some modest involvement of organized labour. With much broader labour and citizen involvement in shaping the objectives and in sharing the fruits

54

of success, democratic socialists could build on this consultative tradition.

None of this is meant to ignore other important values. Shaping an environmentally protective economy is clearly important. When I speak of "fair shares for all," I mean not only sharing fairly among the living but also with future generations. Fortunately, a transition from a goods-producing economy to one with greater reliance on knowledge-based industries need not put extra stress on the environment. Indeed, it may reduce the stress.

These speculations are far from a blueprint for action. They do, however, suggest strategies that simultaneously address our goals for a productive economy and our commitment to a sharing and compassionate society.

In conclusion, let me summarize. Democratic socialism in the 1990s will continue to emphasize "fair shares for all." "Welfare socialism" has not run its course. Implementing a fairer tax system and repairing the ravages of right-wing wrecking crews, who have governed provinces such as Saskatchewan, will continue to provide urgent tasks.

Democratic socialism will continue to emphasize a free society. Groups representing the disadvantaged will continue to need the aid of government so that many muted voices are heard, speaking from positions of strength to government and to other interest groups in society. All governments – including socialist governments – need external watchdogs and advocates for change. Clearly, it should be a policy of government to finance advocacy groups, which then turn around and hammer the hand that fed them. That is good social policy.

Democratic socialists will continue to recognize that life is not solely a matter of our daily bread. We will therefore continue to champion the needs of Canadians acting through their governments to protect our environment, encourage opportunities for cultural expression, assist developing countries, and play our full role in enhancing the prospects for lasting peace.

These distributional goals for an equitable society I take as given among democratic socialists. The hard new thinking required of us is our answer to two questions. How do we make Canada internationally competitive, receptive to imports from developing countries, and do this without savaging Canadian working people? How do we offer all Canadians greater opportunities to participate in a rapidly changing – sometimes threatening but certainly exciting – Canadian economy?

H E N R Y   M I L N E R

4

What Canadian Social Democrats Need To Know about Sweden, and Why

INTRODUCTION

This essay is intended for those who care about social equality in this country and want to do something lasting about it – even if it means dirtying their hands in muddy political waters. I mean to be provocative; I have little interest in social democracy as after-dinner conversation. The point, said Marx, is to change the world, not just to interpret it. Ironically, Marxism, which indirectly has a major influence on contemporary Canadian social democratic thinking, has inhibited Canadian social democrats from changing the world! Now that Marxist-inspired socialism has proven itself so dramatic a failure in Eastern Europe and the Soviet Union, we can turn to the building of a socialist vision free of Marxist baggage.

What I intend to argue is that the most relevant example of building a workable socialism without Marxism is what the Swedes did long ago – as have others in northern Europe. The post-war British left has been unable or unwilling to pull it off (see Jenkins, 1988). Here in Canada we have never tried, except – partially and fleetingly – in the Prairies and Quebec.

It is consistent with their world view for Marxists to reject the Swedish approach to politics. It violates the fundamental tenet of their credo that class interests are irreconcilable. Many in and around the NDP, who perceive themselves as anything but Marxists, implicitly accept this Marxist tenet about class irreconcilability and have failed to pursue, or even really to examine, the social democratic alternative. The essence of a social democratic – as distinct from a Marxist – credo is faith that a principled reconciliation of classes is feasible or, in other words, that collective political activity can achieve an acceptable degree of equality without seeking to eliminate private employers who hire salaried workers and who exchange goods and services in markets.

While Canadian social democrats express superficial admiration for Swedish accomplishments, they make little effort to understand how they came about. They leave their followers with the impression that the Swedish approach is inapplicable to Canada. Attentive Canadians are likely to see and hear repeated comparisons to Sweden, in which Canada invariably comes out the worse. Yet, if they look for analysis, it is available only from the right or the Marxist left (e.g., Gill, 1989), both of which have their own separate reasons for dismissing the Swedish "model." In dismissing the relevance of Swedish experience to Canada, Canadian socialists are in effect dismissing social democracy.

This is not a play on words. Social democracy means democratic egalitarianism. The levels of economic productivity, equality at work, and social guarantees achieved by the Swedes are the best Canadians can hope to achieve for a long way down the road. To realize that this is so, Canadian socialists should leave their academic lecture halls, put down their union songbooks, and look at the day-to-day lives of "ordinary" (to use the NDP's favourite adjective) Swedes. Socialism cannot be based on utopian theories of the perfect man, nor on the peaks of worker solidarity achieved at moments of social activism. Scandinavian achievements in combining egalitarian communal goals with a respect for individual liberty, and the pragmatic pursuit of economic self-interest by workers and owners within private firms, cannot be dismissed. Quite the opposite, they force us to look at our very notion of change, of melding theory and practice.

Ironically, it is the Marxists with their utopian agenda who are often cited to prove that social democracy is unrealistic and inapplicable to Canada. In dismissing the "fallacy" of the "exportability" to Canada of European systems based on social partnership, Stephen Brooks (1989, pp. 234-35) in his introductory public policy textbook approvingly cites Leo Panitch, a Marxist. Reportedly, Panitch was also influential in the Macdonald Commission's refusal to consider such approaches seriously. In light of the immense changes under way in Europe – dismantling command economies in the East, planning economic integration in the West – it is surely absurd for us as social democrats to accept uncritically the negative opinion of Marxists and conservatives on the "exportability" of what is, undeniably, the most successful of social democratic societies.

In a democratic society, lasting changes that substantially improve the lives of ordinary people can come only as the result of gradual, consensual choices. There are no shortcuts to social democracy.

Human beings are the object of social democratic goals, but also their subject. Social democratic reforms can achieve their intended egalitarian effects only if complemented by carefully considered, freely made individual choices. At best, winning political power is a step in this direction.

At the level of national politics Canadian socialists have never given much attention to the day-to-day requirements of a social democratic society. One such requirement is the need to pay for generous social programs and income redistribution. In order to gain (probably fleeting) popular approval, NDPers gleefully jumped on the bandwagon against the federal goods and services tax (GST), giving little heed to the dangers of fomenting a tax revolt that erodes popular willingness to fund redistributive programs. It is essential to criticize the Conservatives for unfair tax policies, such as tax-free capital gains for the rich. But what is a "fair" alternative to the GST? Most industrial countries – including social democratic regimes in Scandinavia – impose broad sales taxes (usually described as "value added taxes") like the GST. With few exceptions, left-wing answers to this question remain a vague footnote to the attack.*

I am not asking for self-delusion with regard to social democracy; it, too, deserves critical assessment. But before we criticize, the least we can do is devote some creative talent to thinking about social democratic institutions. One shudders at how many fine minds and idealistic impulses have been deflected by contemporary Marxism from the practical work of identifying the strategic reforms for advancing society toward socialist goals.

---

*When it is fully in place, in 1992-93, the federal government expects to capture $21.9 billion annually from the GST (Wilson, 1990, p. 135). Subtracting the enhanced GST-tax credit for low-income earners, $1.3 billion annually, leaves net revenue of $20.6 billion. What are the alternatives? We could preserve the current manufacturers' sales tax, which will preserve an estimated $20.4 billion in annual revenue. But everyone agrees the present sales tax is more inequitable and induces more distortions than the proposed GST. Theoretically, we could increase personal and corporate income taxes. But the required increases would be astronomical and politically impossible to impose. To realize an additional $20.6 billion from higher personal income taxes would require they rise by a third. To realize an additional $20.6 billion from corporate income taxes would require them to rise one and a half times! If we could generate a social consensus – which the Conservatives are incapable of doing – to balance the budget and pay for our social policies, Canadians would enjoy a significant indirect benefit. Investors would have less fear of inflation and the Bank of Canada would have no excuse to pursue a high interest rate policy. This, in turn, would lower the cost of servicing the public debt, which currently absorbs twenty-five cents of every dollar of Ottawa's expenditure.

CLEARING THE UNDERBRUSH

There is a lot of underbrush to clear away if we are ever to harvest a good crop. We social democrats need freshly cleared intellectual land. We cannot find it in the jargon-filled, convoluted prose of academic Marxist writing, nor in slogan-filled NDP resolution books. We need to work toward the 1990 equivalent of the Regina Manifesto as if there were no NDP candidates to elect, no CLC bureaucrats to reconcile, no feminist, ecological, or other progressive interest group to appease with the correct choice of language. Can we get our strategy out from under our sacred cows?

Our ideals remain those of 1933 when the Regina Manifesto was adopted. But we hopefully have learned not only about the murderous aberration of "actually existing socialism" that was Stalin, but also about the everyday grey frustrations of life under Brezhnev, Jaruzelski, Honecker, and all the rest. In our modest Canadian way, we need to be as ruthless in exploring new ideas as are contemporary Soviets in debating new political and economic options for their country. (For surveys of contemporary Soviet debates, see Åslund, 1989; Nove, 1989.)

Whether in Eastern Europe or Canada, we now know that central planners cannot manage successfully a complex industrial economy. We now know that, even if democratically elected socialist govern-ments could appoint the most unselfish and competent economic managers imaginable, they would in the long run lower our living standard if they attempted the wholesale substitution of political criteria for profit maximization by privately owned firms based on market prices. *Private ownership can take many forms.* In many industries, worker collectives and co-operatives may be more efficient than shareholder-owned firms; and unions can enhance the productivity of shareholder-owned companies. The lesson that we have learned since 1933 is that, subject to important exceptions (collectively known as "market failures" in economics texts), the aggregate wealth of the community is maximized when firms obey the basic rules of markets. Whatever the form of ownership, the managers of firms should seek to maximize profit based on market prices for the prod-ucts produced and for the factors of production, including labour. In turn, the basis for market prices must be the equating of supply and demand in markets where buyers can select among alternate sellers. New firms must be able to enter an industry and – with public aid for the transition – inefficient firms must be allowed to go bankrupt.

We on the left do not need to be convinced of the limits of markets. What is harder for us to accept are the fundamental limits of a planned economy. To paraphrase Sir Winston Churchill's assessment of democracy, individual firms competing in markets may be the worst means of organizing economic activity – except for the alternatives.

Realizing the productive potential of modern industry requires that each firm undertake thousands of discrete managerial decisions with respect to hiring and firing of workers, buying inputs, investing in plant and equipment, etc. Inescapably, many of these decisions entail socially difficult choices; others entail uncertainty with respect to their outcome. Under any economic system, firing workers is a tough decision. While laying off workers may increase productivity, it violates the natural sense of community among workers. However, if firms avoid the issue of productivity and they overstaff, aggregate productivity in the economy obviously suffers. The decision to buy an expensive piece of equipment generates a current cost and may generate no net financial benefits if the future fails to conform to expectations. Again, no economic system can escape costly decisions under conditions of uncertainty, and everyone will – with hindsight – regret some of them.

The authors of the Regina Manifesto entertained unabashed enthusiasm for central planning as the panacea for the woes of capitalist depression. As did far too many on the left in the 1930s, they uncritically hailed the successes of five-year plans in the Soviet Union. They were prescient in insisting that macroeconomic planning was essential to counter instability of aggregate demand. They also realized planning to be necessary to address economic problems where markets, even under ideal conditions, would perform badly – problems such as pollution, the provision of services like education and health, or the organization of industrial research.

But as the twentieth century draws to a close, social democrats must unambiguously understand that well-functioning markets are necessary to realize a productive industrial economy. In general, firms will not make the painful decisions required to realize a productive economy unless their owners face a "hard" financial constraint that forces the firm – be it a humble farm or a large corporation – to bear the financial consequences of decisions made. I repeat, once again, that the owners of the firm need not be financial investors. They may also be workers within the firm or the firm's customers, as with consumer co-operatives.

No centrally planned economy has succeeded in forcing its state-owned firms to respect "hard" financial constraints. Even in countries such as Hungary, where the Communist government abandoned centrally imposed quotas and introduced a significant measure of market discipline on all state-owned firms, the financial constraints remained "soft." Firm managers could, if necessary, obtain subsidies from the state in order to balance accounts. Firms did not go bankrupt; very few new firms succeeded in competing with existing firms. In the case of traditional centrally planned economies, firms too frequently meet their quotas by lowering quality; markets do not function to impose a financial penalty for such behaviour (see Kornai, 1986; Brus and Laski, 1989).

Even with modern computers and the best of intentions, central planners cannot hope to substitute their decisions for those of managers in the field. In order to render the financial constraints on managers "hard," there is unfortunately no substitute for an economy based on firms exchanging goods and services in markets at prices negotiated voluntarily. These firms will realize financial profits when they are efficient and losses – even bankruptcy – when they are inefficient. Price competition among firms, supplemented by some discretionary regulation and progressive taxation, can be relied on to check excess profitability.

An elected social democratic government could proceed to socialize the means of production nonetheless, hoping to persuade the people that there would be no sacrifice in productivity or that any loss of productivity would be worth it because of other achievements, such as greater equality of income. But we know that we would soon face electoral defeat and have our policies reversed – unless, of course, we made sure the people only heard what we had to tell them and could vote only for approved candidates. As social *democrats*, we reject this scenario in advance.

In ruling out major socialization, we evidently do not embrace the neo-conservative objective of the minimal state where market forces rule in all spheres. Yet, as John Richards makes dramatically clear in his introduction, social democrats must engage neo-conservatives in serious debate, just as we do Marxists. Thatcherism is not just a religious cult to be condemned. The British voted for Thatcherism because it seemed the only workable alternative. By 1979, when her Conservative Party defeated the Labour government, the post-war Keynesian welfare state was not doing the job. British per capita incomes were on average only two-thirds those in Germany and France; unemployment and inflation were consistently worse.

Yet the Keynesian welfare state and mixed economy – to use two shorthand descriptions of post-war society – are the starting point for any practical alternative to Anglo-American neo-conservatism. To be blunt, in our new manifesto we must not only be prepared to live with capitalism; we should welcome it where it contributes to the real wealth of the community!

In his important essay on the ills of British society, David Marquand (1988, p. 172) emphasizes a distinction made as early as John Locke, namely that between active and passive property.

The notion of active property – of property justified by the personal abstinence and entrepreneurial flair of the heroic, self-reliant owner manager, who built up his own capital, risked his own substance, hired his own labour, found his own markets and, in the process, created a new and more productive economic system – had a moral appeal extending far beyond the entrepreneurial middle class itself. It had about it an almost Promethean quality, which forced the paternalist, noblesse oblige ethic of the aristocracy onto the defensive, and which the group ethic of the working class could not match. The switch to passive property – to the view of property which makes it possible to treat industrial enterprises like . . . "bits of real estate" – destroyed the moral basis of the industrial order.

The instinct of many on the left is to assume all property has become passive, to deny the significance of active property. To indulge this instinct is to substitute dogma for thought.

If social democrats accept the limits of planning and the benefits of competitive markets in a mixed economy, what remains of our aspirations for an egalitarian co-operative commonwealth? What happens to the impassioned cry for social justice and an end to exploitation? In their place we can only offer the truth as we see it, a comprehensive program composed of concrete policies and the rationale for them. Our manifesto thus begins, in effect, with the realization that we cannot achieve a communal utopia. We do not have policies that can by themselves change people's conditions. Such policies do not exist. In particular, policies that suppress competitive markets will lower, not increase, average wealth. Moreover, they offer no guarantee of equalizing income distribution. In a well-functioning mixed economy, however, markets, in which consumers and private firms engage in voluntary exchange, and the state, in which agencies operate subject to democratic political control, are not in competition but are complementary. Social democrats must reinforce that complementarity. The idea that we can improve overall welfare by using the state against productive private firms is, ultimately, wrong.

As Canadians currently practise politics, the "parliamentary game" is just that, a game. The government proposes; the opposition, self-righteous trumpets blaring, opposes. Within the realm of the possible, we social democrats must rise above this game. We have an obligation to enlist popular participation – at all levels from municipal councils to Parliament, and from Canadians acting both as individuals and through popular-based organizations. If we are successful – a big "if" – the result will be a social democratic Canada. Whatever name we take, we must continue to think of ourselves as a labour-oriented party. We shall continue to stress full employment and base our support on the mobilized majority of Canadian people.

This is not simply a statement of traditional left-wing ideology. Among the structural changes required is that in the future any Canadian social democratic political party must be able to formulate policy independently of organized labour. Both unions and a social democratic party will be prominent in any future Canadian social democracy. But, just as unions in communist countries were traditionally hollow shells that echoed party propaganda and ignored controversial worker demands, there is an analogous danger in the Anglo-Saxon tradition. The British Labour Party was the child of trade unions. One reason for the failure of British social democracy relative to the Scandinavian experience is that the Labour Party has rarely been able to act at arm's length from organized labour. A trade union is the natural response of a group of workers to promote the collective interests of their trade or their industry. Inevitably, these collective instincts run counter to the general interest of society in well-functioning, productive markets. Neo-conservatives see no problem in this conflict; they are on the side of the market.

For social democrats life is not so simple. We recognize the value of unions, both as institutions to promote equality at work and, if well organized, to promote worker satisfaction and hence productivity. But we also recognize the value of competitive markets. Most people, including most union members, appreciate this tension. A social democratic party that denies its existence and fails to define independent economic policy is electorally doomed. Social democracy needs a powerful social democratic party able to effect reasonable compromises between the logic of trade union demands and that of competitive markets.

If we can become such a force, we will be in a position to seek a principled collaboration with private capital in achieving national economic objectives. Our new manifesto should contain language addressed to business circles: "We will support you in your efforts to make your firms more productive, to invest in those activities where profits await. We will co-ordinate in those efforts where needed: research and development, manpower training, long-run resource development. We specify at the outset those areas of overriding national concern – environmental protection, cultural industries, basic human services – where we believe markets cannot adequately provide. We commit ourselves elsewhere in the economy to allow firms to do what they think best, to respond to market signals in deciding what products and services to supply, and how to do so."

In return, we will insist that the benefits of a productive economy be distributed as equitably as possible. We will implement programs to complement, not inhibit, industrial development. We will fairly compensate the "losers" from changes in technology and market prices, through temporary income support and comprehensive on-the-job and in-house retraining. We will settle for no less than full employment – unemployment levels below 3 per cent – one-third the current Canadian level of 9 per cent. We will redistribute through transfers and generous public services, in enhanced access to education and to leisure-time and cultural pursuits, in improved working and environmental standards. We will pursue generous international policies with respect to aid, trade, technology transfer, and refugees.

Our manifesto must be clear that, if elected to office, a social democratic government will not attempt to govern alone. It will promote institutional reforms that allow far more effective collaboration in public policy by relevant interest groups. On many issues business and labour have shared interests and should speak with one voice. We will organize permanent forums, advisory commissions, and agencies where representatives of both will sit.

While we believe there to be a creative role for collaboration, we take seriously the distinction between active and passive property. Tax laws will foster productive industry but will aggressively seek to stamp out "paper entrepreneurship" based on real estate flips, stock exchange manoeuvres, and other types of short-term financial speculation that seemingly took on a life of its own in the 1980s. We take seriously government's role to foster unionization through supportive labour codes. In particular, we will encourage unionization in the private sector to promote a greater equilibrium between work conditions in the public and private sectors.

We intend to reform political structures to enhance political discussion and rational compromise as opposed to rhetorical polarization. One reform that may merit serious consideration – Ontario NDP, please take note – is an electoral system based on proportional representation. If poorly constituted such systems may be unstable, as in Israel, but they have the great virtue of allowing parties representing diverse views to win legislative representation. Because no one party usually enjoys an overall parliamentary majority, coalition governments are the norm. In putting together coalitions, politicians make publicly debated compromise an inherent characteristic of government. Thereby Canadians could be spared the worst of the "black-and-white" parliamentary charade according to which there are but two sides – one right and the other wrong – to political debates. (Proportional representation would also lessen the regional polarization of Parliament. The present first-past-the-post electoral system frequently allows a party to capture a near monopoly of seats from a region in which it commands a plurality of voter support. Throughout most of our generation our electoral system has, for example, eliminated Liberals from western Canada and New Democrats from Quebec.)

Given traditional attitudes, Canadian business leaders will likely be little interested in the structured partnership we propose – unless they feel it is in their interest. But businessmen are pragmatic. If we can win solid, visible electoral support from "ordinary Canadians" and are able to effect a new relationship with organized labour, business leaders will pay attention. So, the first task is to rally the majority of "ordinary Canadians." Since our manifesto promises neither the usual pie in the sky nor the stirring old left-wing rallying cries, how do we win a large constituency? How do we break through the various vicious circles that preserve the status quo. Using imported British Labour Party traditions, the NDP cannot expect to break through to majority status, but it can assure itself of 15-20 per cent of the vote. Canadians are accustomed to strident politicians feigning indignation over the hot topic of the day. Would Canadians pay attention to a new breed of aspiring politician who talks in depth about issues and complex policies to deal with them?

To free ourselves from these vicious circles is the reason for evoking the politics of 1933, a world where possibilities had yet to be closed off. In 1933 the political consciousness of most Canadians was not trapped by Madison Avenue sales techniques. J.S. Woodsworth did not have to break his speeches into seventeen-second sound bites and scramble after photo opportunities.

I indulge the luxury of imagining that Canadians may still be willing to think about the complexities of "actually existing social democracy." More particularly, that means a willingness to look seriously at those countries that have painstakingly constructed social democratic societies. With that goal in mind, I spent a year in Sweden studying just such a system. I offer below an abbreviated version of what I learned – and have discussed at length in a recent book, *Sweden: Social Democracy in Practice*.

THE SWEDISH "MODEL"

Sweden was in the news early in 1990 when the Social Democrats, who have been in power for fifty-three of the past sixty years, were temporarily forced out of office during a two-week government crisis. The five other parties had ganged up against the government's draconian anti-inflation package: a two-year wage, price, and rent freeze and a restriction on strikes and lockouts. While the crisis was soon over, the Social Democrats remained, at 36 per cent, lower in the polls than at any point in recent memory.

Yet the fundamentals remain sound. Sweden can boast of genuinely full employment, thriving manufacturing exports, a budget surplus, and a per capita income that ties it for third place (behind Switzerland and Japan). In addition, it rates well on non-economic indices contributing to "quality of life": average longevity, absence of poverty, high educational achievement, a clean environment, low crime rates, physical fitness. Nor is the main problem the high taxes that pay for these amenities. A recent reform is lowering the maximum marginal income tax rate to 50 per cent. Admittedly, the reform was introduced because the government feared that high tax rates were inciting too much tax evasion and reluctance to work. Yet Swedes still avoid taxes less than people in most low-tax countries, and they remain basically convinced that the large chunk of national income spent on public services yields fair value. Sweden's equivalent to the proposed Canadian goods and services tax is, incidentally, levied at a rate of 24 per cent.

At the heart of what is right and wrong with Sweden is full employment. Ola Ullsten, Swedish prime minister during part of the brief "bourgeois interlude" of non-Social Democratic rule and later ambassador to Canada, put it as follows:

> If there is anything unique about Sweden . . . I think it is . . . the political commitment to full employment. And that commitment is embraced by all political parties, by business and indeed by unions. Has it worked? Yes, I think it is fair to say that it has. Not without problems and disappointments. Nor without sometimes heated discussions about the means. Nor does everyone get a job when and where he or she wants a job. And indeed we do have regional disparities and individuals for whom there will always be a problem finding suitable employment. (Ullsten, 1988)

Sweden's unemployment rate has been below 2 per cent since 1987. This means, almost literally, that everyone works, for Sweden also has the highest labour force participation rate in the Western world. Almost all women work. Disabled people, who elsewhere would be classed unfit for work, are integrated into the labour force. Sweden admittedly has the associated problems of a tight labour market. Employers are short of skilled workers, and nominal wage increases exceeded 10 per cent in 1989. For 1990, Sweden's rate of inflation is expected to reach 11 per cent, a rate above that of all Sweden's major trading partners except Britain. (One-third of 1990 Swedish inflation is a one-shot rise due to implementation of the tax reform.)

Most other countries would find this situation enviable. They would simply – as *The Economist* (3 March 1990) urged – reduce inflation by doubling unemployment and still enjoy unemployment rates among the lowest in the Western world. But increasing unemployment violates a fundamental social democratic principle shared, as Ullsten makes clear, by many who are not Social Democrats. Namely, Swedes are committed that each citizen receive a decent income and that each contribute by work to the betterment of society. So, rather than allow unemployment to rise, the Social Democrats sought to enlist business and labour behind a tough anti-inflation wage and price freeze.

Full employment is a matter of social principle *and* of practical economics. For Swedish social democrats it is the linchpin of the economic system. It contributes to industrial efficiency because workers, reassured by genuine full employment and backed by the manpower training policies (jointly run by government, business, and labour), are less afraid to change jobs, to allow uncompetitive industries to shut down, and to move to expanding industries employing the latest technology. And full employment underpins the welfare state, since it means no "welfare backlash" from workers resenting the support of idle workers with their taxes. Sweden spends slightly more on labour market programs than does Canada (2.7 per cent of GDP in 1987 compared to 2.2 per cent in Canada). But whereas 75 of every 100 dollars Canada spends on labour market programs are for income maintenance (primarily unemployment insurance), only 30 of every 100 kronor Sweden spends on such programs are for income maintenance (Economic Council of Canada, 1990).

At its most rudimentary, the Swedish "model" as it developed in the 1950s consists of three operating principles: full employment, international industrial competitiveness and free trade, and the welfare state. Full employment is attained through the justly famous "active labour market policies" – massive investment in training and retraining, mobility grants, and, as the last resort, public works. International competitiveness arises from an economy open to international competition and from the "solidarity wage policy." Under this policy wages in all sectors rise more or less at the same rate, a rate based on the average productivity growth of industries facing international competition. Over time, Swedish income disparities have been significantly reduced. Sweden has the lowest level of income inequality (and of poverty) among Western nations (Ringen, 1987). The solidarity wage policy also has the effect of accelerating elimination of comparatively inefficient firms and sectors – by preventing their survival through payment of low wages.

The political economy of a centralized wage-bargaining system is the subject of a rich literature often termed "(neo)corporatist" (see, for example, Goldthorpe, 1984). Calmfors and Drifill (1988) provide a simple typology of wage-bargaining systems. At the laissez-faire pole, characterized by firms individually bargaining over wages with individual workers or small unions, wages and prices are constrained because firms cannot pass wage increases on in higher prices without losing substantial sales. At the corporatist pole, characterized by centralized bargaining between federations of unions and employers, both sides are conscious of the effect of their decisions on the aggregate economy. Unions will usually restrain wage increases from a knowledge that high nominal wage increases will be dissipated by higher prices. In the case of Sweden, unions bargain in the full knowledge that international competition means that wage gains beyond the rise in productivity are paid for in jobs lost due to imports from countries with lower costs. Centralized bargaining inhibits employers from setting off an inflationary wage spiral by outbidding each other for labour skills in scarce supply.

Although the decentralized pole has undesirable features from a social democratic perspective – weak unions and high wage inequality – either pole may provide an economy with relative wage and price stability. The worst wage-price inflationary spirals arise in the "no man's land" in the middle (such as Britain's system) where neither constraining force is operative.

Under the Swedish version of the corporatist system inflation has usually been kept down, while workers and capital have been encouraged to move to high-wage "sunrise" sectors. It is not state bureaucrats who pick winners; success results from decisions by individual firms, in response to market prices, including the solidarity wage policy. Full employment programs ease the transition from old to new jobs; so does the knowledge that entitlements (such as pensions) will be maintained. Since the Swedish welfare state provides unrivaled universal public services irrespective of income, job changes do not entail the risk of sacrificing good education, child care, recreation, and housing.

Underlying Swedish institutional arrangements is a social partnership between labour and capital, built on encompassing structures. This partnership has enabled Sweden to operate at unemployment rates far lower than in most industrial countries, while avoiding wage-price inflationary spirals. LO, the largest national trade union federation, and SAF, the employers' federation, share a common interest in holding down inflation. They have been able, for the most part, to work together to stabilize wages and prices, realizing that if Swedish prices rise faster than those of rivals it spells economic disaster. This partnership has not arisen spontaneously; it has required hard political work. Here again is Ullsten, with the assessment of a senior politician:

A tight fiscal policy to avoid inflationary effects of full employment means high taxation, which isn't popular in any circles. Trying to keep business [on] a tight leash [using] high social fees, strict
labour laws and various claims on company profits, isn't easily
advocated either. Nor is it as easy as it sounds to get people to
accept the realities behind the eloquent terms of "labour force
mobility". It often means being uprooted from places where you
want to stay and from occupations it took you a lot to learn. . . .
(Ullsten, 1988)

Actual performance never corresponded perfectly to the model,
but it came close enough – until the recession of the late 1970s when
Swedish inflation exceeded the OECD average and international competitiveness suffered. Ironically, this occurred at a time when "bourgeois" non-social democratic parties were in power. When the Social
Democrats returned to power in 1982, they won the consent of the
unions for a major currency devaluation. Unions did not obtain wage
increases to offset the price increases arising from devaluation of the
krona. Everyone became, in effect, poorer, but Swedish exports
became competitive again.

The "crisis" of spring 1990 arose because the government sought
to avoid replaying the scenario of a decade ago. Wage earners felt they
still had to regain fully ground lost due to the earlier devaluation.
Worse, in a context of very low unemployment and labour shortages,
workers whose relative incomes have declined resent those who are
getting ahead of them. Secondary school teachers and bank employees launched major strikes. In this context the government proposed a
wage and price freeze combined with a ban on strikes. The central
labour federations proved unable to deliver the needed labour support
for such tough controls. The watered-down version that did gain the
needed support – mandatory price freezes and voluntary wage
restraint – can only be stopgap. If the Swedish model is to continue,
the old partnership will have to be adapted. Can it be expected to do
so?

Sweden is in much better economic shape in 1990 than in the
previous crisis of 1979–80. Then as now, many critics pronounced the
death of the Swedish model. But it bounced back. Admittedly, the
critics could be right this time. Despite the fact that Swedish social
democracy has delivered on its promises, the partnership underlying
the system is inherently fragile. As Ullsten says, it persists thanks to
intelligent political work.

In the short term little will change. The opposition parties are
divided. Only the Conservatives question the system's underlying
principles; the Liberals and Centrists do not. Thus, even with a

change of government in 1991, which seems probable, the essential everyday workings of Swedish social democracy will remain in place for years to come. But what of the long term?

I remain confident that the Swedish model will survive. My prognosis rests on the fact that beneath the current discord and self-criticism are a widely held understanding and acceptance of the trade-offs that make social democracy work. This underlying sensibility is invisible to the foreign journalists who fly in for a week, speak to articulate, self-critical Swedes – whose national characteristic is that they don't mince words – and write exposés on "Sweden-in-crisis." Yet it is there to see. Swedes understand how their society works. Swedes, including trade unionists, respect managers and entrepreneurs who manage "active" capital. They do not respect "passive" capital – the fast-buck speculator or stock exchange manipulator. Everyone recognizes that investing financial and human capital in better products and services is a legitimate activity; investing in slick TV commercials to seduce Swedes into buying those products is not.

When the need arises, Swedes are able to assess their immediate interests in the light of the larger interests of their society. Unthinkable in Canada, Swedish labour and business collect statistical data together and jointly publish quarterly reports on wage trends. The fifty-page pre-election booklet distributed to visiting journalists is written jointly by the five parties – from Communist to Conservative. Members of Parliament are seated by region, not party. In contrast to our first-past-the-post elections, Swedes employ proportional representation. This means that all major views are expressed in elected assemblies; it also means few cases of one party with an absolute majority of seats, and therefore coalitions and continuous compromise are required to govern. On the other hand, Swedish politicians feel less bound to gloss over real differences than do our politicians. The outcome is a high level of rational decision-making and a supportive popular political culture.

This brings me to the question of political culture. Without a supportive political culture, social democratic policies are unsustainable. In general, social democrats in Canada place far too little emphasis on institutions that disseminate information and transmit values. Let me start with the importance of education.

Swedish education is free to the very highest level; there are no financial impediments. On the other hand, under the solidarity wage policy, there is comparatively little financial reward for those with higher educational credentials. University students are career-oriented and practical and, since universities give preference to applicants returning after an interlude in the work world, students tend to be older.

From earliest childhood and throughout life, learning and living are integrated. The Swedish child's school day is integrated with the activities of neighbourhood leisure-time centres; for older children it is co-ordinated with youth recreation centres, libraries, music schools, and sports clubs. Students must acquire between six and ten weeks of practical work experience – part of which must be in jobs normally associated with the opposite sex – during the nine years of comprehensive schooling. The upper secondary schools provide access to university to those in the vocational as well as academic stream. Even students in the academic stream undergo annual two-week work-experience programs. Those in the vocational programs spend almost half their three years in on-the-job training. The intake capacities of post-secondary programs are closely linked to labour market demand.

Work-study programs are but one example of the close links between industry and education. Sweden's high level of spending on research and development – over 2.5 per cent of GNP, compared to 1.8 per cent for Japan and 1.3 per cent for Canada – is well known. Less well known is that three-fifths of this R&D is financed by private industry, much of it taking place in the thirty-one collaborative private-public technological research institutes.

Sweden pioneered in extending the lower boundaries of formal schooling with its extensive child-care system, which in turn has fostered participation of women in the labour force. Sweden deserves to be better known for pioneering adult education. Ten per cent of Sweden's world-leading per capita spending on education goes to adult education. At any given time, about 25,000 adults are taking municipally run courses to complete their schooling. These are supplemented by state-subsidized courses provided, along with general interest "study circles," by the ten adult education associations. These adult education associations are sponsored by major interest groups – unions, political parties, co-operatives, pensioners' organizations, etc. In total they annually organize about 300,000 "study circles" attracting 2.5 million participants. (Sweden's population is 8.5 million.) All employees have the right to leaves of absence to upgrade skills and are eligible for allowances to replace lost income. This right is above and beyond participation in union-sponsored education courses, taken by roughly 40,000 workers annually.

There are other aspects to Swedish cultural policy. Local public libraries annually lend out nine volumes per person. Library services are provided in hospitals and seniors' residences and in workplaces through union "book ombudsmen," with free home pick-up and delivery for shut-ins. The employers' federation and trade union federations both sponsor cultural activities and popular theatre. Subsidies are allocated to all 100 daily newspapers, except those leading in their respective markets. Newspaper readership is double that in Canada (Milner, 1989, ch. 6).

In these and other ways, Swedish institutions bridge the gap between expertise for the few and knowledge for the many more successfully than in Canada. One relevant example is business management and economic policy. In Canada both union and management contrive to segregate the managers from the managed. The management side jealously preserves the "managerial rights" clause within collective bargaining agreements while union leaders shun any responsibility for management decisions. Universities grant professional degrees in management and imply that, without a Master's in Business Administration, no one is competent to manage. In Sweden, by contrast, practical business knowledge is stressed from school to trade-union training courses. Co-operatives, which run major supermarket and department store chains, work with the adult education associations and mass media to educate consumers. Both trade union and employer federations hire first-rate academic economists. Academic economics has a more practical bent than in Canada. The result of all this is that a pragmatic understanding of "how the world works" is surprisingly widespread among Swedes and has in turn contributed to Swedes' remarkable success in agreeing on what problems need to be tackled and in finding means to resolve them.

Viewed from the perspective of wage increases in a tight labour market, contemporary labour relations appear strained. But that is only part of the story. Sweden has been at the forefront among industrial countries in the use of computers and robotics. Labour-management co-operation has significantly eased major labour market adjustments that are, as Ullsten insisted, inevitably socially painful. The growth of shipyards in newly industrial countries such as Korea has destroyed the comparative advantage of high-wage shipyards such as Sweden's. Both labour and management can take credit for the adjustments whereby workers, who in 1982 were building ships at Kockums in the southern port city of Malmo, are now building Saabs in the same plant. The world showcase for job redesign is the new Volvo plant at the former shipyard of Uddevalla, near the Norwegian border.

Volvo, the largest firm in Sweden, provides an important case study of the potential benefits to workers of effective labour-management collaboration. In the late 1960s, the management of Volvo won union support to transform the work structure. The assembly line was eliminated in its new plants. Small teams of workers undertake all stages of vehicle production; they also order parts, schedule time off, and even recruit and train new team members. The position of team supervisor-inspector is rotated each week among members. Volvo's co-determination agreement with its employees stipulates that the choice of production strategies, adoption of new systems of production and investment, and personnel matters associated with them go first to the seven-member works committee, composed of the four top union officials and the three most senior executives. Volvo conducts a biennial survey of its employees, the results of which form the basis of group discussions in which all employees participate. In the past twenty years Volvo has flattened its managerial pyramid, cutting its headquarters staff from 1,800 to 100 persons and breaking down distinctions between blue and white collar, skilled and unskilled, and between supervision, quality control, and production.

The economic incentive for a decentralized participatory managerial style at Volvo is – as elsewhere in the Swedish economy – the great difficulty of attracting workers in a tight labour market. The alternative to consensual management is to entice employees of rival firms with higher wages, thus breaking wage solidarity, initiating an inflationary wage-price spiral, lost exports, devaluation of the krona, etc. While major Swedish firms do invest abroad – to assure access to foreign markets and to utilize lower-cost labour – the managerial style of their domestic factories has permitted an enviable combination of high worker satisfaction, high labour productivity, and high wages.

In concluding this section, I emphasize one important difference between Sweden and Canadian cultural communication. Not only do Swedish institutions provide the means of disseminating required knowledge effectively, they do *not* provide for communicating the antithesis of rational communication: commercial television. With the exception of imported cable telecasts, Sweden has no commercial radio or television. Radio and television programs are broadcast by four autonomous subsidiaries of the Swedish Broadcasting Corporation, which in turn is entirely outside government control. It derives revenue from annual licence fees charged to owners of television sets. The average Swede watches only 104 minutes of television daily, compared to 225 for the average Canadian. Forty per cent of regular program hours on the two television channels are information rather than entertainment-oriented. Subtitled (not dubbed) imported shows make up a similar percentage.

As long as Swedish popular culture is substantially free of television-based commercialism, the system is likely to remain secure. (There is, at present, ongoing discussion of introducing a small measure of commercial broadcasting.) Swedes will doubtless continue to tell visitors about their problems, and that the problems are worse than in the past. But Swedes will not, I believe, undermine their system through the unthinking short-term choices of narrow interest groups. When need be – as in adjusting to the new Europe – they will be able to bring the big economic picture into view and act accordingly.

CANADIAN PROSPECTS

Here in Canada the cultural dimension can only make a social democrat pessimistic. How can we envisage a practical social democratic society, given the hold of consumerism fostered by commercial television? To be consistent, we should argue to phase out commercial television – foreign and domestic. To do so would constitute electoral suicide, since Canadians appear wedded to it. At best, we might reduce the amount of television imported from any one foreign country and, in the CBC, replace most U.S. programs by those from countries with less commercial cultures.

At this point I return to Quebec, about which I am less pessimistic. First of all, its culture benefits from the admittedly porous shelter from American commercialism provided by language. But it is also a matter of Quebec enjoying greater social cohesion because its people are more homogeneous, less spread out geographically, and fewer in number.

To understand Quebec's potential, one first needs to break out of the 1970s mindset. As I write in the summer of 1990, polls reveal that up to 60 per cent of Quebecers favour sovereignty. Some leading Quebec businessmen, Liberal and Conservative stalwarts, many of whom fought for the "non" in the 1980 referendum, are now talking of sovereignty as the only post-Meech solution. How can this be? Most of us on the left had in the 1970s an implicit theory of change. Change in Quebec would come through the linking of progressive forces in a popular movement. Those in unions, in community action groups, intellectuals and artists all shared a sense of building that movement. Albeit sovereignty and a French Quebec were goals of *le combat*, they were but *le début* – interim objectives on the way to a fundamental transformation of Quebec into a home-grown democratic socialism.

Arrayed against "us" progressives were the business elite and federalist politicians, in Quebec City and in Ottawa. Up to 1982, we accepted the Parti Québécois as a valuable, if suspect, ally. The break came in the wake of the serious recession of 1982. Large deficits in the provincial budget compelled the PQ to bargain aggressively with public-sector unions; double-digit inflation prompted the unions to bargain equally aggressively. The results were bitter public-sector strikes in the winter of 1982-83, a kind of civil war within the supposed alliance of progressive forces. As with any civil war, each side experienced an acute sense of betrayal. Trade unionists denounced their former PQ allies as *fascistes*. PQ leaders muttered about the hypocrisy of well-paid teachers spouting Marxist slogans to justify salary demands that could only be paid for by cutting programs to the truly poor.

The public concluded "a pox on both your houses." People turned away from the "progressive forces." They looked again to the Liberals, led by a resurrected Robert Bourassa, and to an emerging Francophone business elite. In doing so, the public may not have been far off the mark. We intellectuals, political activists, and public-sector unionists had been very good at expressing ideals and writing programs but had proved incapable at the pragmatic task of carrying them out. Our implicit theory of change was simply not good enough; we needed more appropriate ideas.

There are clear indications that now, at the beginning of the 1990s, organized labour is itself moving toward a new position. Not only the leaders of the Quebec Federation of Labour (FTQ) and the small, moderate Federation of Democratic Unions (CSD), but even those in the radical Confederation of National Trade Unions (CSN) now express support for Scandinavian-style co-operation (*concertation*) with management and are abandoning the quasi-Marxist rhetoric of class conflict that still punctuates the discourse of most English-Canadian unionists. "The province of Quebec is," as Kumar and Ryan (1988, p. 15) observe, "an anomaly in the area of consultation where labour, management and government appear to have a strong, shared understanding for working together."

An obvious recent example of this Quebec "anomaly" is provided by the highly publicized Forum sur l'Emploi conducted in November, 1989, in Montreal (Milner, 1989b). Claude Béland, president of the Mouvement Desjardins (Quebec's large credit union federation), presided. Sponsors of the Forum included all the trade union federations, the Quebec Chamber of Commerce, the Quebec section of the Canadian Manufacturers' Association, and many other *corps intermédiaires*. Fifteen hundred representatives of unions, employers, different levels of government, and community organizations gathered to discuss how to achieve full employment: adaptation to new technology, work organization, role of entrepreneurship, and government planning. Representatives of Swedish labour and business were well received when they insisted that truly full employment at stable prices cannot be achieved without a large measure of collaboration between labour and management in firm management and in administration of government labour market policies. The godmothers of this exercise in *concertation* were Diane Bellemare and Lise Poulin-Simon, economists who, inspired by the Scandinavian and Austrian experience, have published two influential books on full employment (1983,1986) – books unfortunately yet to be translated into English.

Another indication of Quebec's "anomaly" is seen in public attitudes toward international free trade. Quebec trade unionists opposed the Canada–U.S. free trade agreement in 1988, but many did so half-heartedly, without the passion evident among English-speaking union leaders. Quebec opinion – among union leaders as among other interest groups – is sensitive to the risks of job loss posed by exposure to international markets, but it is less inclined than in the rest of the country to see protectionism as a solution. Why the difference? One explanation is that Quebec labour has more faith that government and business will effectively work together to compensate "losers" from free trade. In Quebec, as in Scandinavian society, there is an acceptance of the logic that the economy should take advantage of the benefits of free trade, provided that the "losers" are not forgotten.

Similarly, there has developed an acceptance in business circles that the state is not their natural enemy and that, especially in a small economy like Quebec, the state must facilitate consolidation into firms large enough to compete internationally. There exists in Quebec a range of financial institutions that are collectively owned and blur the distinction between labour and capital. One such example is the Fonds de Solidarité, which currently has $275 million invested in fifty-eight companies. Controlled by the FTQ, it encourages union members to invest collectively. Provincial and federal governments provide a tax incentive to investors in the Fonds. La Caisse de Dépot, the provincial government pension-based investment fund, has $40 billion in assets and is a key financial investor in the province.

None of this means that the political forces capable of realizing a social democratic Quebec – within Confederation or not – are in place. A self-conscious European-style social democratic labour party is missing. The fledgling Quebec NDP cannot fill the gap. It is too much held in sway by the neo-Marxist ideas of a former generation and has yet to come to terms with the economic reality of the 1990s. Nor, at present, can the Parti Québécois. Too many of its members remain beholden to a dogmatic and defensive nationalism. If and when such a party emerges, it could very well find a public – and even a labour movement – open to the kind of program outlined earlier in this essay.

Of course, some in Quebec welcome not only access to American markets but also America's neo-conservative approach to public policy. But they are far from a majority, and they will be opposed. Left-wing Canadian nationalists have reacted to recent Quebec developments with bitter nostalgia and bewilderment (e.g., Resnick, 1989). How could Quebecers support free trade, vote for Mulroney, and give such respect to their business elite? Such a response ignores the limitations of the "progressive forces" that we have discussed above and vainly expects social change to follow the fading road map of an aging "New Left." In conclusion, we would do well to remember the admonition of Kolakowski, a prominent Polish philosopher and political dissident:

> The trouble with the social democratic idea is that it . . . has no prescription for the total salvation of mankind, it cannot promise the fireworks of the last revolution to settle definitely all conflicts and struggles. It has invented no miraculous devices to bring about the perfect unity of man and universal brotherhood. It believes in no final easy victory over evil.
>
> It requires, in addition to commitment to a number of basic values, hard knowledge and rational calculation, since we need to be aware of and investigate as exactly as possible the historical and economic conditions in which these values are to be implemented. It is an obstinate will to erode by inches the conditions which produce avoidable suffering, oppression, hunger, wars, racial and national hatred, insatiable greed and vindictive envy. (cited in Jenkins, 1988, p. 142)

REFERENCES

Åslund, A. (1989). *Gorbachev's Struggle for Economic Reform*. Ithaca, New York: Cornell University Press.

Bellemare, D., and L. Poulin-Simon (1983). *Le Plein Emploi: Pourquoi?* Montréal: Presses de l'Université de Québec.

Bellemare, D., and L. Poulin-Simon (1986). *Le Défi du Plein Emploi*. Montréal: Albert Saint-Martin.

Brooks, S. (1989). *Public Policy in Canada: An Introduction*. Toronto: McClelland and Stewart.

Brus, W., and K. Laski (1989). *From Marx to the Market: Socialism in Search of an Economic System*. Oxford: Clarendon Press.

Calmfors, L., and J. Drifill (1988). "Bargaining Structure, Corporatism and Economic Performance," *Economic Policy*. No. 6 (April).

Economic Council of Canada (1990). *Good Jobs, Bad Jobs: Employment in the Service Industry*. Ottawa: Supply and Services Canada.

Economist, 3 March 1990. "A Change of Course: A Survey of the Swedish Economy."

Gill, L. (1989). *Les Limites du Partenariat*. Montréal: Boréal.

Goldthorpe, J.H., ed. (1984). *Order and Conflict in Contemporary Capitalism*. London: Oxford University Press.

Jenkins, P. (1988). *Mrs. Thatcher's Revolution: The Ending of the Socialist Era.* Cambridge, Mass.: Harvard University Press.

Kornai, J. (1986). "The Hungarian Reform Process: Visions, Hopes, and Reality," *Journal of Economic Literature*, XXIV, pp. 1687–1737.

Kumar, P., and D. Ryan (1988). *Canadian Union Movement in the 1980s: Perspectives from Union Leaders.* Kingston, Ontario: Queen's University Industrial Relations Centre.

Laporte, J. (1983). *Les Syndicats et la Gestion Participative.* Montréal: Agence D'ARC.

Marquand, D. (1988). *The Unprincipled Society: New Demands and Old Politics.* London: Fontana Press.

Milner, H. (1989a). *Sweden: Social Democracy in Practice.* Oxford: Oxford University Press.

Milner, H. (1989b). "Le Forum sur L'Emploi: A Sign of Things to Come in Quebec?" presented at the meetings of ACSUS, San Francisco (November).

Nove, A. (1989). *Glasnost in Action.* London: Unwin Hyman.

Resnick, P. (1989). *Letters to a Québécois Friend.* Montreal: McGill-Queen's Press.

Ringen, S. (1987). *The Possibility of Politics: A Study in the Political Economy of the Welfare State.* Oxford: Clarendon Press.

Ullsten, O. (1988). "A Policy for Full Employment," speech delivered at the conference "Equality and Efficiency" sponsored by University of Alberta and Swedish government.

Van der Berg, A. (1988). *The Immanent Utopia: From Marxism on the State to the State of Marxism.* Princeton, New Jersey: Princeton University Press.

Wilson, M. (1990). *The Budget.* Ottawa: Department of Finance.

LYNN MCDONALD

5   Politics – Left, Right, and Green

NINETEENTH-CENTURY SOCIALISTS SOUGHT TO "BUILD JERUSALEM IN England's green and pleasant land," imagery from William Blake that continued to inspire even in the Saskatchewan dust bowl of the 1930s. Tommy Douglas loved to quote the hymn, especially in times of defeat:

> I will not cease from mental fight
> Nor shall my sword sleep in my hand
> Till we have built Jerusalem,
> In England's green and pleasant land.

Canadians have changed the last line to "In *our* green and pleasant land," but more than editing is needed for socialists contemplating their future prospects. Quite apart from what socialism might mean, where is the green and pleasant land in which to build it? When Blake wrote, in the eighteenth century, there were "dark satanic mills" enough, and more still in the nineteenth century when socialists began to organize. But in neither century did anyone realize that the invisible pollution might be even worse than the belching of the mills. Plentiful food from healthy farms and abundant fish from river and sea could be counted on to arrive in the cities for the industrial population. There was no understanding of the long-term harm caused by chemicals to *all* people on the planet, not just to workers in mill towns. Soil productivity and fish yields were not issues then, let alone global warming, disappearing ozone, radioactive wastes, and other toxic garbage.

For the founders of modern socialism the problems were *social*; among all schools of socialism the primary economic problem was *distribution*. Levels of production became problematic only in times of economic crisis, which would cease with the establishment of social-ism. At times of crisis production was too low; it was unthinkable that it could be too high!

All that has changed. As we approach the end of the twentieth century, we are acutely aware that problems thought to have been solved have not. Even the most thoughtful social democrats of the 1950s and 1960s, such as Crosland (1956), assumed economic growth was benign. Given present knowledge of environmental degradation, early post-war calls for revamping socialism now seem pathetically mistaken. The environment is the issue of the day, and any rethinking of socialism must make this the starting point.

THE ENVIRONMENTAL CRISIS IS FOR REAL

Heading most environmentalists' crisis list is global warming due to rising concentrations of greenhouse gases (such as carbon dioxide) in the atmosphere. The two basic causes of atmospheric change are deforestation and the exponential increase in the amount of fossil fuels being burned. While there is much uncertainty in projecting future atmospheric warming, many of the scenarios are scary (Schneider, 1989). René Dumont, a prominent ecologist, estimates that already the death toll from global warming has reached one million people per year. He estimates that, without warming, the ten million annual death toll from famine would be one million lower. Atmospheric warming may melt polar ice, raise ocean levels, and inundate large areas of coastal settlement, such as Bangladesh. Some agricultural regions may become too hot and dry for cultivation. All kinds of delicate connections may be disrupted. Forest species adapted to a certain temperature may, in the space of a few decades, find them-selves in the wrong latitude. Migrating birds, which normally arrive at their breeding grounds at peak times for insects, may starve as the insects' breeding cycles change. The loss of species, already occurring at an unprecedented rate from forest clearing, may be exacerbated.

Global warming is only the first crisis. Radioactive wastes are accumulating with no known means of permanent disposal. Dioxins from pulp mills on the Pacific coast have forced the closure, not of the mills, but of the shrimp fisheries. In Ontario and Quebec acid rain is killing maple forests and sterilizing lakes. Overfishing by both Cana-dian and foreign boats has decimated Atlantic cod stocks and is clos-ing down the fishery.

It is difficult to believe in a potential crisis in food production when farmers face gluts and depressed prices, but the experts tell us it is there. Wasteful use of irrigation water is building up salt deposits that threaten soil productivity. The run-off from soils treated with chemical fertilizers, pesticides, and herbicides endangers water supplies. High-energy, high-chemical farming methods encourage farmers to abandon traditional crop rotations and cultivation. The result can amount to "mining the soil" – leaving it destitute of organic fibre and liable to erosion. The modern tendency to seed one variety only of one crop in a region poses risks from loss of genetic diversity.

NUCLEAR POLITICS

The nuclear issue breaks down the usual patterns of political divisions. The governments that have opted out of a nuclear future include both social democratic (Sweden and Norway) and conservative (Italy and Switzerland). The United States has effectively abandoned nuclear power for the best of corporate reasons: even with massive subsidies and protection against lawsuits, the costs are just too high. Britain, in late 1989, effectively opted for a non-nuclear future, ironically thanks to Mrs. Thatcher's plans to privatize the electricity-generating industry. The real costs of nuclear generation were uncovered and no one would pay.

The governments that are still pro-nuclear span the ideological rainbow from the Soviet Union (their only response to Chernobyl is a different choice of reactor), to France (socialists are expanding both the domestic industry and are continuing weapons testing in the South Pacific), to right-wing military governments (South Korea and, until recent elections, Brazil) and left-wing Marxist regimes (China, Cuba, and Romania under Ceausescu).

In Canada all three major parties have in the past promoted nuclear power, and two of them still do. The federal Crown corporation, Atomic Energy of Canada, is aggressively marketing its new, smaller, "friendlier" reactors, of a size suitable for every university, hospital, and small town. The Ontario Liberals became moderately anti-nuclear when in opposition, but once in office they permitted the Darlington nuclear plant to open and were neutral on Ontario Hydro's proposal for ten to fifteen new reactors.The recently elected Ontario NDP government is making a major commitment to demand-side conservatism and independent supply. It remains to be seen whther these good beginnings mark an end to Ontario Hydro's penchant for nuclear power.

In the case of the Soviet Union and France no public hearings are necessary before construction of a nuclear facility. In Canada, nuclear projects have been exempted from environmental assessment, but public opinion counts for enough that the industry, using tax subsidies, advertises massively. Nuclear proponents have the gall to cite protecting the environment as an argument for expansion. The alternative, they claim, is dirty coal, global warming, and acid rain. They ignore the fact that nuclear generation itself causes global warming and that uranium processing contributes to acid rain.

Public ownership has done nothing to safeguard the public interest against the nuclear industry, as the French, Soviet, and Canadian examples all show. A vigilant public, on the other hand, has been key in reversing pro-nuclear policies in Sweden, Austria, Norway, Italy, and Switzerland. It is no coincidence that the countries that have voted nuclear out all enjoy strong democratic institutions.

POLLUTION – FOR PROFIT OR FULFILLING THE PLAN

That the search for maximum profits encourages capitalist firms to ignore costs borne by others is only too obvious. If pollution does not immediately affect the corporate accounts, why bother? It is also obvious that the desire for profit encourages firms to cheat on pollution regulation. The result, for most members of the industrialized capitalist world, is a high standard of living, at the expense of environmental quality for future generations. Much of the apparent success of capitalism in producing wealth comes from living off environmental capital, what Harold Macmillan called "selling the family silver." The failures of capitalism will be only too real when the next generation has to start paying the clean-up costs.

Deterioration of the environment is no less serious, however, in the publicly owned, centrally planned economies where there is not even the short-run benefit of a high standard of living. Thanks to the greater ability of these governments to suppress citizens' groups and control the media, the problems are much less known.

The Destruction of Nature in the Soviet Union, a detailed exposé by a Soviet official using a pseudonym (Komarov, 1978), documents both the serious mistakes made by Soviet planners and the thoroughness of the measures to prevent public disclosure. It reports findings from official bodies, including ignored recommendations against certain projects because of environmental hazard. It shows how military requirements have been used to stifle public information and to set aside environmental protection regulations. Lake Baikal in Siberia is the world's largest in volume, and formerly one of the world's cleanest. A cellulose plant was built on Lake Baikal to supply fibre for tires for heavy bombers. In the end, the tires were made elsewhere with petroleum products, but the lake's water was polluted by the mill. As strategic materials, lead and zinc are subject to no environmental controls. In the great Soviet power projects, built in the 1930s under the control of the secret police, protection of the environment received about as much attention as did the health and safety of the labourers in

82

the Gulag. Siberian forests have been clear-cut and not replanted – as in Canada. Chemical pesticides and fertilizers are used massively in farming, including some banned in the West. Leaching into drinking water is a serious problem. Maximum permissible concentrations of various toxic substances are established, but in many cities these are routinely exceeded – by factors up to one hundred. Birth defects have increased markedly. The Sea of Azov had the most productive fishery in the world but is now polluted from pesticide run-off and petro-leum extraction, and the water level itself has been lowered by exces-sive irrigation. There is almost no fishery left and the beaches are unfit for use. As in Western countries, strict laws on the environment were eventually adopted but have been infrequently and haphazardly enforced. Factory managers find it more important to fulfil their quotas than to respect environmental standards – even if they incur occasional fines.

In Poland over a quarter of agricultural land has been contaminated by heavy metals from industry. There are smelters from which no workers live long enough to receive their pensions. In Cracow the corrosion of the city's old beautiful statues is the urban face of acid rain; in northern Czechoslovakia are dead forests, the rural face. In the Baltic states pollution from heavy industry introduced by Russian planners is a major grievance of Baltic nationalists.

Ecoglasnost movements have emerged across the Soviet Union, but the environment seems to be the last area in which Soviet reformers want *perestroika*. Perhaps understandably. Environmentalists form part of the threat to the Soviet state. In hopes that local autonomy will ensure that past mistakes are not repeated, they have frequently allied themselves to nationalist movements in calling for political auton-omy. And for the Russians, living in a cold harsh climate, the green-house effect does not seem such a bad idea. Furthermore, the Soviets want to extract and sell their fossil fuels as fast as they can – to earn hard currency and a softer life.

Anti-nuclear activists in the West can sympathize with their Soviet counterparts on the short-sightedness of decision-makers. "Before it even produces one kilowatt of energy," Komarov (1978, p. 103) laments, "an atomic power plant is more costly to the natural envi-ronment than all other forms of energy production." Even with the most modern equipment, some radioactive strontium and cesium escape. To produce a few kilograms of uranium, thousands of tons of sulphuric acid are used, in one of the dirtiest of industrial processes. All this was said before Chernobyl, when the Soviet Union had only one major nuclear disaster to answer for – the explosion of nuclear wastes at Chelyabinsk, in the Ural Mountains. That disaster required the evacuation of people as far as 200 kilometres away, and parts of the region are still uninhabitable. The number of victims is still an official secret, as are environmental reports on damage to soil, water, plant, and animal life (Medvedev, 1979; Haynes and Bojcun, 1988). Scientists discussing the resulting genetic damage report their results as if an experiment had been conducted!

Why do centrally planned economies permit so much environmental degradation? Soviet environmentalists cite a number of reasons. "Fulfilling the plan," it seems, takes as much precedence over protecting the environment as maximizing short-run profit does under capitalism. Managers – whether in communist or capitalist economies – will usually prefer to pay a fine rather than stop production and correct an environmental problem. Soviet forest managers face quotas both for tree-cutting and reforestation. Guess which ones are routinely met and which not? The Soviet economy has no incentives for finding new uses for unwanted by-products. For example, the fluorine emitted in the production of polyethelyne film is a toxin that kills the taiga, the subarctic evergreen forest of Siberia. Although it has industrial uses, quotas for fluorine are established in a separate ministry from the one responsible for polyethelyne. The result: no inducement for the managers of the polyethelyne plant to capture and sell the fluorine.

FAILED THEORIES

Apart from the aberrations of central planning, some of which are correctible, the problem has its genesis in the very heart of the communist system, in the labour theory of value. Karl Marx, the "godless atheist," was thorough in his atheism but not so in his materialism. While earlier exponents of the classical economic theory of value, such as David Ricardo, allowed some role for land and resources in creating value, for Marx human labour alone counted. The commodities produced from natural resources – from the soil, forests, fish, minerals, and so forth – acquired value only when labour was added in the process of production. In a primitive economy the animal hunted has no value but that labour the hunter expends in the chase. Marxist economists under the spell of the labour theory of value simply do not see the condition of the natural environment as relevant. Marx was typical of nineteenth-century socialists in failing utterly to see the potential for harm in the physical processes of production. He saw well what profit-maximizing capitalists in the chemical industry, to take one example, did to their workers; his writing reveals no suspicion that the industry could indirectly cause harm by its emissions. Under socialism, apparently, the chemical industry would not pollute.

84

Objects with literally no value will obviously be underpriced. Clean water in the Soviet Union, for example, is cheap and squandered. No value is attributed to it, because no social labour went into producing it. With clean and dirty water priced alike, there is no financial incentive to spare clean water for essential uses and to use dirty water for, say, irrigation and industrial uses. Relatively clean water is routinely wasted in industrial uses and truly clean water has become a rarity. More fundamentally, Soviet environmentalists blame a "domination of nature" theme in Communist ideology. Stalin's proclivity for heavy industry was only the worst manifestation. Lenin shared the same obsession, as indeed have most philosophers and natural scientists until recently.

The concepts of gross national product and national income (the two are numerically equal, the one measuring the value of goods and services, the other the income earned from their sale) are used throughout the capitalist world as a general economic indicator. They reflect many of the same intellectual blind spots as the Marxist labour theory of value. Gross national product admittedly includes some benefits derived from the natural environment. Thus it includes rent earned on arable farmland and the income from sale of minerals. But it remains essentially a measure of the value of labour expended in the economy – wages and salaries to measure labour expended directly, and depreciation to measure labour expended indirectly in the "using up" of manufactured capital goods. Gross national product does not measure the "using up" of natural resources. National income does not rise upon discovery of oil and gas reserves, nor is it reduced by the running down of old reserves.

When we consider the "using up" of non-marketed environmental goods, national income accounts are even more perverse. They measure restorative work on the environment as a productive service, but the underlying "using up" of the environment goes unrecorded. As an example, consider the 1989 oil spill by an Exxon tanker in Alaska. The wages, salaries, and profits earned by labour and capital devoted to clean-up are included in the state's income accounts for the year. If this labour and capital had been employed elsewhere in Alaska at similar rates, the gross state product would have remained the same. But this is bizarre; it implies no value to the forgone output from the labour and capital diverted to clean-up. If this labour and capital had been unemployed, the gross state product actually rose due to the accident!

When people ask if our standard of living will decline if we take environmental protection seriously, they usually have in mind the volume of consumer goods. Asked if life would be more pleasant with cleaner air and water, more swimmable beaches, fewer polluted fish, and more singing birds, most agree. Yet there is no generally accepted way to measure any improvements of this sort in our standard of living, to include them in national income accounts (*Economist*, 1989, p. 53). Pollution indices exist, of course. Mortality rates measure the worst effects, and social scientists have attempted to construct more subtle environmental measures to amend national income accounts. Access by public transport to a swimmable beach would score high on any environmental measure of mine.

An environmental audit – of the forests, fish stocks, soil quality, state of wilderness areas, nonrenewable resources, drinking water, and air – would be a good start. Annual reports would provide the data for people to hold officials to account for their environmental stewardship. At election times voters could assess the performance of the government. Are there more or fewer trees, better or worse soil quality, cleaner or more polluted water? Employees and owners of corporate shares could use comparable information in collective bargaining and at shareholder meetings. Parks departments would report on the birds and beasts, flowers and trees under their care, not just on the number of visitors and dollars spent.

Common to both capitalist and communist economies is a failure to recognize *physical limits*. Economics in the nineteenth-century was scorned as the "dismal science" because early economists, like Thomas Malthus and David Ricardo, took account of the natural limits on human activity. Later economists shed that realism and developed models of easy substitutability among natural resources, manufactured capital goods, and labour in the production of goods. If, for example, the supply of arable land is fixed, that poses no problem in these models to an exponentially growing population. Farmers can always satisfy demand, at "reasonable" cost, by applying more capital and labour to the existing fixed supply of land.

The naiveté of these models is now under attack. As one representative critic has written, economic theory that permits endless growth must be rejected because it "essentially ignores the second law of thermodynamics: in any closed isolated system, available energy and matter are continuously and irrevocably degraded to the unavailable state" (Rees, 1989, p. 3). Conventional economic growth models ignore the downstream consequences of pollution and are silent about the scarcity of resources. Rees emphasizes that all modern economies depend crucially on stocks of non-renewable material and energy resources. Consequently, they continuously degrade and consume the very resource base that sustains them. What these models call production is really consumption. Contrary to conventional economic theory, sustainable development with the prevailing pattern of resource use is not even theoretically conceivable. There is no equilibrium in the relationship between our industrial economies – capitalist or communist – and the environment.

Ecosystems, by contrast, seem to be inherently self-sustaining. Unlike economic systems, they are driven by an external source of free energy, the sun. Solar energy, through photosynthesis and direct warming of the earth's surface, sustains virtually all biological activity. Over the last two centuries of industrialization there has been an explosive accumulation of manufactured capital, a steady rise in material living standards, and exponential population growth. This could not have happened without the intensive use of fossil fuel deposits. Yet the second law of thermodynamics holds; this expansion was purchased at the cost of a permanently degraded resource base.

Throughout much of the nineteenth century economists subscribed to the "iron law of wages," according to which wage levels in the long run would inevitably remain at the level of subsistence. Before any consensus could emerge in favour of a welfare state, this conventional wisdom of nineteenth-century economics had to be overturned. The changes in economic thinking required now are of the same magnitude as ridding conventional wisdom of the "iron law of wages." Making recourse to the theory of thermodynamics is one means to make the change; undoubtedly there are others.

While the majority of the left have ignored environmental matters, a minority has been more enlightened. Narodism in late nineteenth-century Russia was a back-to-the-land form of socialism, derided by "scientific" socialists as hopelessly naive and backward looking. In 1895 Austrian socialists formed a Friends of Nature association. It still runs shelters for hikers and engages in environmental advocacy. It was a sort of socialist hiking club, to get the workers out of the pubs and gambling dens. Karl Renner, a leading Austrian Marxist and later president of his country, was an early member. The anarchist Peter Kropotkin published *Mutual Aid* in 1902. Although it is more human-centred than present-day radical ecology, it is a classical environmental statement of the continuities across all forms of life. John Stuart Mill, an economist with feminist and some limited socialist leanings, did work on a zero growth society. Mill was an advocate for the environment, including wildlife protection and species diversity, and was an opponent of monoculture.

Virtuous resolutions on the environment abound in NDP resolution books – federal and provincial. Predictably, New Democrats are against pollution and for a healthy, clean environment. Yet there are anomalies. Leading the list is energy prices – where the NDP seeks simultaneously low prices, lots of jobs in the petroleum industry, and a safe clean environment without global warming or acid rain. It is worth recalling that the issue on which the minority Conservative government fell in 1979 was an 18¢/litre gasoline tax introduced by then Finance Minister John Crosbie ("short-term pain for long-term gain"). The NDP introduced the non-confidence motion that toppled the government. More recently, environmentalists have argued for a "carbon tax" on hydrocarbon fuels as a means to reduce use of these fuels and hence reduce greenhouse gases. The NDP in 1989 joined with Conservatives and Liberals to vote against a proposal for such a tax.

A typical example of muddled NDP thinking on this subject is a 1987 resolution that flags the problem of a "depressed world price" of petroleum products and calls for "fair and competitive gasoline prices" and more energy megaprojects, including the tar sands and offshore oil. The NDP shares the general misconception that oil and gas are "produced" by investment in exploration. There is no appreciation that non-renewable resources are finite, and that future generations have as much claim on them as ours. As recently as the 1988 federal election, the federal NDP proposed a reduction in unleaded gasoline prices, against the advice of every researcher consulted. When the federal government announced agreement in principle to proceed with the Hibernia development on the Newfoundland banks, the response of the federal NDP caucus was to complain that federal government guarantees were too weak! Admittedly, a year later, when the government introduced legislation, the NDP caucus stressed environmental risk instead.

If the NDP had been more prescient on global warming and acid rain, it might have made little difference to actual policy. By contrast, the party's pro-nuclear stance in Saskatchewan has left its mark in radioactive tailings, deserted mining towns, and toxic lakes. The Saskatchewan NDP actively promoted the uranium industry since the 1950s, falling for Eisenhower's "atoms for peace" proposals as much as liberals, conservatives, and socialists everywhere. The NDP's intransigent pro-nuclear position in Saskatchewan lost the party the support of some of its most dedicated supporters and thereby contributed to the defeat of the Blakeney government in 1982. The provincial party reversed its position immediately after that election.

Also on the party's demerit list is the federal caucus's failure to give prominence to the environmental consequences of the free trade agreement. This was consistent with the decisions of the leadership to downplay generally the free trade issue. Former party leader Ed Broadbent, incidentally, justified the party's low profile on environmental issues on the grounds that polls showed the party had credibility on the issue in any event. Resolutions were submitted to the 1989 federal convention to establish a "green caucus" but they never made it to the convention floor for debate.

Among the party's environmental credits is the role of the federal

NDP, especially of Tommy Douglas, in creating the federal Department of the Environment. The Barrett government in British Columbia deserves credit for establishing an agricultural land reserve to preserve agricultural land and restrict the urban sprawl of metropolitan Vancouver. It was model environmentalism, much needed in a province long on scenic beauty and short of arable land. Once in office, Social Credit weakened the legislation but dared not do away with it altogether. More recently, the British Columbia NDP has begun to consider how to apply "sustainable development" to the provincial economy. A series of NDP-sponsored private member's bills introduced in the 1989 legislative session pose an ambitious agenda. They would create an environmental protection fund, increase pollution penalties, prohibit the dumping of toxic materials in coastal waters, phase out pulp mill pollution, reduce forest wastes, establish a royal commission on forest resources (and issue no new cutting leases until it reports), encourage value-added forest product uses, ban ozone-depleting substances, ensure environmentally sensitive spending by government, protect "whistle blowers" (who reveal environmental lawbreakers), secure freedom of information on the environment, monitor spills, promote recycling, and reduce lead levels in drinking water. In Yukon the NDP government led by Tony Penikett loans money interest-free to homeowners for an energy audit and retrofit. While federal and provincial governments stall, New Democrat members of Toronto's City Council have led the way in adoption of a plan to reduce carbon dioxide emissions. And as mentioned above, energy conservation is among the most prominent priorities of the new Ontario NDP government.

PRACTICAL REMEDIES

Some of what needs to be done to save the planet is both obvious and easy. We can legislate mandatory environmental assessments and audits, and strengthen environmental protection legislation. We can phase out over the next thirty years the domestic nuclear industry, giving ourselves adequate time to improve energy efficiency and to find safer alternatives. Citizens support the use of tax incentives to reduce pollution – for example, eliminating subsidies for chemical fertilizers, augmenting subsidies for preservation of wildlife habitat on farms, for preservation of genetic diversity of crops, etc.

Some of what needs to be done is obvious but costly. To reduce consumption of hydrocarbon fuels, environmental groups have advocated a "carbon tax" based on their relative addition to greenhouse gases. Thus, relatively clean-burning natural gas should be taxed more lightly than gasoline, coal, or fuel oils. It is difficult but not impossible to raise domestic Canadian petroleum prices while the Americans continue their low-price gas-guzzling ways. A second obvious reform is to remove greenhouse gases by growing more trees. It is hypocritical of us to condemn Brazil for destruction of its tropical forests while we Canadians continue to cut more trees than we replant. A related matter is the designation of more land as conservation areas. Designation of 12 per cent of our territory, as recommended by the Brundtland World Commission on the Environment and Development, would be a challenge, but surely one within our capacity.

Studies have repeatedly shown that it is cheaper to invest in conservation and thereby reduce energy demand by a given amount than it is to invest in energy megaprojects to increase supply by a comparable amount. A 1984 study estimated that Canada could reduce energy consumption by 30 per cent – by means of better insulated homes and factories, more efficient transportation, etc. The cost to conserve this amount of energy worked out to be $20 (in 1990 Canadian dollars) for the energy contained in a barrel of oil. Even at world oil prices prevailing before Iraq's invasion of Kuwait this was below the cost of imported offshore oil and far below the cost per barrel of energy from megaprojects such as Hibernia or tar sands. Incidentally, the same report calculated at $60 the cost for a nuclear plant to produce the amount of energy contained in a barrel of oil (*Economist*, 1990).

Given these relative costs, why do we not see more investment in conservation? There are at least two reasons. First, the perverse nature of politics. Despite green rhetoric, politicians are far more prone to subsidize increased energy supply than reduced energy demand. Investments in new supply are usually big – big dams, big coal mines, big pipelines, big offshore oil and gas platforms. These investments generate large profits for the construction firms involved, high wages for construction workers, taxes for the relevant provincial and municipal governments, plus income and employment in related industries. An equal dollar investment in energy conservation may well yield more jobs but these jobs will be in a thousand small projects geographically dispersed across the country – building triple-pane windows, retrofitting a house, insulating hot steam pipes in a factory, installing a heat exchanger in a pig barn, improving a city's bus system. It goes without saying that the regionally concentrated interest groups lobbying for subsidies for a megaproject – chambers of commerce, construction unions, and local politicians – will usually be more effective than any counter-lobby on behalf of conservation.

A second reason is human psychology. People value a dollar today far more than the uncertain prospect of two dollars five years hence. If we think of conservation investment as a cost yielding future benefits in the form of lower energy bills, then most consumers and business people appear unwilling to invest unless they expect very high returns. Regulatory bodies expect energy supply projects to yield an annual rate of return (after allowing for inflation) of only 5-10 per cent. On the other hand, business people and consumers expect energy conservation to yield a minimum annual rate of return of at least 25 per cent. More and better information on the benefits of conservation can help, by lowering the uncertainty surrounding new conservation technologies, but we should also be prepared to regulate tougher standards on ourselves.

In yet other areas there is no consensus among environmentalists as to what needs to be done, but some indications can be given. A Royal Commission on Lifestyles and the Environment could elicit new ideas for conservation and pollution reduction. Hearings across the country would stimulate all manner of community and professional organizations to rethink their own responsibilities. Businesses, consumers, unions, churches, parents, and teachers all have something to contribute. Values, as much as practicalities, have to be reconsidered in the light of the environmental crisis. Educational institutions must become part of the solution – from kindergarten on up. This will require changes in curriculum, in library resources, and in teacher training. In universities and colleges new courses on the environment are needed, not only in the natural sciences, but in sociology, economics, politics, philosophy, theology, literature, and such professional studies as engineering, law, business administration, and tourism/recreation.

Some of the questions facing us are tough, intellectually and morally. Even under optimal environmental policy, can the world continue economic growth without serious environmental harm? What about population growth? Can people in the "two-thirds" world improve their living standard without our cutting back on ours? What are our responsibilities to preserve non-renewable resources for future generations?

The New Democratic Party can and should become – in fact though not in name – the green party of Canada. It should play the role on the environment it so honourably and effectively did for half a century on social policy. The NDP – and the Co-operative Commonwealth Federation (CCF) before it – originated ideas, demonstrated their feasibility at the provincial level, and conducted public education until the "old-line" parties implemented them. Certainly no other major party will ever pursue green politics with the passion it needs. The Conservatives have discovered the environment for public relations purposes but have yet to make a decision that would upset their corporate supporters or the American government. The Liberals are not much better. Although the recently defeated Ontario Liberal government pioneered some waste management policies, the same party remained pro-nuclear and favours energy megaprojects as much as the Conservatives.

A separate Green Party is not a viable option for a country without proportional representation. In European countries with proportional representation, the Green Party can elect members to parliament and force "red-green" alliances with social democrats. In Canada, increased votes for a separate Green Party would likely mean fewer NDP votes, without green victories. It would allow more Conservatives and Liberals to sneak through in four-way fights.

Environmentalists outside the NDP are sceptical, and wonder if Canadian social democrats can become truly ecological, abandoning the human-centred approach to life that has been as much a part of socialist history as of the surrounding culture. This, make no mistake about it, means *animal rights*, recognizing an equal entitlement to a place in the world for all species. The great majority of New Democrats are no more ready for brother toad and sister wolf than were the contemporaries of St. Francis of Assisi. Radical environmentalists should, nonetheless, join the NDP and educate us. They, like New Democrats, should not give up on "ordinary Canadians." The "deep ecology" debate must go on in the NDP as elsewhere in society.

To assist in consciousness-raising, I close with a quotation from Robert Burns's poem to a mouse, on its nest having been turned up with a plough:

> I'm truly sorry man's dominion,
> Has broken nature's social union,
> And justifies that ill opinion, which makes thee startle,
> At me, thy poor, earth-born companion, and fellow-mortal!

Several stanzas bemoan the wrecking of the mouse's preparations for the Scottish winter, to end with sentiments as relevant to environmentalists today as to mice then. Foresight may indeed be vain and the best-laid plans of mice and us "gang aft agley":

> Still thou are blest, compared with me!
> The present only toucheth thee:
> But och! I backward cast my eye, on prospects drear
> And forward, though I cannot see, I guess and fear!

REFERENCES

Crosland, C.A.R. (1956). *The Future of Socialism*. London: Jonathan Cape.

Economist, 26 August 1989, "Getting physical."

Economist, 6 January 1990, "Money to burn."

Haynes, V., and M. Bojcun (1988). *The Chernobyl Disaster*. London: Hogarth.

Komarov, B. (1978). *The Destruction of Nature in the Soviet Union*. White Plains, New York: Sharpe.

Medvedev, Z.A. (1979). *Nuclear Disaster in the Urals*. New York: Norton.

Rees, W.H. (1989). "Energy Policy and the Second Law: Time to Ante Up," presented to Seventh Canadian Bioenergy Seminar, Ottawa.

Schneider, S.H. (1989). "The Changing Climate," *Scientific American*, CCLXI:3 (September).

6

Self-Management in a Planned Economy: Recent Catholic Social Theory

IN THE SIXTIES, THE GROWING MISERY IN MANY THIRD WORLD COUNTRIES and the cry of the people struggling for liberation deeply affected ethically concerned persons and their institutions in the First World, including the Christian churches. The major Christian organizations, such as the Geneva-based World Council of Churches, several Roman Catholic episcopal conferences, the Vatican, the (Protestant) National Council of Churches of the United States, and the Canadian Council of Churches, experienced a conversion of heart and mind and adopted a new, more critical social perspective. They extended their compassion and solidarity to Third World peoples and condemned First World economic and political domination. This was accompanied by an extensive literature, including official ecclesiastical documents, that dealt with social ethics and economic justice from an identification with society's victims. This literature analysed in critical fashion the cultural impact of contemporary capitalism and, in particular, the impact of the market system with its centre in the North on the people in the less developed countries of the South.

In the seventies and eighties, the turn to monetarist policies widened the gap between rich and poor in the developed capitalist countries, created new standards of chronic unemployment, multiplied the homeless and the hungry in the big cities, and produced a culture of poverty in an ever growing underclass. The Christian churches again composed official documents in which they sided with the poor against the rich and lamented the emergence of a neo-conservative middle-class culture that legitimated the indifference of the comfortable and well-to-do to the suffering of others.

In this paper I wish to look at the surprising shift to the left in official Roman Catholic social teaching, especially the encyclicals of

Pope John Paul II and the pastoral messages of the Canadian bishops, and analyse their ethical critique of present-day capitalism and their recommendation of an alternative economy that combines central planning with industrial self-management. It deserves to be mentioned that an analagous evolution of social theory has taken place at the World Council of Churches (Duchrow, 1987).

TRADITIONAL CATHOLIC TEACHING

Traditional Catholic social teaching, in keeping with Leo XIII's encyclical, *Rerum novarum* (1891), promoted a corporatist vision of society (Dorr, 1983). Catholic social teaching was critical of liberal capitalism because it surrendered the economic well-being of society to the impersonal forces of the market, because it promoted individualism and utilitarianism, and because it allowed the rich, the owners of industry, to exercise undue power in society at the expense of the great majority. At the same time Catholic social teaching firmly condemned socialism. The reasons given for this condemnation were three: the secular spirit of the socialist movement, the class conflict fostered by socialist parties, which undermines the unity and cohesion of society, and the socialist opposition to private property.

What Catholic social teaching advocated was strong government in the hands of high-minded men, located above the conflicting class interests, who would promote the common good of society (including religion), guide and contain economic development, and protect the poor against exploitation by the rich. Behind this stood a "Tory" vision of an organic society. Still, the Catholic social teaching of 1891 defended the formation of labour organizations.

Quadragesimo anno, Pius XI's depression encyclical of 1931, went so far as to recommend a corporatist organization of the economy (*Seven Great Encyclicals*, 1963, p. 148). Owners and workers in the same field of production were to unite in distinct corporations, and the different corporations in turn were to form a national economic council that would plan and balance the economy in favour of the well-being of all. Mussolini showed some interest in this idea. Yet these recommendations were so far removed from the economic debate in the Western democracies that political scientists paid no attention whatever to Catholic social teaching.

In the sixties, thanks to Pope John XXIII and the Vatican Council (1962–65), we observe an important evolution of Catholic social teaching. A few years later liberation theology strongly affected the social teaching of the Latin American Bishops Conference (1968) at Medellin, Colombia, which in turn influenced the 1971 World Synod of Bishops held in Rome and subsequently the encyclicals of Pope

Paul VI (see Baum, 1987, pp. 3–31). In the eighties, Pope John Paul II, in critical dialogue with Marxism in his native Poland, brought Catholic social teaching into conversation with the political and economic debates going on in Western and Eastern European society. It is this papal social theory I wish to examine.

LABOREM EXERCENS

Relying on the biblical story of creation and on social philosophy reflecting Marxist thought, the papal encyclical, *Laborem exercens* (1981), proposed a definition of human beings as workers (Baum, 1982, p. 96). This was new in Catholic social teaching. Humans differ from animals because humans alone must produce the historical conditions of their survival by labour. Beavers and other animals work, it is true, but they do so by instinct. Humans are guided in their work by their intelligence. Humans have to invent their world.

The encyclical distinguished between the "objective dimension" of labour, the finished product, and the "subjective dimension" of labour, human self-realization (*ibid.*, pp. 102–06). Humans build the world, and in doing so they constitute themselves. Since humans are spiritual beings, the encyclical insists on the priority of the subjective over the objective dimension. Primacy must be given to human self-realization, not to the material product. Whenever this priority is violated, whenever goods are produced under conditions that inhibit the self-realization of workers, the right order of God's universe is inverted.

Reflecting on human "subjectivity," the encyclical concludes that, thanks to their great dignity as humans, workers are entitled to participate in the decisions affecting the organization of labour and the use of the goods they produce (*ibid.*, pp. 106–08, 122–25). When workers are prevented from exercising these responsibilities, i.e., prevented from being "subjects," they become the "objects" of production and "alienated" from their human vocation and from what rightly belongs to them.

This theory of workers' subjectivity is critical of both capitalism and communism. In capitalist countries the decisions regarding the work process and the use of capital are made by the owners and/or managers of the industries, and in communist countries these decisions are made by the appropriate office of the state bureaucracy. In both systems workers suffer alienation. We note that John Paul's social encyclicals are always critical in both directions, critical of what he calls "liberal capitalism" and "Marxist collectivism."

In this context, the encyclical uses the phrase, "the priority of labour over capital" (*ibid.*, pp. 116–19). This expression has several meanings.

It refers to the principle mentioned above, namely that production must respect the subjectivity of the workers. A slightly extended meaning is that capital, especially industrial production, must be at the service of labour. In running the industries, priority must be given to the well-being of the workers. "Workers," in the encyclical, refers first to manual labour and beyond that to all men and women employed in industry – white-collar workers, the cleaning staff, the engineers, and even the salaried managers. (The encyclical rejects the Marxist distinction between productive and unproductive labour.) And since, according to the encyclical, the workplaces in today's society are interrelated and in fact depend on commercial, financial, political, and social institutions, the whole of society must be understood as labouring. The priority of labour over capital means, therefore, that corporations must serve the well-being of the workers they employ and the whole of the society to which they belong.

In this context, the encyclical offers a provocative definition of capitalism. If an economic system violates the priority of labour over capital, it is "capitalist," even if it wants to be known by another name (*ibid.*, p. 107). What is implied here is that even if the Eastern European countries present themselves as socialist, they deserve to be called state capitalist since they do not respect the priority of labour.

How can society assure that capital actually serves labour? Experience has taught us, the encyclical argues, that the nationalization of industry is no guarantee that it will be run in the service of labour. A government may decide to nationalize an industry to enhance its power, accumulate capital for war production, or compete successfully on the world market. In this context, the encyclical significantly modifies the Catholic understanding of private property.

The older Catholic social teaching defended the right of private property against socialist theory. But the Catholic concept of property was derived from the feudal order where ownership consisted largely of land and hence differed significantly from the modern, liberal concept of property, which refers mainly to productive machinery and capital investment. Even in the older Catholic social teaching, private property never implied the right to use and dispose of goods as one liked; private property always included the social responsibility to take care of the land and distribute from it to those in need. Property was private, but its use was common.

In continuity with this tradition and in response to the contemporary situation, *Laborem exercens* modifies the concept of property. Property, whether private or public, is here seen as conditional.

Isolating the means of production as a separate property in order to set it up in the form of "capital" in opposition to "labour" – and even to practise exploitation of labour – is contrary to the very nature of these means and their possession. They cannot be possessed against labour, they cannot even be possessed for possession's sake, because *the only legitimate title to their possession* – whether in the form of private ownership or in the form of public or collective ownership – *is that they should serve labour* and thus by serving labour that they should make possible the universal destination of goods and the right to common use of them. (*Ibid.*, p. 123. Emphasis added.)

What follows from this is that there is no perfectly safe form of ownership. No form of property guarantees that capital will be used in the service of labour and the community as a whole. According to *Laborem exercens*, the greatest likelihood that the priority of labour over capital will be respected occurs when firms are owned by the workers themselves. Ultimately, the encyclical argues, it is the destiny of workers to become themselves the owners of the giant workbench at which they labour (*ibid.*, p. 123). But even this is no final guarantee of justice. Society will always have to remain watchful.

While John Paul II is critical of capitalism and communism, he does not recommend revolution, neither in the West nor in the East. Writing in 1981, he believed that the two systems could be reconstructed. He argued that the historical agent for this reconstruction in West and East is the labour movement as it becomes conscious of its historical vocation in industrial society. Since the workers have been turned into objects and suffer alienation, and though the majority are society's victims, they have the conscience and the consciousness to hear the call of justice to organize, exert political pressure, and initiate social transformation. In this struggle the workers should be supported by all citizens who love justice, including the Church itself. The Pope thus called for "the solidarity *of* labour and *with* labour" (*ibid.*, p. 110). The encyclical here replaces the deterministic theory of class conflict, proper to scientific Marxism, with a voluntaristic theory, a specifically ethical one, of preferential solidarity with the labour movement.

The tone of *Laborem exercens* is hopeful. It was written at a time when the Polish Solidarity movement promised to be the agent of social reconstruction in that country. Yet while the encyclical emphasizes the political vocation of the workers and their right to co-manage and eventually to co-own the industries, it does not belittle the responsibility of the central government for the economic well-being of society. Catholic social teaching has always sought a balance between centralizing and decentralizing institutions, even though – ironically – the organization of the Catholic Church itself has become increasingly centralized in the papacy.

Catholic social teaching proposes two contrasting principles, called "subsidiarity" and "socialization" (Dorr, 1983, p. 327). Subsidiarity is the moral principle that protects small communities or organizations from being interfered with or dominated by higher powers. In church teaching, subsidiarity has been an ethical argument against excessive state power and thus against existing state socialisms. Subsidiarity is the Catholic term for "small is beautiful." By contrast, socialization is a moral principle that demands that, whenever a small community or organization is unable to take care of its needs, higher powers must intervene to co-ordinate joint efforts to help. In church teaching this principle has been used to justify the right and duty of the state to interference in the national economy. The two principles together can be translated as "small is beautiful, big whenever necessary." The two principles were applied in *Quadragesimo anno*, Pius XI's encyclical of 1931, to justify the right of the state to nationalize privately owned corporations whenever the power of these institutions was so big that it prevented the state from protecting society's economic well-being (*Seven Great Encyclicals*, 1963, p. 156).

John Paul II does not hesitate, therefore, to recommend a planned economy in his very first encyclical (*Redemptor hominis*, 1979, nn. 15–16). In a world of scarcity, he argues, the production and distribution of goods must be guided by a long-range plan, democratically controlled, that fosters the well-being of all. In *Laborem exercens* he briefly mentions that the socialization of the economy must at the same time protect the subsidiarity of people and their institutions (Baum, 1982, pp. 124–25). Yet the encyclical makes an extensive use of the centralizing and decentralizing principles in its treatment of unemployment.

John Paul II distinguishes between the "direct" and the "indirect employer" (*ibid.*, pp. 127–29; cf. Mihevc, 1989). The "direct employer" is the person or group of persons that makes a contract with the worker regarding work and wages. In contemporary society this work contract is influenced by several societal factors, such as legislation on the conditions of employment, training available at schools, systems of transportation, housing close to the place of work, and so forth. These social factors the Pope calls the "indirect employer." Because of the interrelatedness of all institutions in industrialized nations, the indirect employer is society itself. Issues of employment and unemployment touch the whole of society, and the whole of society is responsible for them.

The distinction between the direct and the indirect employers allows John Paul II to be critical in both directions, critical of former Communist governments in Soviet bloc countries that disregarded the role of the direct employer, limited the freedom of workers to choose or change their job, and inhibited the economic initiative of the citizens; and critical of Western capitalist countries that disregard the role of the indirect employer, rely on direct employers to overcome the lack of jobs, and resign themselves to scandalous levels of structural unemployment.

Why, we may ask, is the encyclical more critical of Western capitalism than of Eastern communism? In other papal documents we find severe judgements on Communist society. Yet *Laborem exercens* pays special attention to capitalist society because John Paul II believed that in the seventies world capitalism had entered a new phase, replacing the more benign Keynesian period with a new, more brutal phase that would widen the gap between the rich and the poor and exercise a devastating impact on the less developed countries.

THE CANADIAN CATHOLIC BISHOPS

In no Western, capitalist country has the Catholic hierarchy been as concerned with social justice and as critical of contemporary capitalism as in Canada. Throughout the seventies, responding to Catholic and ecumenical groups and organizations and collaborating with Protestant church boards, the Catholic bishops of this country became deeply concerned with the issue of faith and justice and promulgated a series of progressive pastoral messages. In the eighties, influenced by the encyclical *Laborem exercens*, the Canadian bishops became more radical in their teaching. In December, 1982, they published the controversial statement, "Ethical Reflection on the Economic Crisis," which recognized the crisis of world capitalism and its entry into a new, more brutal phase (Sheridan, ed., 1987; Baum and Cameron, 1984).

The relatively brief, though densely written "Ethical Reflection" outlined the changes in the structure of capital in Canada to account for increasing unemployment and poverty and then proposed, for public debate, various alternative models of economic development. What has occurred in the world, according to the bishops, is an "intensification" of capital in ever-expanding and all-devouring transnational corporations, a "concentration" of capital in the metropolitan areas, producing massive regional inequalities, an "internationalization" of capital allowing the shifting of industries to parts of the world where labour is cheap and governments prevent workers from organizing, and finally – in Canada – the increase of "foreign ownership." Added to this is the turn to new, capital-intensive technology, i.e., to automated production, without any plans for providing alternative jobs for laid-off workers. What is taking place over the entire world, according to the bishops, is an effort to rebuild the economy around privately owned giant corporations whose aim is to

maximize profit and whose power is so great that national governments are obliged to serve the corporate interests.

The bishops point to the devastating consequences of this new
phase of capitalism. Everything is left to impersonal market forces.
(Catholic social teaching appreciates the market as a useful economic
institution, but it always held that the market must be embedded in a
culture of self-restraint and be regulated by public policy.) At the
present, the bishops argue, the aim of government is to dismantle the
institutions that have protected the human community in the past.
With privatization and deregulation, governments create a clean playing field for private corporations. According to the verdict of the
bishops, "as long as technology and capital are not harnessed by
society to serve basic human needs, they are likely to become an
enemy rather than an ally in the development of peoples" (Baum and
Cameron, 1984, p. 10).

What is being played out on the world level is the rough game of
global competition, into which the nations are drawn, often against
their will. National economies must be competitive. Mr. Trudeau told
us that we have "to tighten our belt" and a little later Mr. Mulroney
reminded us that the Canadian economy must become "lean and
efficient." According to the Canadian bishops, "the renewed emphasis on the 'survival of the fittest' as the supreme law of economics is
likely to increase the domination of the weak by the strong, both at
home and abroad" (*ibid.*).

What are the alternatives proposed by "Ethical Reflections"? We
note that the bishops do not speak as economists: they offer *ethical*
reflections on the economy, based on biblical values. Their proposed
alternatives are not blueprints for innovative institutions: what they
try to do, rather, is to initiate a public debate on Canada's economic
future and stretch people's imagination of the possible. Our imagination has become impoverished, the bishops argue, when we believe
that the only choice available for society is between capitalism and
communism.

Following the lead of *Laborem exercens*, the social reconstruction
proposed by the Canadian bishops calls for two contrasting economic
policies, one centralizing – demanding more planning on the national
level – and the other decentralizing – demanding greater diversifica-
tion of ownership and expanded regional initiatives. While critical of
the industrial megaprojects undertaken by the federal government,
the bishops ask nonetheless that the government "promote the self-
sufficiency of Canada's industries, strengthen the manufacturing and
construction industries, create new job-producing industries in local
communities, redistribute capital for industrial development and provide relevant job-training programmes" (*ibid.*, p. 14). At the same

time, the bishops also call for the decentralization of capital and regional economic activity. Here their proposals include self-reliant models of economic development, community ownership and control of industries, and new forms of worker management and ownership. To render the less developed regions in Canada more self-reliant the bishops also encourage local production to supply basic needs and labour-intensive industries using appropriate forms of technology (*ibid.*, pp. 15–16). The tension between central planning and vigorous regional development is here seen as protecting personal freedom and economic initiative in society.

Reconstructing the economy along these contrasting lines is a societal project that differs significantly from liberal capitalism and Marxist socialism. Yet it also differs from social democracy, which, like most socialisms of the past, has operated out of a centralizing imagination. The social democratic state was here seen as the solution of all social and economic problems. It is worth noting, however, that at its foundation the Co-operative Commonwealth Federation saw itself as a made-in-Canada socialism that supported co-operatives, favoured various forms of collective ownership, and integrated a decentralizing principle into its economic policy. There is a certain affinity, I am prepared to argue, between the original social philosophy of the CCF and contemporary Catholic social theory.

The important, difficult technical question of how to connect democratically controlled central planning with regional initiatives and co-operatively owned industries is not touched upon in the ecclesiastical documents. For some critics, this is reason enough not to take the bishops' proposals seriously. Still, I would argue that the answer to this difficult question is not simply a technical one to be resolved by economic science: the answer depends in part on one's vision of society. Where does one see the great danger for society? In the hegemony of the market? Or in bureaucratic control? The thrust of Catholic social teaching distrusts the impersonal forces of the market and favours instead reliance on human, rational planning, ever to be reviewed, but never to be forsaken.

On his visit to Canada in 1984 John Paul II fully supported the pastoral statements made by the Canadian bishops. He even repeated their provocative statement.

The needs of the poor have priority over the wants of the rich; the rights of workers are more important than the maximization of profits; the participation of marginalized groups has precedence over a system which excludes them. (*Ibid.*, p. 6; Baum, 1987, pp. 88–103)

He supported the need for greater planning around natural resources and food production, including international co-operation, and he encouraged the development of alternative forms of economic development (co-operative or community-based) and explicitly condemned economic imperialism.

SOLLICITUDO REI SOCIALIS

In 1987 John Paul II published *Sollicitudo rei socialis*, his second encyclical dealing with social and economic justice (Baum and Ellsberg, eds., 1989; Baum, 1988). Here he focused on the plight of the Third World and laid the blame for it on the developed countries of the North, including the West and the Eastern bloc. Again the Pope excoriated "liberal capitalism" and "Marxist collectivism," both as systems and as ideologies. He demonstrated the devastating impact of the Cold War, "the logic of the two blocs" (Baum and Ellsberg, eds., 1989, pp. 20–21), on the underdeveloped countries of the Third World.

Let us take a brief look at the manner in which this encyclical proposes the double emphasis on central planning and decentralizing economic development.

Sollicitudo recognizes the global interdependence of all national economies. Yet, according to the encyclical, this interdependence is mediated through economic agreements and financial institutions set up by the capitalist powers, for their own advantage, to the detriment of the poorer nations. Under these conditions interdependence becomes a system of economic oppression. What is needed, the encyclical argues, is the restructuring of interdependence from a commitment to solidarity. This involves economic planning on the international level. Yet even on the national level planning is necessary to protect the resources of the earth, save the natural environment, convert military industries to peaceful production, and stop the present economic trend in capitalist countries toward increasing unemployment and housing shortage and the accompanying culture of poverty.

This attack on capitalist ideology and the liberal prejudice against economic planning is balanced by a long paragraph blasting the over-bureaucratization of the economy in the Eastern European countries. People have the right, the human right, to economic initiative. Humans are meant to be the subjects of their lives.

> Experience shows us that the denial of this right . . . diminishes, or in practice absolutely destroys the spirit of initiative, that is to say the subjectivity of the citizens. . . . In the place of creative initiative there appears passivity, dependence and submission to the bureau-

cratic apparatus which, as the only "ordering" and "decision-making" body . . . of the totality of goods and means of production, puts everyone in a position of absolute dependence, which is similar to the traditional dependence of the proletariat in capitalism. This provokes a sense of frustration or desperation and predisposes people to opt out of national life, impelling many to emigrate and also favouring forms of "psychological" emigration. (*Ibid.*)

Compared to *Laborem exercens*, the mood of the *Sollicitudo* is dark. When we consider the growing hunger and misery in the South, the ever-increasing production of nuclear arms in the North threatening human survival, and the ecological devastation of the entire globe caused by the maximization of production, we must conclude, John Paul II argued, that our civilization is "oriented toward death rather than life" (*ibid.*, p. 23). Will we have time to change our ways? What is demanded, the encyclical argues, is a moral conversion to human solidarity, to "the logic of solidarity," beginning preferentially with the poor and oppressed.

This takes me at the end of this paper to a dimension of Catholic social theory, present from its beginning, that receives detailed attention in *Sollicitudo*. What is required for the transformation of society, including its economic system, is not only the reconstruction of institutions but also and at the same time an ethical conversion.

The accent on the ethical dimension has frequently been used for conservative or even reactionary political purposes. Catholics have often given the impression that if only people became more generous and virtuous, then the problems of society would disappear and there would be no need to change the inherited institutions. Having been exposed to such a "moralizing" of political and economic issues, Catholic populations have often been difficult to mobilize for radical social action aimed at the transformation of society.

Yet the call for ethical conversion made in more recent Catholic social teaching, very strongly in *Sollicitudo*, has an altogether different meaning. It affirms a crucial point, neglected in secular political theories, that the reconstruction of political and economic institutions will not achieve the anticipated result unless the participants acquire the appropriate consciousness, unless people experience a renewal of the spirit, unless men and women transcend the individualistic and utilitarian mind-set induced by the market system and learn to care for one another and feel responsible for the well-being of all. What is required is an ethical conversion.

Liberal political and economic theory abstracted from the ethical dimension, proclaiming that people could free themselves from the old stories of virtue, guilt, and care for the common good and rely on enlightened self-interest alone. Even the liberal defence of welfare capitalism consisted of utilitarian arguments. Mitigating the gap between rich and poor was to create a peaceful environment propitious for production and commerce; offering higher wages to workers was to turn them into customers and thus extend the commodity market. While Marxism criticized the self-interest produced by the market system and anticipated that the revolutionary struggle would transmute egotism into social solidarity, Marxist socialist theory assimilated nonetheless the reigning utilitarianism, except that now the significant enlightened self-interest was a collective one, the material class-interest of the proletariat. Political theories on the right and on the left betrayed a singular indifference to ethics.

At present this indifference to ethics is seen in the development theories devised for Third World countries by capitalist and socialist political scientists. From their perspective poverty is a purely economic concept, and thus, depending on their ideological orientation, they invent development schemes that promise to overcome the economic handicap.

According to Catholic social theory, supported by some secular political theorists – for instance, a thinker like Karl Polanyi – poverty is not a purely economic concept. The material poverty inflicted on people profoundly humiliates them, dislocates them against their will, and undermines their cultural integration. Thus, a development scheme envisaged in purely economic terms may not be helpful at all: it may even increase the people's humiliation, their dislocation and cultural disintegration. Only a development scheme that protects the cultural identity and respects the collective personality of the people is ethically acceptable: and only such a scheme has a chance of succeeding.

According to Catholic social theory, articulated in *Sollicitudo* (*ibid.*, pp. 26–36), all projects of social reconstruction, in underdeveloped countries and in the developed North, must pay attention to the ethical dimension. Enlightened self-interest, individual and collective, is important and not to be despised, but it is not enough; it must be accompanied by a conversion to solidarity, beginning preferentially with the poor and the oppressed. Without special solidarity with the weak and great respect for the common good, the best system will not work well.

Since we are forced to think in global terms today, we may well ask the question why workers and other disadvantaged groups struggling for greater justice in their countries of the North should be concerned about justice for the impoverished masses of the South. Why should they extend their solidarity to Third World struggles? Is enlightened collective self-interest sufficient reason? It is very difficult, if not impossible, to argue for global solidarity on the basis of a utilitarian ethic. According to Catholic social theory the ground for global solidarity is the unity of the human family: we belong to one another, we support one another, we are responsible for one another, we are like a single family where the suffering of one induces the suffering of all, and we are willing to make personal sacrifices so that all be well. Without a conversion to solidarity, the encyclical argues, masses of peoples in the South will be doomed. But can such an ethical conversion be purely secular? Or will it inevitably involve a religious dimension? Must one believe in a gracious, originating divinity before the unity of the human family becomes concretely felt in the heart and generates global solidarity, beginning preferentially with the poor and oppressed? *Sollicitudo* suspects that this may be the case.

REFERENCES

Baum, G. (1982). *The Priority of Labor*. New York: Paulist Press.

Baum, G. (1987). *Theology and Society*. New York: Paulist Press.

Baum, G. (1988). "The Anti-Cold War Encyclical," *The Ecumenist*, 26 (July-August), pp. 65–74.

Baum, G., and D. Cameron (1984). *Ethics and Economics*. Toronto: James Lorimer.

Baum, G., and R. Ellsberg, eds. (1989). *The Logic of Solidarity*. Maryknoll, N.Y.: Orbis Books.

Dorr, Donal (1983). *Option for the Poor: A Hundred Years of Vatican Social Teaching*. Maryknoll, N.Y.: Orbis Books.

Duchrow, Ulrich (1987). *Global Economy*. Geneva: WCC Publications.

Mihevc, John (1989). "Self-Reliance and Basic Human Needs," in C. Pratt and R. Hutchinson, eds., *Christian Faith and Economic Justice*. Burlington, Ont.: Trinity Press.

Seven Great Encyclicals (1963). New York: Paulist Press.

Sheridan, E.F., ed. (1987). *Do Justice!* Toronto: Jesuit Centre for Social Faith and Justice.

JOHN RICHARDS

7
Playing Two Games at Once

> When everyone is both worker and owner it's like you're playing
> two games in your mind at once.
>
> Chris Haines (quoted in Faustmann, 1988), worker director,
> Lamford Forest Products, New Westminster, B.C.

AS ANYONE INVOLVED IN UNION ACTIVITY KNOWS, THE 1935 WAGNER ACT
was a key piece of Franklin Roosevelt's New Deal legislation. The
importance of the Act is to have codified those public policies, such as
union certification, that provide state support for collective bargaining. Under pressure from Canadian unions in the 1940s, Ottawa and
the provincial governments each adopted variants of the Act.

The purpose of this essay is to "get beyond" the Wagner Act and
explore alternatives in industrial relations. I shall argue the need for a
new social contract that – while recognizing the importance of collective bargaining – enables a significant measure of worker participation in management. Easier said than done! The Wagner Act is
revered – by union leaders in both Canada and the United States – as
the Magna Carta of organized labour. To suggest that union leaders
"get beyond it" is for many of these leaders proof of unpardonable
apostasy.

It is important to understand that the Wagner Act constituted a
kind of social contract in North America among leaders of business,
government, and labour. After World War Two all sides more or less
came to accept it as a framework within which to resolve industrial
conflict. It also ushered in the "golden decade" of American unions,
during which union density (the unionized proportion of the labour
force) more than doubled. Canadian union density lagged behind that

Table 1
Union Density: United States, Canada, and British Columbia

Year	United States*	Canada*	British Columbia**
1935	13.5%	14.5%	—
1940	22.5	16.3	—
1945	30.4	24.2	38.9%
1951	31.7	28.4	46.0
1955	31.8	33.7	49.1
1960	28.6	32.3	50.1
1965	30.1	29.7	43.2
1970	29.6	33.6	43.5
1975	28.9	36.9	43.9
1980	23.2	37.6	42.9
1981	22.6	37.4	43.1
1982	21.9	39.0	46.3
1983	20.7	40.0	45.6
1984	18.8	39.6	42.9
1985	18.0	39.0	42.8
1986	17.5	37.7	40.0
1987	17.0	37.6	39.8
1988	17.0	36.6	37.6
1989	16.4	36.2	36.7
1990	—	36.2	37.7

*Percentage of paid nonagricultural workers belonging to a union.
**Percentage of paid workers belonging to a union; excludes agricultural paid workers before 1976.

SOURCES: U.S. data: cited in Industrial Relations Centre (annual). Canadian data: Labour Canada (annual). British Columbia data: British Columbia Ministry of Labour (annual).

in America until the 1950s, when density was approximately one-third in both countries (see Table 1). For the last two decades, however, American business leaders have been increasingly critical of collective bargaining. Many have in effect cancelled the contract embodied in the Wagner Act, and they have succeeded in pushing union density back to levels prevailing in the mid-1930s.

Canada has not experienced any analogous decline. Indeed, Canadian union density slowly rose until the early 1980s. Still, obvious questions need to be posed. Canada followed American union density up in the 1940s; will it follow it down now? Canadian union density has either declined or remained static in each year since 1983. Is this the beginning of a downward trend? Is it just a short-term fluctuation around a stable average? Or is it a short-term fluctuation from the rising trend of the last half-century?

A FEW THOUGHTS ON POLITICAL CULTURE

Much as we try to be analytic about industrial relations, any left-wing discussion of this subject is embedded in beliefs about the sanctity of labour and in mistrust of corporate management. Before I proceed to the central argument, let me be explicit about the set of beliefs I imbibed from my prairie roots in Saskatchewan.

Saskatchewan is the one political jurisdiction in North America for which social democratic government has been the norm. The New Democratic Party and its predecessor, the Co-operative Common-wealth Federation, governed for thirty-one of the thirty-eight years between 1944 and 1982. The NDP suffered a humbling defeat in 1982 and lost again in 1986, although it had recovered sufficiently by then to win – narrowly – the popular vote. The NDP's electoral base in the prairie provinces is essentially a left populist farm-labour alliance. Farmers are small businessmen, keen to improve their net income by cutting expenses, including wages that enter, directly or indirectly, into their expenses. The potential for conflict with union members intent on raising wages via collective bargaining is obvious, and in most jurisdictions the two do not cohabit politically.

Why they have usually been willing to do so in Saskatchewan has fascinated left-wing academics since the prominent American sociologist, Seymour Martin Lipset, chose it as the topic of his doctoral thesis in the 1940s (Lipset, 1950). The explanation in his thesis, which I think basically correct, is that on the Prairies the NDP (and its predecessor, the Co-operative Commonwealth Federation) has been part of the same North American political culture that extends back to the People's Party of the 1890s and earlier. It dispensed with much of the rhetoric and ideology of European socialist parties. Instead, it employed a populist ideology that sought to minimize class and racial distinctions among "the people" and to concentrate political wrath on loosely defined "vested interests," elites dominating the "old-line parties" and major financial and industrial corporations.

A similar explanation underlies the electoral success of the Manitoba NDP, which governed for fifteen of the nineteen years between its initial victory in 1969 and its defeat in 1988. Ed Schreyer's election as Manitoba NDP leader just prior to the 1969 provincial election symbolized an end to the scholastic debate among socialists over the historical significance of the 1919 Winnipeg General Strike. Schreyer, a Roman Catholic of German descent who had represented a rural riding as a Member of Parliament in Ottawa, transformed the Manitoba NDP. While it retained a central place for the union movement, the party ceased to be a "labour party" in the British tradition. After 1969 the working-class ridings of North Winnipeg were no longer the core; the party became a much broader "populist" coalition. What it lost in ideological purity, it obviously gained in electoral success.

The farm-labour marriage on the Prairies is a pragmatic one that, from the perspective of any socialist intellectual, has frequently lacked political direction. But despite pragmatic compromises, governments in this left populist tradition have established many of the progressive precedents in Canadian public policy – as much in labour law as elsewhere.

The Saskatchewan Trade Union Act of 1945 gave Canada's most rural province the most pro-labour legislation of any North American jurisdiction at the time. Saskatchewan public-sector workers thereby gained, for example, the right to bargain collectively and to strike two decades earlier than elsewhere in Canada. Saskatchewan's 1972 Occupational Health Act has served as the basic model for occupational health and safety legislation. A front-page story in *The Globe and Mail* (22 February 1988) written shortly before the NDP's defeat in Manitoba concluded that "Manitoba's labour legislation is the most pro-union in the country (with the possible exception of Quebec)." NDP initiatives in Manitoba included first-contract legislation, the first Canadian legislation on equal pay for work of equal value, the highest provincial minimum wage, a provision for final-offer arbitration, strict regulation of union decertification, and a powerful occupational health and safety program.

The farm-labour marriage has at times been stormy. Provincial NDP and labour supporters often bicker, public-sector collective bargaining frequently being the irritant. Saskatchewan and Manitoba NDP leaders have been compelled to live their own version of Chris Haines's dilemma, "playing two games at once," reconciling support for unions and collective bargaining with pursuit of economic efficiency and the need for the support of non-union voters.

In Saskatchewan in particular, successive CCF-NDP cabinets encouraged a tradition of professional public administrators who behaved as public entrepreneurs innovating in social and economic policy. They simultaneously resisted, more effectively than in most provinces, the pressure of special interest groups – including unions – to introduce programs of dubious net social value. Thus arose the irony that on many dimensions of interprovincial comparison of government size – such as civil servant to population ratios – Saskatchewan under the NDP was *below* the national average.

Beyond the Prairies social democratic government in Canada is so rare that unions cannot draw on a local tradition of "playing two games at once." Instead, many union leaders feel instinctively that exercise of the management function – in either the private or public sector – is in principle suspect. Not surprisingly, the Canadian union response to change in labour law has often been a retreat into "militant conservatism," into a defence of past advantages won. But this may be a self-defeating strategy for unions and their political allies. The Wagner Act was a significant advance fifty years ago; its limitations are now too important to ignore.

Class conflict pervades Canadian industrial relations; one aspect is mistrust by the managed of those who do the managing. Mistrust is equally present among those on the other side. If surveyed, a clear majority of Canadian businessmen and managers doubtless would express the hope that Canadian unions experience the secular decline of their American counterparts. Such attitudes have encouraged conservative provincial governments, notably in British Columbia and Alberta, to undertake legislative changes that may indeed lower Canadian union density to American levels.

One final detour. The argument in this essay refers extensively to public opinion surveys. Many criticize them as tools whereby corporations and politicians manipulate us as passive consumers or voters. Simultaneously, many dismiss survey results as superficial, unable to tell us anything useful about the complex relationships of politics. I sympathize with the first critique but not the second. Surveys are expensive to conduct well and good-quality surveys can only be bought by those with money. The second critique is true to the extent that good political leadership cannot be reduced to a set of answers to an opinion survey. But this critique too often serves as a device to avoid facing up to what people actually think. Survey results may be inaccurate for many reasons, but in general good surveys do depict accurately what people think at the time the survey is undertaken.

The second critique leads into a complex question: should social democrats base their policy on majority opinion? Where government policy implicates directly the personal moral integrity of politicians, the answer is clearly "no." On matters such as abortion and capital punishment we expect politicians to apply their personal morality. Another reason for answering "no" is that, as participants in a social movement, we hope in the future to shift public opinion. However, when the public resists our message for an extended period stretching into decades, we social democrats are open to the charge of sectarian irrelevance if we fail to examine closely why the public continues to entertain "non-socialist" thoughts.

With this prologue, the argument can be summarized in the following four points.

1. *Ambivalent public attitudes.* Public attitudes toward collective bargaining and unions are basically similar in Canada and the United States. In both countries a majority support the principle of collective bargaining to determine wages and the need for due process to resolve

individual worker grievances, but in both countries there exists much scepticism about many aspects of collective bargaining. The Wagner Act model of industrial relations enjoys only limited public support and, accordingly, conservative politicians face only limited opposition to legislation that erodes collective bargaining.

2. *The "two faces of unions."* Unions have both a "monopoly and collective voice face." Unless social democrats recognize explicitly that unions are *both* the "collective voice" of organized workers *and* a special interest group seeking to redistribute income from non-union to union members, electoral support from non-union households will be tenuous.

3. *Trends in Canadian union density.* Recent evidence from British Columbia – where union density has declined significantly since 1982 – suggests there are no unique social or political characteristics within Canada to prevent our unions from following their American counterparts down in the 1990s, much as they followed them up in the 1940s.

4. *Worker participation in management.* Many workers want to participate more extensively in management and to exercise more individual authority over their work environment than collective bargaining agreements have traditionally afforded. The general public, union members included, does not share the left's innate mistrust of worker participation in management. However difficult it is for unions to "play two games at once" – to engage simultaneously in collective bargaining and to participate in corporate management – it is probably a necessary condition for their future growth that they do so.

AMBIVALENT PUBLIC ATTITUDES

As illustrated in Table 1, Canadian and American union densities have diverged over the past quarter-century, and by the 1980s Canadian density was twice the American level.

Some writers, for example Lipset (1986), explain this divergence in terms of a difference in political culture between citizens of the two countries. Americans allegedly possess a much stronger commitment to classic liberal values, including the "right to work" – the right to enter into individual contracts between employer and worker without the constraint of collective bargaining. Arguing in the "cultural fragment" tradition, Lipset perceives contemporary Canadians to be the carriers of imported "collectivist" political cultures – whether the commitment to "peace, order, and good government" of nineteenth-century colonists who had earlier rejected the American revolution, or the class-based union solidarity of twentieth-century British working-class immigrants. For Lipset, "collectivist" New Deal legislation such as the Wagner Act is an aberration arising in a period of extreme political crisis; the secular decline of union density constitutes an institutional adaptation to basic American political culture.

But are Canadian attitudes really that different from American? Survey results indicate that, in general, attitudes on both sides of the border are remarkably similar. Table 2 compares Canadian and American attitudes toward unions along four dimensions: (1) confidence in leaders; (2) general approval/disapproval; (3) union power; and (4) satisfaction of union members and desire of the non-unionized to join a union.

In the first four polls the identical question was posed, eliminating problems of responses varying with wording. As measured by the per cent having "a great deal of confidence," Canadians and Americans are about equally sceptical of union leaders. The only difference implied by these four polls is that Canadians may be more sceptical of corporate executives than are Americans. But both Canadians and Americans express more confidence in them than in union leaders.

We should not conclude from the first dimension that either Canadians or Americans disapprove in general of unions. Gallup's question (poll 5), posed for over fifty years, shows some decline in approval among Americans since the 1930s, but Americans still approve of unions by a margin in excess of two to one. Three similar questions posed to Canadians (6a, 6b, and 7) show a majority positive response but somewhat *less* approval than among Americans. Note the sharp divergence between union and non-union workers and their families.

A closely related dimension is public perception of power exercised by unions. Poll 8 suggests that about half of the American public think unions too powerful; that proportion has declined somewhat in the past two decades as actual American union density has declined. Given the present differences in union density between the two countries, unions doubtless are more powerful in Canada than in the United States. Therefore it is not surprising that polls 10 and 11a show a higher proportion of Canadians (half to two-thirds) concluding unions to be too powerful. Again, there is a significant divergence between union and non-union families.

The final dimension compares member satisfaction with performance of his or her union, and the desire of the non-unionized to join a union. Again, attitudes of Canadian and American workers are remarkably similar. Roughly three-quarters of American union members are "somewhat or very satisfied" (12a). If we distribute the "fair" responses equally between the positive and negative responses in poll 13a, then about seven out of ten Canadian union members think their union does a "very good or good" job of representing their interests. Similarly, only one-third of non-union workers in the United States

Table 2
Public Attitudes Toward Unions, Canada and United States

I. Confidence in leaders

How about the people who run (. . .)? Would you say you have a great deal of confidence in them, only some confidence, or hardly any confidence?

	great deal	only some	hardly any
	(percent)		
United States			
1. Harris (quoted in Lipset, 1986)			
Major companies			
American public, average 20 polls, 1966–85	24		
Unions			
American public, average 20 polls, 1966–85	15		
2. National Opinion Research Center (quoted in Lipset, 1986)			
Major companies			
American public, average 10 polls, 1973–84	26		
Unions			
American public, average 10 polls, 1973–84	13		
Canada			
3. Decima (quarterly)			
Multinational corporations			
Canadian public, average 8 polls, 1981–82	12		
Union members, average 5 polls, 1981–82	11		
Union families, average 8 polls, 1981–82	10		
Non-union families, average 8 polls, 1981–82	13		
Unions			
Canadian public, average 11 polls, 1981–84	10		
Union members, average 11 polls, 1981–84	18		
Union families, average 11 polls, 1981–84	14		
Non-union families, average 11 polls, 1981–84	7		
4. Richards and Mauser (1986)			
Multinational corporations			
Vancouver public, 1985 (n = 335)*	20	57	17
Union workers in Vancouver, 1985 (n = 96)	19	58	20
Non-union workers in Vancouver, 1985 (n = 156)	20	59	13
Unions			
Vancouver public, 1985 (n = 335)	10	43	44
Union workers in Vancouver, 1985 (n = 96)	17	47	35
Non-union workers in Vancouver, 1985 (n = 156)	7	41	48

Table 2 — *(Continued)*

II. General approval/disapproval of unions
United States
5. Gallup (quoted in Lipset, 1986)
   In general, do you approve or disapprove of
   labor unions?

	approve	disapprove
American public, 1936	72	20
American public, 1947	64	25
American public, average 2 polls, 1957	70	16
American public, 1967	66	23
American public, 1978	59	31
American public, 1985	58	27

Canada
6. Angus Reid (1987)
   a. First, generally speaking, do you think labour
   unions in Canada have had a positive or negative impact on individual working Canadians?

	positive	negative	no effect
Canadian public, 1987 (n = 1,504)	52	39	2
Union workers, 1987 (n = 322)	70	23	2
Non-union workers, 1987 (n = 700)	49	43	2
Federal voting intentions, June, 1987			
Conservative (n = 292)	46	46	2
Liberal (n = 360)	53	39	2
NDP (n = 458)	63	30	2

   b. And would you say labour unions in Canada
   have generally had a positive or negative impact
   on the country as a whole?

Canadian public, 1987 (n = 1,504)	46	44	2
Union workers, 1987 (n = 322)	61	29	2
Non-union workers, 1987 (n = 700)	42	49	2
Federal voting intentions, June, 1987			
Conservative (n = 292)	34	58	2
Liberal (n = 360)	43	48	2
NDP (n = 458)	59	33	2

7. Gallup (1984)
   Generally speaking, and thinking of Canada as a
   whole, do you think that labor unions are a
   good thing or a bad thing?

	good thing	bad thing	don't know
Canadian public, 1979	50	35	16
Canadian public, 1984 (n = 1,051)	51	35	14
Union families, 1984	72	17	11
Non-union families, 1984	43	42	15

Table 2 — *(Continued)*

III. Extent of union power

United States

8. Opinion Research Corporation (quoted in Lipset, 1986)
   Please tell me which one statement best
   describes the way you feel about labor unions in
   this country: (1) Labor unions today are not
   strong enough. I would like to see them grow in
   power. (2) Labor unions today have grown too
   powerful. I would like to see their power
   reduced. (3) The power that labor unions have
   today is about right. I would like to see it stay
   the way it is.

	not strong enough	too powerful	about right
American public, 1971	14	55	24
American public, 1976	9	52	28
American public, 1985	20	46	31

Canada

9. Angus Reid (1987)
   There is often discussion about what types of
   things organized labour should or should not be
   doing. For example, donating money to political
   parties like the NDP. Do you yourself think
   labour unions should or should not be involved
   in that area?

	should	should not	don't know
Canadian public, 1987 (n = 1,504)	20	71	9
Union worker, 1987 (n = 322)	20	72	8
Non-union worker, 1987 (n = 700)	20	73	7
Federal voting intentions, June, 1987			
Conservative (n = 292)	12	81	7
Liberal (n = 360)	18	73	9
NDP (n = 458)	31	62	7

10. Decima (1986)
    Some people say that unions in Canada have
    become too powerful. Others say that unions
    are necessary in Canada to protect workers from
    exploitation. Which one of these views best
    reflects your own?

	too powerful	necessary
Canadian public, June, 1981	52	40
Canadian public, June, 1982	61	31
Canadian public, December, 1984	53	41
Canadian public, December, 1985	50	45
Canadian public, December, 1986	50	45
Union members, December, 1986	28	66
Union families, December, 1986	36	58
Non-union families, December, 1986	59	36

Table 2 — *(Continued)*

11. Gallup (annual)

a. Do you think that labor unions are becoming too powerful, are not powerful enough or are about right?

	too powerful	not powerful enough	about right
Canadian public, 1979	68	7	19
Canadian public, 1984 (n = 1,051)	62	6	27
Union families, 1984	47	12	37
Non-union families, 1984	68	4	23

b. In Canada political parties can receive donations from unions and corporations. In your opinion should both unions and corporations be allowed to donate to political parties, unions only, corporations only or should neither of these organizations be allowed to donate funds?

	both	unions only	corporations only	neither
Canadian public, 1986 (n = 1,040)	38	3	8	37
Union members, 1986	38	2	8	44
Non-union members, 1986	38	3	9	35

IV. Union workers' satisfaction with their union/Non-union workers' desire to join union

United States

12. Quinn and Staines (1979), Institute for Social Research, University of Michigan

a. All in all, how satisfied are you with your union or employees' association – very satisfied, somewhat satisfied, not too satisfied, or not at all satisfied?

	somewhat or very satisfied	not at all or not too satisfied
American workers belonging to a union, 1977 (n = 540)	73	27

b. If an election were held with secret ballots, would you vote for or against having a union or employees' association representing you?

	for	against
American workers neither belonging to a union nor covered by a union contract, 1977 (n = 1,265)	33	67

Canada

13. Angus Reid (1987)

a. How good a job would you say your labour union does of representing your interests?

	very good or good	fair	poor or very poor
Canadian union members, 1987 (n = 322)	55	27	16

b. If you had your choice, regardless of whether or not you are working and regardless of what type of job you hold, would you prefer to belong to a labour union or would you rather not?

	would prefer	rather not	don't know
Canadian non-union workers, June, 1987 (n = 700)	29	62	9

*n refers to the number of respondents sampled.

want to belong to a union (12b), slightly more than the proportion among Canadian workers (13b).

Table 3 summarizes the results of more detailed questions on attitudes toward collective bargaining from a survey conducted in Vancouver. While several methodological caveats must be kept in mind, these results obviously suggest public scepticism toward many collective bargaining practices. As expected, union members give more favourable responses, but they are far from satisfied.

However critical people may be of union leaders (question 4), questions 3 and 7 suggest that a majority clearly subscribe to the idea of countervailing power. Unions are necessary to counter the power of employers in determining wages and working conditions, and to prevent employer favouritism. The majority also favour public-sector workers retaining some rights to strike (11 and 12). Question 2 implies that a majority – even within the subset of union members – think unions are partially responsible for unemployment, by forcing wage rates above market-clearing levels. Question 5 suggests disagreement with the principle of the union shop. (Responses on this issue would be expected to vary considerably, depending on wording. A more pro-union response would have been elicited with an alternate wording, e.g., "Given that a majority of workers have democratically chosen to form a union, the minority of workers who disagree should be free to decide whether or not to join.") Similarly, seniority, a principle embedded in most collective bargaining agreements, does not enjoy majority support (6). Employer intervention in any way in his employees' decision to unionize has been a fundamental unfair labour practice. This restriction on employer intervention does not apparently enjoy majority support (8), even among union members. Question 10 suggests decertification procedures are perceived to be too difficult. The final question in this table (13) illustrates a general willingness to accept government overriding the collective bargaining process.

With access to survey results such as the above, it is not surprising that conservative provincial governments have been willing to incur labour's wrath and legislate to weaken state support for collective bargaining.

THE "TWO FACES OF UNIONISM"

As Freeman and Medoff, economists generally sympathetic to the union movement, have long insisted, unions have two faces: "a 'monopoly wage-setting' face, with generally harmful effects to the overall efficiency of the economy; and a 'collective voice/management response' . . . face with generally positive effects on the operation of the economy" (Freeman, 1986, p. 178). Unions raise wages, which in

Table 3
Public Attitudes toward Collective Bargaining, by Union Status*

	total sample (n = 335)		union workers (n = 96)		non-union workers (n = 156)	
	agree	disagree	agree	disagree	agree	disagree
1. The growth of unionism has made our democracy stronger.	59%	41%	65%	35%	56%	44%
2. Union demands often contribute to unemployment.	64	34	54	45	68	30
3. When it comes to determining wages and working conditions, the employers' power needs to be balanced by unions.	71	29	81	20	65	32
4. Union leaders usually represent the best interests of their members.	44	55	56	43	37	63
5. Every worker should be free to decide whether or not to join the union where he works.	89	11	82	19	91	8
6. In a case of layoffs the best person should be kept on the job regardless of seniority.	71	24	66	32	76	19
7. Without unions workers would have little protection against favouritism by management.	66	32	79	20	58	39
8. Employers should have a say in the decision by their workers to unionize.	61	37	57	39	65	34
10. At present it is too difficult for unionized workers to get rid of their union if the majority don't want it.	75	16	69	24	79	11
11. In general public sector workers – such as teachers, bus drivers and civil servants – should continue to have the right to strike.	60	38	77	23	54	43
12. Public sector workers in essential services – such as policing, firefighting and nursing – should continue to have the right to strike.	56	42	69	31	54	43

Table 3 — *(Continued)*

13. The government should be more willing to legislate an end to strikes and lockouts that cost the economy a great deal.	75	18	69	29	84	15

*Percentages may not total 100 per cent due to omission of "don't knows." Reported results have been aggregated from a four-element range extending from strongly disagree to strongly agree. Results in the first two columns are from the total sample; the remaining results are from the subset of the sample who are currently working for a wage or salary or have done so in the last five years.

The survey was conducted by telephone interviews in the spring of 1985 on a representative sample of adults in the greater Vancouver region. The sample was selected using probability sampling techniques, and 335 completed the interview. Interviews were conducted by students at Simon Fraser University. The first caveat is that the issues involved in the questions are complex, so that subtle changes in wording might make large differences in how people respond. To have greater confidence in the inferences drawn from this study, the results of alternative question wording should be examined. Second, the study was conducted by relatively inexperienced student interviewers. Third, while the survey was designed to be representative of attitudes in the Vancouver region, it may not be generalizable to all of Canada. Finally, surveys can, at best, assess only imperfectly the degree of conviction by which people hold their positions. It is easy to say yes or no to hypothetical questions.

SOURCE: Richards, Mauser, and Holmes (1988).

turn generates a modest misallocation of resources due to the consequent shrinkage of employment in the union sector and excessive substitution of machinery for labour. This negative effect on productivity is offset by the ability of unions to improve working conditions and thereby lower employee turnover and increase productivity. Furthermore, unions reduce inequality of wages and lower profits, particularly in sectors where a measure of monopoly power would otherwise permit a high rate of profitability. Freeman (1986, p. 200) has offered the following summary of the empirical evidence:

Perhaps the most sensible conclusion to draw from the evidence is that the economy functions best when there are both union and non-union sectors. Competition reduces the "monopoly wage" costs of unionism and encourages the positive aspects of unionism. Competition keeps non-union firms from taking advantage of their workers and forces them to adopt union-initiated work practices and modes of pay favored by employees to maintain their non-union status. . . . An economy is likely to operate efficiently when there is a sufficient number of union and of non-union firms to offer alternative work environments to workers, innovation in workplace rules and conditions, and competition in the marketplace.

Poll results imply that intuitively people understand this dual role of unions. They would probably be more comfortable with the NDP were its leaders more explicit on the subject. However supportive people are toward unions, they fear that a political party, particularly the NDP with which the unions are affiliated, will unduly abet the "monopoly face" of unionism. Consider poll 9 in Table 2, pertaining to union contributions to the NDP. By over three to one, Canadians oppose such contributions. There is no significant difference between the response of union and non-union workers, and even NDP supporters disapprove by a ratio in excess of two to one. It is worth noting that Canadians are about equally suspicious of corporate contributions to political parties as they are of union contributions (11b).

TRENDS IN CANADIAN UNION DENSITY

British Columbia's experience during the 1980s illustrates that political decisions can significantly reduce union density, and that any cultural differences between Canada and the United States offer little guarantee against union erosion. If any Canadian province possesses Lipset's "collectivist" pro-labour culture, it is British Columbia. Its work force has long been among the most unionized of Canadian provinces. Union leaders exercise great influence within the councils of the provincial NDP; furthermore, the NDP – and before it, the Co-operative Commonwealth Federation – has been a powerful influence in provincial politics. None of this prevented an ideologically conservative provincial government from weakening the legislative basis for collective bargaining and contributing to a significant decline in provincial union density over the decade. From the peak in 1982, density has fallen 8.6 percentage points. In relative terms it is as if one in five union members became non-union (see Table 1).

The causes for union growth and decline are complex. Without any legislative change, British Columbia union density would probably have fallen due to large productivity gains and the consequent lower employment in the highly unionized forest sector. Individual legislative changes have not been draconian; each has precedents elsewhere in Canada. Cumulatively, however, the provincial Social Credit administration has legislated to increase the cost of union organizing, to lower the cost to employers of resisting unionization, and to diminish the effectiveness of the strike as a bargaining tool. To illustrate, consider two of these legislative changes.

Prior to The Labour Code Amendment Act of 1984, a union local could be certified if it "signed up" over half the total number of workers within the proposed bargaining unit. That statute introduced the American practice of certifying a union only after a government-sponsored election among workers within the bargaining unit indicates majority support for collective bargaining. Canadian employers have lobbied for elections on the grounds that elections delay certification and permit the employer to state the anti-union case. For precisely the same reasons unions have lobbied against certification elections. On this change the government enjoyed overwhelming support – overall, 85 per cent of the public approved, 10 per cent opposed; among union members 75 per cent approved, 24 per cent opposed (Richards and Mauser, 1986, p. 176).

The British Columbia Industrial Relations Reform Act of 1987 constituted an important break with the Wagner Act tradition, as both its authors and the provincial labour movement recognized. Corporate executives within long-unionized sectors such as construction now perceive a non-union environment as a feasible "achievement." Of symbolic importance, the Act relabeled the provincial Labour Relations Board, subsuming it as one of two divisions within the newly created Industrial Relations Council. The other division has extensive investigation, mediation, and arbitration powers. The Act permits parties access to courts for damages caused by wildcat strikes, prohibits secondary boycott agreements and non-affiliation agreements except in construction, and eases successorship requirements for employers. The Council enjoys powers to force elections among striking workers on employers' final offers, to call cooling-off periods during strikes/lockouts, and to restrict secondary picketing.

WORKER PARTICIPATION IN MANAGEMENT

Worker participation in management may enhance productivity – for example, by lowering the costs to management and labour of implementing new technology. That is a separate matter. The argument here is that a new social contract embodying worker participation in management is a good idea because workers want it. The argument is simply that current collective bargaining practices do not adequately satisfy workers' desire to participate in management.

While union density may fall due to unfavourable legislative changes enacted by a conservative government, it may also fall because people choose to work in a non-union environment. Kochan, an industrial relations expert generally sympathetic to the union case, has extensively studied the growth since the 1950s of non-union "human resource" industrial relations systems in American industry. Many major companies have developed sophisticated personnel programs that apparently satisfy employee demands better than does traditional collective bargaining. Union leaders often perceive such programs as devices to weaken unions – and, indeed, that may be a motivation for employers to introduce quality circles, broad job descriptions that permit workers to vary tasks, flexible work schedules, counselling for substance abuse, etc. However, to the extent that declining union density reflects workers freely choosing a non-union work environment, union leaders need to reassess traditional collective bargaining. Kochan's conclusions on the growth of non-union "human resource" industrial relations systems are worth quoting:

> . . . previous systems of personnel administration based on collective approaches were inappropriate. Instead, personnel policies geared toward individual motivation and career goals rose in importance. Personnel staffs with training in psychology and the behavioural sciences were more suited to these policies and problems than were industrial relations staffs. . . . The newest industries, the newest firms in existing markets, and the newest plants in existing firms increasingly tended to be non-union. In other words, no longer were unions an inevitable fact of life and no longer was it necessary for management to accept their existence. . . . During this period the labour movement also generally rejected worker participation efforts and other programs that might have led to fundamental alterations in collective bargaining . . . . most unionists were sceptical of these efforts and opposed their expansion, seeing them as anti-union ploys designed to undermine the role of the union and the sanctity of the collective bargaining agreement. (Kochan, 1986, pp. 43-44)

In general, collective bargaining resolves reasonably well workers' interests in redistributing corporate revenue. Collective bargaining, however, has not proved adequate as a means to encompass workers' interests in management, whether at the immediate worksite level or at the level of corporate planning. A simple but suggestive poll result is that 65 per cent of Canadians agreed, and only 25 per cent disagreed, with the statement: "I would like to take a more active part in the decisions which affect the future of the company I work for" (Decima, 1983, p. 158). Union members were more desirous of such participation than the average.

Table 4 provides evidence on union performance by specific functions. Canadians think unions perform well with respect to bargaining wages and fringe benefits, much less well with respect to functions entailing some union assumption of managerial responsibility: job training for members, ensuring company survival, eco-

Table 4
Public Assessment of Union Performance by Specific Function

Many people say that unions have different responsibilities. I'd like you
to tell me, for each one, what kind of job you think unions are doing.
How about doing everything they can to (. . .) Would you say unions
are doing an excellent, good, only fair, or poor job?

	excellent	good	only fair	poor
1. get higher salaries for their members				
Canadian public, average 5 polls, 1982–86	20%	45%	24%	11%
Union members, 1986	16	49	25	10
2. get more fringe benefits such as longer vacations and greater pension coverage for their members				
Canadian public, average 5 polls, 1982–86	17	57	26	9
Union members, 1986	13	51	29	7
3. ensure job security for their members				
Canadian public, average 5 polls, 1982–86	14	43	27	16
Union members, 1986	13	47	23	18
4. ensure that their members have greater access to job training programs				
Canadian public, average 5 polls, 1982–86	7	34	37	19
Union members, 1986	10	30	37	22
5. ensure that their members have a safer and more enjoyable work environment				
Canadian public, average 5 polls, 1982–86	14	46	29	12
Union members, 1986	13	46	29	13
6. ensure the economic survival of companies				
Canadian public, average 5 polls, 1982–86	4	21	34	41
Union members, 1986	5	22	38	34
7. co-operate with government and private industry to plan the economic future of the country				
Canadian public, average 5 polls, 1982–86	3	19	35	42
Union members, 1986	4	27	40	29

SOURCE: Calculated from data in Decima (1986).

nomic planning. The differences in assessment by the general Canadian public and union members are remarkably small.

More can be learned from the Vancouver survey introduced earlier. In the same survey, borrowing the methodology of a survey of British workers (Heller, 1979), we posed a series of questions to compare actual and desired levels of influence at work (Table 5). We divided management decisions into three categories: personal decisions (e.g., hours of work, job duties, holiday scheduling); administrative decisions (e.g., hiring and firing, selection of supervisors); and major policy decisions (e.g., financial investment and planning, introduction of new technology). For each category of decision we invited respondents to describe their actual and desired situation by choosing from a four-element continuum ranging from "no influence" to "complete control."

Table 5 suggests collective bargaining, as practised, does not meet workers' demand to influence decisions at work. The difference between desired and actual levels of influence has an intuitive meaning as "degree of frustration."★ Results from the survey also suggest a strong willingness to support industrial relations innovations that enhance worker ability to exercise influence at work. We posed questions about a particular reform, codetermination,★★ to introduce a

★We also conducted multivariate regression analysis to isolate the effect of individual characteristics on respondents' responses. In addition to union status we identified four other characteristics: age, gender, education, political preference (measured by voting in 1983 provincial election). The more rigorous regression results confirmed the simple tabulated evidence that unionization does not address worker desires for greater influence at work. Sceptics will always respond to results such as these that we have not asked respondents to make trade-offs, that people will always want more influence provided it is costless. Ideally, respondents should be posed the following type of question: "If you were offered work in another firm that enabled you to exercise as much influence over work as you desire, and was in all other respects the same as your present job, how large a wage cut would you accept in order to take it?" This is, in the jargon of cost-benefit economists, an example of "contingent valuation" cast in terms of maximum willingness to pay. Alternatively, questions could be posed in terms of minimum compensation demanded to move from the respondent's ideal to his actual situation: "If you worked in another place of employment that allowed you as much influence over work as you desire, how much of a wage increase would you demand to move to your actual job?"

★★In a narrow sense "codetermination" refers to the West German industrial relations practice, initiated by the British occupation administration after World War Two, whereby employees of large firms select half the members of their firms' supervisory level boards of directors. (West German firms have a two-board structure. The supervisory level board selects the managing board.) More generally, codetermination refers to any industrial relations system under which both employees and financial owners select members of boards of directors.

Table 5
Average Level of Actual and Desired Influence at Work,
by Union Status

	*total, all workers (n = 261)**	*non-union (n = 96)*	*union (n = 156)*
Personal decisions: actual influence	1.273**	1.388	1.073
desired influence	1.798	1.850	1.726
Administrative decisions: actual influence	.864	1.032	.594
desired influence	1.385	1.516	1.179
Major policy decisions: actual influence	.660	.829	.392
desired influence	1.224	1.323	1.083

*These questions were posed only to those who are currently working for a wage or salary, or who have done so in the last five years. Provincial political preference is the respondent's vote in the 1983 provincial election.

**Numbers display the mean response (actual and desired influence) for each subset of respondents: no influence (0), a little influence (1), a lot of influence (2), complete control (3). For example, since the values in the second row are in all cases larger than those in the first row, we can say that the typical worker, regardless of social characteristics, desires more influence over personal decisions at work than he or she has at present.

SOURCE: Richards, Mauser, and Holmes (1988).

fairly specific proposal and render the idea of greater influence less abstract to respondents.

We presented respondents with several of the standard arguments for and against codetermination. One argument in favour is that workers thereby obtain more and better information about their firm, which enables them to consider the long-run implications of their demands. A second argument in favour is that codetermination requires managers to pay more attention to the implications of management decisions on their workers. Our respondents overwhelmingly think codetermination would increase workers' access to relevant information about their firms and that this would increase efficiency (Table 6, statement 1). Overwhelmingly, they also think firms "would operate better because managers would take workers' interests more into account" (3).

A conservative counterargument suggests that workers have no interest in efficiency and that the presence of their representatives in the board room would block the ability of managers to make efficient decisions and consequently would lower firm profits and wages (Furubotn, 1978). A large majority of respondents reject this argu-

Table 6
Attitudes toward Codetermination

Questionnaire preamble: Today, workers have some influence on decision-making through unions and collective bargaining. Recently, some have proposed that workers also elect representatives to company boards of directors. I'm going to read four statements about this idea. For each would you say whether you agree or disagree.

	agree	dis-agree	don't know
1. The company would operate more efficiently because workers would be better informed about the company.	90%	9%	1%
2. The company would be less profitable because the worker representatives would prevent managers from making efficient decisions.	22	75	3
3. The company would operate better because managers would take workers' interests more into account.	83	15	2
4. Having worker directors would weaken the willingness of workers to bargain hard for wage increases, and this would make workers worse off.	15	79	7

These statements were posed to all respondents, whether or not they were working (n = 332).

SOURCE: Richards, Mauser, and Holmes (1988).

ment (2). Finally, some left-wing critics fear codetermination as a form of "class collaboration" that will sap worker commitment to collective bargaining for maximum wages. As with the right-wing objection, this argument was rejected by a large majority (4). The proportions are not reported, but union workers rejected it as consistently as did the non-unionized.

Table 7 contains the results from questions on support for legislation to enable codetermination. Overall, nearly five out of six in the sample think workers on the boards of large companies would be a "good thing" (Table 7, question 1). This is somewhat higher than the result (71 per cent "good thing," 14 per cent "bad thing") obtained by Gallup in 1977 in a national survey using a question with the same wording (*The Gallup Report*, 1977). Support for this idea extends fairly uniformly across supporters of the different political parties. Division of the sample according to the electoral choices in the 1984 federal election produced only minor variations. Predictably, Conservative supporters favour the idea somewhat less than supporters of the

Table 7
Support for Codetermination, by Union Status and Federal
Political Vote in 1984

1. In general do you think it would be a good thing or a bad thing if workers in large companies were able to elect members on the board of directors? (posed to total sample, n = 333)

	good thing	bad thing	don't know
total sample	82%	15%	4%
union status			
union	88	9	3
non-union	79	18	3
federal vote, 1984			
Conservative	80	15	5
Liberal	90	8	3
NDP	90	10	0

2. What proportion of directors do you think workers should be able to elect? (posed to those answering "good thing" to no.1, n = 272)

	under 10 per cent	one-third	one-half	a majority	don't know
total sample	29%	46%	18%	6%	2%
union status					
union	29	44	17	10	1
non-union	30	47	16	6	2
federal political preference					
Conservative	32	48	15	4	0
Liberal	28	43	20	3	5
NDP	17	57	15	9	2

SOURCE: Richards, Mauser, and Holmes (1988).

Liberals and NDP, but the differences are not large. Female workers favour the idea somewhat more than male workers; unionized workers somewhat more than the non-unionized.

An important supplementary question to pose is the degree of participation at the board level that people want workers to exercise. Those who thought codetermination a "good thing" were asked their opinion on the appropriate proportion of directors that workers should select (question 2). Do they want worker representatives restricted to a nominal proportion? Do they want parity? What support exists for the radical idea that workers dominate, and be able to elect a majority of board members? Overall, and for all identified groups, the mode is that workers select one-third of board members. (This corresponds to the fraction employed in codetermination laws in several European countries.) Three in ten want only nominal worker representation of less than 10 per cent; one in four want workers to achieve parity or majority status. Predictably, a higher proportion of Conservative supporters want nominal worker representation than do supporters of the NDP. If we eliminate those wanting only nominal worker representation (29 per cent of 82 per cent), there is still a majority, four out of seven, in favour of codetermination.

Finally, we conducted a statistical test that attempts to reduce responses to a small number of fundamental underlying attitudes. Two stood out as by far the most important: attitudes toward collective bargaining and desire for influence at work. The first in importance (in terms of ability to explain the correlation among results) was attitudes toward unions and collective bargaining. People were fairly consistent in having either pro- or anti-union attitudes. For example, if they agreed with pro-union statements (e.g., "Without unions workers would have little protection against favouritism by management"), they typically disagreed with anti-union statements (e.g., "Union demands often contribute to unemployment").

The second fundamental attitude was the extent of desired influence at work. This attitude proved to be statistically independent of the first. People's ideas about participation are not closely linked to their attitudes toward collective bargaining. People do not perceive worker participation either as a substitute for collective bargaining or as a logical extension of present collective bargaining practices. It is another dimension to industrial relations, important on its own terms. It is not a proxy for either pro- or anti-union attitudes. It may be used as the basis for anti-union strategies by management; it can equally serve as a basis for new union strategies to increase the scope of union activities beyond traditional collective bargaining.

CONCLUSION

Canadian unions find themselves in a situation analogous to that faced by American unions during the decade after passage of the Taft-Hartley Act in 1947. American unions vigorously lobbied against passage of this legislation, which curtailed powers afforded to unions by the Wagner Act. Conservative politicians and corporate executives in Canada are beginning to envision an industrial relations environment in which formerly highly unionized sectors may successfully resist unionization and in which legislative support for collective bargaining can be weakened. If Canadian unions are to escape the depressing fate of their American comrades, a necessary – if far from sufficient – condition is probably that they respond positively to the public demand for greater participation in management of the workplace.

Collective bargaining is not enough; unions must learn to "play two games at once."

REFERENCES

Angus Reid Associates (1987). *Public Opinion Regarding Organized Labour.* Winnipeg.

British Columbia Ministry of Labour (annual). *B.C. Labour Directory.* Victoria: Province of British Columbia.

Decima Research Ltd. (quarterly). *The Decima Quarterly Report.* Toronto.

Decima Research Ltd. (1983). "In-depth Analysis: Changing Patterns in the Work Place," *The Decima Quarterly Report.* Toronto (Summer).

Decima Research Ltd. (1986). "In-depth Analysis: the Workplace," *The Decima Quarterly Report.* Toronto (Winter).

Faustmann, J. (1988). "When Workers Turn Bosses," *Report on Business Magazine* (March).

Freeman, R.B., and J.L. Medoff (1984). *What Do Unions Do?* New York: Basic Books.

Freeman, R.B. (1986). "Effects of Unions on the Economy," in S.M. Lipset, ed., *Unions in Transition: Entering the Second Century.* San Francisco: ICS Press.

Furubotn, E.G. (1978). "The Economic Consequences of Codetermination on the Rate and Sources of Private Investment," in S. Pejovich, ed., *The Codetermination Movement in the West.* Lexington, Mass.: Lexington Books.

The Gallup Report (1977). "7-in-10 Approve Worker Reps on Board of Directors," Toronto: The Canadian Institute of Public Opinion (January).

The Gallup Report (annual). Toronto: The Canadian Institute of Public Opinion.

The Globe and Mail. "Labor and politics 'fused' in Manitoba," 22 February 1988.

Heller, F., *et al.* (1979). *What do the British Want from Participation and Industrial Democracy?* London: Anglo-German Foundation for the Study of Industrial Society.

Industrial Relations Centre (annual). *The Current Industrial Relations Scene in Canada,* ed. by P. Kumar *et al.* Kingston, Ont.: Queen's University.

Jamieson, S. (1987). "Industrial Relations Reform Act, 1987," Vancouver: Department of Economics, University of British Columbia (mimeo).

Kochan, T.A., *et al.* (1984). *Worker Participation and American Unions.* Kalamazoo, Mich.: W.E. Upjohn Institute for Employment Research.

Kochan, T.A., *et al.* (1986). *The Transformation of American Industrial Relations.* New York: Basic Books.

Kumar, P. (1986). "Union growth in Canada: Retrospect and Prospect," in W.C. Riddell, ed., *Canadian Labour Relations.* Volume 16 of studies commissioned by Royal Commission on the Economic Union and Development Prospects for Canada. Toronto: University of Toronto Press.

Labour Canada (annual). *Directory of Labour Organizations in Canada*. Ottawa: Supply and Services.

Lipset, S.M. (1950). *Agrarian Socialism*. San Francisco: Berkeley University Press.

Lipset, S.M. (1986). "Labor Unions in the Public Mind," in Lipset, ed., *Unions in Transition: Entering the Second Century*.

Quinn, R.P., and G.L. Staines (1979). *The 1977 Quality of Employment Survey*. Ann Arbor: Institute for Social Research, University of Michigan.

Richards, J., and G. Mauser (1986). "Attitudes towards Unions and Worker Participation in Management," in J. Richards and D. Kerr, eds., *Canada, What's Left? A new social contract pro and con*. Edmonton: Newest Press.

Richards, J., G. Mauser, and R. Holmes (1988). "What do Workers Want? Attitudes Towards Collective Bargaining and Participation in Management," *Relations Industrielles*, XLIII,1, pp. 133-52.

LARRY PRATT

8   Up from Nationalism

Patriotism having become one of our topicks, Johnson suddenly uttered, in a strong determined tone, an apophthegm, at which many will start: 'Patriotism is the last refuge of a scoundrel.' But let it be considered, that he did not mean a real and generous love of our country, but that pretended patriotism which so many, in all ages and countries, have made a cloak for self-interest.

– James Boswell, *The Life of Samuel Johnson*

INTRODUCTION

I love my country too much to be a nationalist, wrote Albert Camus in the midst of the Second World War. A man, he said in his "Letters to A German Friend," published clandestinely during the Nazi occupation of France, should be able to love his country and still love justice. There are means that cannot be excused in the name of the nation, and no nation can be justified by a blind, unswerving love and obedience: to love one's country enough to fight for it, it is necessary to demand a great deal of it, to be severe with it, and sometimes to prefer justice to it. Because the Germans had refused to demand anything from their country but the power to enslave others, they would lose their terrible war, Camus told his German friend. "This is what separated us from you; we made demands."

   Like Camus, I love my country too much to be a nationalist. I think nationalism is easier to reconcile with the demand for power than the demand for justice. There is not much in nationalist doctrine, aside from the illusion that a world based on the principle of national self-determination would be free of war and inequity, that speaks to issues of justice; almost by definition, nothing in it speaks to humanity at large. A nationalist is someone who, above all else, wants power – power, that is, for his own kind. Every nationalist grouping claims to have a moral legitimacy based on its own unique history and circumstances, but the claim is invariably accompanied by demands that have far less to do with justice than with old-fashioned *Realpolitik*. All nationalists agree in this much at least: that every people that considers itself to be a "nation" has the right to set up its own sovereign state and to use it to promote the nation's interests. The struggle for power seldom ends there, however; sovereign statehood once attained, nationalism often inclines through irredentism, or the desire to "liberate" others of the same nationality, to imperialism, or the will to rule others (Wight, 1986, p. 147). This is simply another way of stating that nationalism, however much it professes to be defensive or reactive in purpose, frequently becomes expansionist when it combines a sense of mission with the military and economic elements of state power. And, further, it is not just the great powers that have used nationalism as a weapon for aggrandizement: India did so against Portuguese Goa; Nkrumah's Ghana attempted to do so in West Africa; Nasser's Egypt, Assad's Syria, and Saddam Hussein's Iraq have all tried to mobilize Arab nationalism to promote the hegemony of their own states in the Arab world.

The principle of national self-determination asserts the right of every self-conscious nationality to form its own state. However, some nationalist groups have chosen to pursue power and their other goals within federal political systems; the concept of two nations within a decentralized Canadian federal state, for example, has long been the preference of many Quebec nationalists and some English Canadians. But such a solution requires a willingness and capacity on both sides to negotiate compromises on a host of difficult and sometimes intractable issues, such as language rights, and to do this on a more-or-less continuing basis. The rejection of the Meech Lake Accord, a realistic and relatively modest document, in June, 1990, provided plenty of evidence of the lack of support for such a conception in the rest of Canada. Whether the rest of Canada will acquiesce in the alternative of a Quebec with significantly more of the attributes of a sovereign state remains to be seen, but whichever way the issue is resolved it will be resolved by power. To argue that nationalism is basically about power politics rather than, say, distributive justice is not to deny that those who dislike nationalism and wish to defeat nationalist policies are also self-interested and engaged in a power struggle. But what I *do* deny is that nationalism occupies the moral high ground on conflicts over, for instance, free trade with the United States; or that nationalists act on behalf of all members of the nation when they demand cultural and economic protection.

Economic nationalism, that "pretended patriotism" which Samuel Johnson rightly identifies as a cloak for self-interest, is part of the same will to power: those domestic interests threatened by world markets are enabled to use the powers of the sovereign state to shield themselves and to protect their turf – at the expense of their fellow citizens. The nature of the nationalist appeal is to find external causes for problems and thus to avoid painful internal trade-offs and change: American economic nationalism, for instance, singles out Japan and other Asian states as the external source of its domestic economic ills, but the strategy only obscures the true nature and origin of the disease and does nothing to start the patient on the road to recovery. At a minimum, nationalists attempt to shape economic activity so as to industrialize and increase the primacy of their own nation-state: economic nationalism, like its forerunner, mercantilism, views the world economy as a battleground for states in conflict over wealth and power.

The remaining sections of this chapter are devoted to a critique of nationalism: the first part examines the history of this modern ideology and the role of intellectuals in its dissemination; the second attempts to explain its tremendous psychological appeals; and the third explores the nature of economic nationalism. Throughout the chapter, it must be understood, I will be critiquing nationalist doctrine and ideas *in general*; it is nationalist ideology as it has evolved over the last two centuries, not its specific applications to particular countries, that requires a critical examination. What *are* these ideas that so many people still accept as common sense, where do they come from, and what are their implications in today's world?

A central assumption in what follows is that Canadians are much too credulous and naive in dealing with the rhetoric and substance of nationalist claims. One source of this tendency is obvious: our fears and insecurities in the face of American power and wealth have driven many Canadians to accept nationalist ideas and remedies as the sole alternative to the *Pax Americana*. Living next door to the world's most powerful nation-state, itself prone to excesses of national chauvinism, we have had good cause to worry about Canada's survival and independence, and, despite the support of business for the free trade agreement with the United States, many Canadian interest groups are still craving protection from American economic and cultural penetration and from shifting world market forces. Support for the welfare state has typically been articulated in nationalistic terms, free trade being viewed as a great solvent of unique national institutions and social programs. Beyond this, as will be shown later, nationalism exerts powerful psychological incentives for a society to use the sense of external threat as a bond to hold itself together and channel its destructive instincts: from this standpoint, the United States is an indispensable source of Canada's unity and integration. Depending on the circumstances, then, nationalism can act as an agency of moral cohesion – a crucial element in the domestic unity and external power of any state.

But, as the saying goes, those "who sup with the devil should use a long spoon." Nationalism has another, far less positive side, and it is this that Canadians (among others) need to think harder and longer about. As Camus might have put it, we need to demand more of our nationalists, if only because they claim to speak for Canada and its true interests. A critical re-examination of nationalist ideas, assumptions, and public policies is long overdue in both English Canada and Quebec. Unfortunately, many of Canada's intellectuals, who might be expected to lead such an exercise in critical thinking, are themselves deeply committed to nationalism and are in no position to be objective about it: indeed, they are a significant part of the problem. Since the 1960s, a significant section of the intellectual class in English Canada has embraced a very pessimistic, even defeatist, anti-American nationalism as a kind of ersatz religion; this fearful, enervated group could hardly be expected to abandon its beliefs and opinions in the face of a few unwelcome facts.

In what follows, it will be argued that the satisfaction of nationalist grievances at the expense of existing states introduces a profound instability into international politics, and that the principle of nationality itself, with its metaphysical criteria for statehood – language, culture, race, history – appeals to what is irrational and potentially violent in political life. Nationalism emphasizes the beauty of the particular, the ugliness of the universal. It makes a cult of language, local culture, and prejudice. The survival of the national group is precarious, for it is always faced with external threats to its existence. Germans can be truly Germans only if they live together in the same state. Jews can only be true Jews when they are restored to Palestine. The Québécois are perpetually threatened with decay into third-rate North Americans, and thus require the full powers of a sovereign state. And so forth. Only a homeland matters. Nationalism rejects the possibility of a real international society. Anything that tempts us to believe in universal, cosmopolitan ideas or a timeless set of truths is preaching uniformity, and uniformity is death; life is only to be found in one's own language, culture, tradition, and local feelings. The man who is cut off from his own or puts his loyalty to class or religion above his loyalty to his nation is finished, useless, without rights of any kind, "worse than dead," in Rousseau's words. For the whole is greater than its parts and the freedom of an individual is realized only through his absorption in his nation and its destiny.

Such, it will be argued, is the doctrine of nationalists the world over. As an ideology capable of mobilizing and regulating human beings, it has had few rivals. Whether it is an appropriate model for political organization at the end of the twentieth century is another matter. Many people are rightly questioning the meaning of both nationalism and traditional sovereignty in the face of ecological dilemmas of a world-wide nature and a world economy that is manifestly beyond the control of even the greatest powers, and one of the questions they are raising is why our political systems must continue to fragment at a time when the forces of economic and technical change are unifying the globe as never before. That is really the question I wish to raise in this essay, and I want to begin by trying to explain where nationalism came from, what its doctrine means, and why it has been so strikingly successful. While I shall give examples of nationalist movements and policies, my real subject is the *ideas* of nationalism and the ways in which these ideas are used and manipulated by those who seek power and wealth.

WHAT IS NATIONALISM?

Men and women need communities, and they can develop very strong attachments to them. This is not nationalism. Nationalism, a modern phenomenon, needs to be distinguished from *patriotism* (*patria – fatherland*), love of one's country or state, a willingness to defend it; and from *xenophobia*, a dislike or fear of foreigners. Patriotism, the positive loyalty to one's homeland, and xenophobia, the negative reaction against foreigners, appear to be universal sentiments that can be found in the ancient writings of, for example, Thucydides and in the artifacts of every known culture. But such sentiments do not constitute nationalism. When the Greek city-states combined under Sparta's leadership to defeat the great Persian invasion in the fifth century B.C., they did so to defend their communities and their ways of life. Although they fought for their independence, they were not motivated by what we would now call Greek nationalism. When the Persians had retreated, the Greek states dissolved their alliance and went back to fighting one another: no Greek nation appeared (nationalism has *not* been an automatic or spontaneous reaction to great power aggression). The Greeks interpreted their victory as one of free men over despotism, not as an expression of national pride. Patriotism and xenophobia are potentially dangerous sentiments that need to be moderated, but they do not come complete with ideological roadmaps, theories of language and race, or a plan for restructuring the international relations of states.

Before the age of nationalism, the idea of patriotism (passionately brought to life by Machiavelli in his *Discourses* and developed by many republican writers up to the eighteenth century) also was associated with the defence of liberty, constitutional rights, self-government, and the struggle against tyranny; it embodied, in other words, an idea of the duties of citizenship going well beyond simple loyalty to one's country. The English Tory Samuel Johnson, whose famous "apophthegm" opens this chapter, also defined "patriot" in the 1755 edition of his *Dictionary* as "one who maintains and defends his country's freedom and rights," but also noted its use "ironically for a factious disturber of the government" (Dietz, 1989, p. 185). Patriotism as civic virtue, standing for political equality and social justice, was the essence of what the Chartists, unionists, and Dissenters defended as "the rights of Englishmen" against the oppressive conditions of early industrial capitalism.

In contrast, nationalism is a European doctrine that is no more than 200 years old. Nationalism refers to the will of an historically self-conscious people to attain self-government. It is the idea that every "nation" should have its own state and that the international states system should be based on nationalist principles. Nationalism, an invention of intellectuals and radical politicians, derives from the era of the French Revolution and the resistance to French hegemony that followed that great upheaval, especially in the lands of Germany, in the early nineteenth century. It has been seen as an offshoot of the Romantic revolt, an aspect of the German-led reaction against the principles and aesthetics of the French Enlightenment – against, that is, rationality, objectivity, cosmopolitanism, and the idea that there are universal moral laws that can be readily discovered by each of us (Berlin, 1981, pp. 10–15).

Against the Enlightenment ideal of a cosmopolitan Europe or world society governed by reason and universal laws, the first true nationalists, influenced by thinkers such as Rousseau and Edmund Burke, asserted the specificity of each society, the individual's organic links to his own people, and the rule of soil, blood, and the national will. What nationalism rejects is in some ways more illuminating than what it claims to stand for, and part of what it rejects, I wish to emphasize, is the idea that there is a true international society, that the peoples and societies of the world are in any authentic sense interdependent, or that their relations ought to be based on moral obligations and law as well as on interest and power. Early nationalists explicitly denied the view of eighteenth-century policital economists that the well-being of the individual is dependent on the well-being of the human race (List, 1885, p. 121). Nationalism denied that men and women have "duties beyond borders" or that class, gender, or other ties can have priority over loyalties to the nation: Burke's argument that the inherited rights of an Englishman are worth far more than the abstract rights of man championed by the French revolutionaries was central to the nationalist credo.

While internationalists from Grotius in the seventeenth century through Saint-Pierre, Voltaire, Kant, Bentham, and their successors in the peace movements of the last century and a half have stressed the need for limits on sovereignty, the role of a common morality and law, and the creation of international institutions capable of mitigating anarchy, nationalists have viewed international relations as the realm of the struggle for power, inevitable conflict, and war. It is disconcerting to realize that for nationalists, historical progress consists in the movement from the cosmopolitan and universal to the triumph of the autarkic nation-state; any weakening of national sovereignty in favour of supranational institutions or other forms of internationalism is a case of history marching in the wrong direction. The nation-state, in effect, is the supreme achievement of history: its purpose is not to transcend itself but to preserve itself and increase its power and resources relative to those of its rivals.

Nationalist doctrine holds that mankind is naturally divided into separate, distinctive, and readily identifiable "nations," that nations must constitute sovereign states, and that there are no valid members of international society save those based on national self-determination (Kedourie, 1985, p. 73; Wight, 1986, p. 85). These ideas have been so thoroughly incorporated into our everyday political discourse that they are seldom questioned. But however familiar and natural they may seem, this is an ideological portrayal of a world that does not exist and has never existed, and indeed would have seemed absurd to earlier political thinkers. It is, in the most literal sense of the word, a delusion – a false but fixed belief. Like most doctrines, it takes no heed of the myriad social, cultural, and political complexities of the existing world; rather, it wishes them away.

Under the most rudimentary analysis, the language and thought behind nationalism reveal themselves to be inconsistent and irrational (albeit, for reasons discussed below, extraordinarily appealing). For example, what are nations? According to those European writers who formulated many of the central ideas in the doctrine in opposition to French rationalism, nations are historically self-conscious groups of people distinguished from one another by criteria such as language, territory, race, culture, customs, laws, and shared history, and who have willed their right to self-determination through struggle and war. These conservative intellectuals, greatly influenced by Burke's florid attacks on the French revolutionaries and his appeals to the organic and irrational nature of society, defined the nation as spirit, soul, and the will striving for self-realization. The nation is what gives the individual his meaning, his breath of life, his sense of belonging – things that are beyond rational understanding and must be felt. "Our fatherland is with us, in us," said Leopold von Ranke, Germany's greatest nineteenth-century historian (and not, it must be noted in fairness, a man much devoted to the nationalist movement; Ranke was cool to German unification for most of his life and, like Goethe, was little more than a cultural nationalist [Ranke, 1981, p. 4]). Ranke wrote:

> Germany lives in us. We enact it, whether we choose to do so or not, in every country we enter, in every zone. We stand upon it from the very beginning and cannot escape it. This mysterious something that informs the lowest among us as well the highest – this spiritual air that we breathe – precedes any form of government and animates and permeates all its forms. (Meinecke, 1970, p. 205)

Nationality, Friedrich Meinecke wrote in his *Cosmopolitanism and the National State*, "is a dark, impenetrable womb, a mysterious something, a force arising from hidden sources that is incorporeal itself and permeates the corporeal. The richness of personal and individual being arises from it." The language, like the phenomenon of nationalism itself, is irrational and violent.

If nationality is the womb from which our individuality derives, for most nationalists language is the genetic code that divides us and sets the struggle of nations in motion. Language is certainly the most visible, and arguably the most dangerous and divisive, of the attributes that allegedly divide humanity into nations. Language is the test by which a nation is known to exist. "A group speaking the same language is known as a nation, and a nation ought to constitute a state" (Kedourie, 1985, p. 68). The philosopher, J.G. Fichte, argued in his influential *Addresses to the German Nation*, delivered in 1807-08 in the wake of Prussia's crushing defeat at the hands of Napoleon at Jena in 1806, that "we give the name of people to men whose organs of speech are influenced by the same external conditions, who live together, and who develop their language in continuous communication with each other." A nation is defined by its original language, says Fichte, and its speech must be constantly cleansed of foreign words and expressions, since the purer the language, the easier it becomes for the nation to realize itself. The real boundaries of a national state are those that correspond to the linguistic map: it is not because men dwell between certain mountains or rivers that they are a people; they dwell together because "they were a people already by a law of nature which is much higher" (Kedourie, 1985, pp. 69–70). The nation, Fichte is saying, is (or must become) a homogeneous linguistic unit with borders that overlap with the geographical distribution of groups of people speaking the same language, which is to say, the nation is an expanding, dynamic force. Germany, if we follow this logic, is entitled to incorporate or liberate peoples of the German nationality suffering under foreign oppression in, say, Poland.

According to one view of nationality, the nation is the sole representative of the sovereignty of the people, and it acknowledges no other rights or privileges or claims. The individual has no existence apart from his participation in the general will of his nation. The collective rights and interests of the group will always prevail over those of the individual or of minorities, for the whole is prior to and more important than its parts. Rousseau, reacting to the partitions of Poland by the great powers in the late eighteenth century, wrote in his *Considerations on the Government of Poland* (1772) that education "must give souls a national formation, and direct their opinions and tastes in such a way that they will be patriotic by inclination, by passion, by necessity. When first he opens his eyes, an infant ought to see the fatherland, and up to the day of his death he ought never to see anything else." His love of country "is his whole existence; he sees nothing but the fatherland, he lives for it alone; when he is solitary, he is nothing; when he has ceased to have a fatherland, he no longer exists, and if he is not dead, he is worse than dead" (Rousseau, 1772, p. 176).

If the idea of the soul acquiring "national formation" seems bizarre, to nationalists seeking Poland's salvation from Russia and the other European powers it represented the necessary rejection of all universal values and ideas. "National education" teaches us that although we ourselves may be mortal, our nation is immortal; so long as we have the fatherland, so long as we realize our individual freedom through our participation in the collective will of the nation-state, we achieve a kind of immortality. If our nation is suppressed, as Poland was when it was partitioned by the great powers, our souls can only be born again through its liberation – that is, through politics. Although Rousseau is too complex and contradictory a thinker to be labelled a nationalist, this doctrine exalts politics and reduces the individual human being to expendable cannon fodder: the individual who is "worse than dead" without his nation now exists only to be mobilized by the national state and kept distinct and separate from other peoples, above all from the civilized, homogenized "Europeans" detested by Rousseau. "Incline the passions of the Poles in a different direction, and you will give their souls a national physiognomy which will distinguish them from other peoples, which will prevent them from mixing, from feeling at ease with those peoples, from allying themselves with them ..." (Rousseau, 1772, p. 169). Nationalism is a reaction against the idea of a universal and cosmopolitan international society; in Rousseau's advice to the Poles, however, we can first see the nation as a surrogate for religious faith, as a route to moral salvation in a world irredeemably corrupted by the forces of modernization.

From the 1790s onward, the highly centralized nationalist state was feared on the grounds that it could draw on an all-encompassing total power because of its new capacity to mobilize all of the "moral forces" in the population, to conscript all industry and tax wealth at unheard-of levels, and to put huge armies of soldier-citizens into the field against its opponents. The appearance of such revolutionary changes in France quickly taught its enemies they would not long survive unless they followed the French example. War is a violent teacher, and especially so when waged by whole peoples. The era of limited wars fought by professional armies was over; that of total wars waged by entire nation-states had begun.

France, the "nation in arms," was first to discover the latent moral energy of its population when in August, 1793, the revolution proclaimed something close to total mobilization in a famous law: "The young men shall fight; the married men shall forge weapons and transport supplies; . . . the old men will have themselves carried in to the public squares and rouse the courage of the fighting men, to preach hatred against kings and the unity of the Republic." What France's enemies faced was the dynamic power of the idea of nationality when fused with the autonomous state. Carl von Clausewitz, the young Prussian officer who is remembered as the philosopher of war, called it a force "that beggared all imagination. Suddenly war again became the business of the people – a people of thirty millions, all of whom considered themselves to be citizens." With the full weight of the nation thrown into the balance, "nothing now impeded the vigor with which war could be waged, and consequently the opponents of France faced the utmost peril" (Clausewitz, 1976, pp. 592–93).

Nationalism could only be countered by other nationalisms. The powers ranged against France only escaped destruction and ultimately threw off her hegemony, the historian Ranke later argued brilliantly, because, out of the war and crisis and the conflict of opposing forces, they discovered the real secret of their liberation: "If we are now attacked by a spiritual power, so we must oppose it with spiritual force. The domination which another nation threatens to exercise over us can be countered only by the development of our own nationality. I do not mean an invented chimerical nationality but the actual, essential one which is expressed in the state" (Ranke, 1981, p. 154). The true power of the state, asserts Ranke (p. 152), is to be found less in its military strength or wealth than in the moral and spiritual forces of the age – religion yesterday, nationality today – that breathe life into men and make them begin to fight with some hope. "What would have become of our states if they had not received new life from the national principle on which they were based? Is it convincing that they could exist without it?"

The idea of national self-determination – i.e., that every self-conscious nationality has a right to constitute itself a sovereign state – introduced a fundamentally new and volatile factor into the conduct of international relations. During the nineteenth century, national self-determination "grew into a condemnation of every state that included different races, and finally became the complete and consistent theory, that the State and the nation must be co-extensive" (Acton, 1907, p. 146). Ranke was prophetic when he wrote that nationality had become the leading idea or principle of the era that followed the wars of Napoleon. This doctrine of international legitimacy, which triumphed in the Versailles settlement after World War One and has since been used as an ideological weapon by political leaders as diverse as Woodrow Wilson, Lenin, Roosevelt, Hitler, and Gandhi, can perhaps be seen as the final revenge of the French Revolution against its opponents. Certainly it was part of the revolt against reason. For it is simply untrue that the world is – or ever has been – arranged as the doctrine of national self-determination asserts.

A "Whiggish" nationalist such as John Stuart Mill could argue the principle that: "It is in general a necessary condition of free institutions that the boundaries of governments should coincide in the main with those of nationalities" (Mill, 1962, p. 312). But the attempt to realize this in practice – and Mill at least made exceptions of "dependencies" not prepared for self-government – could only happen at the expense of existing multinational states or empires and long-established diplomatic arrangements, and such a nationalistic attempt was bound to be a cause of perpetual instability and war. What would become of a country, such as Poland, comprised of many peoples and cultures? Europe itself, particularly its eastern areas, was not neatly divided into distinct linguistic, racial, or cultural nations or nationalities, and beyond Europe there were the sprawling, ramshackle empires of Asia and the tribal systems of Africa, though little that resembled the European idea of a modern nation. No matter. Where no nation existed, one could always be "imagined" or invented (Anderson, 1983).

The invention of nationality is the task of the intellectuals. In a pioneering study on emerging nationalisms in Eastern Europe, Czech historian Miroslav Hroch has argued that nationalist movements in this region passed through three stages. The first phase is when a small group of patriotic scholars began to have "a passionate concern" for the study of the language, the culture, the history of "the oppressed nationality." The second stage occurs with the diffusion of national ideas by a larger number of patriotic agitators. And finally, the national "revival" comes when the broad masses are incorporated into the movement (Hroch, 1985, pp. 22–23).

The creation of a national consciousness in areas where peasant populations were indifferent or sometimes very hostile to all forms of secular power usually fell to an urban middle-class elite. By and large, this elite succeeded in achieving its goal of an independent nation-state when it found an external power willing, for its own interests, to support the nationality's claim. But great powers pursue their *own* interests, and alignments change. Thus, an independent Lithuania was the creation of Germany's attempts in 1917 to destroy the Russian empire by creating mini-states it could control; Hitler and Stalin put it under Soviet rule in 1940; and fifty years later when the Lithuanian nationalist movement, led by a romantic professor of music, declared Lithuania's independence, Gorbachev and the leaders of the West declined to recognize it as a sovereign state, preferring to keep the Russian empire intact and to encourage its reform from within. If there is a lesson in Lithuania's struggle, perhaps it is simply that the alignments of great power politics will determine whether and when a people that calls itself a "nation" shall be granted statehood.

FEAR AND THE APPEALS OF CONTEMPORARY NATIONALISM

It is simple enough to write critiques of nationalism. It is less simple to explain its remarkable durability and attractions. No one can deny that there has been a phenomenal resurgence of nationalism, especially (but not exclusively) in the post-Communist world. Why does nationalism – this peculiarly ideological way of looking at the world – persist, and even go from strength to strength, when other ideologies and systems of belief wax and wane? Consider what has happened to Marxism. In a famous essay published on nationality in 1862, the English liberal historian Lord Acton said that "Nationality is more advanced than socialism, because it is a more arbitrary system." Among the subversive theories of his day, he saw nationalism as the most attractive "and the richest in promise of future power" (Acton, 1907, pp. 159, 134). This was excellent prophecy: Acton seems to have grasped the self-destructive nature of socialist strategy when confronted with a more ruthless force.

For all of its tortured rationalizations and efforts to align itself with various nationalisms over the years, Marxism has suffered defeat after defeat at the hands of nationalist movements and governments. In August, 1914, the workers in all European states supported the war aims of their respective governments and went off to slaughter one another. The Polish socialist, Rosa Luxemburg, remarked bitterly that the proud old cry of "Working men of all countries, unite!" had become "Working men of all countries, slit each other's throats!" In the sixties nationalist tensions split the world Communist system, then in the seventies these tensions led to wars between socialist states in Southeast Asia. The resurgence of nationalism and ethnic rivalries in Eastern Europe and in many of the republics of the Soviet Union in the years of the Gorbachev revolution, particularly in the aftermath of the dramatic collapse of Soviet communism in Poland, East Germany, Czechoslovakia, Hungary, and Romania in late 1989, attests to the strength of national sentiment in the face of official socialist ideology. Marxism now has no credibility in the post-Communist world, but traditional nationalism, combined with democratic institutions and right-wing economics, certainly does – at least for now. The U.S.S.R. itself, the last of the great multinational empires, may be disintegrating under the combined pressures of a worsening economic crisis and nationalist upheavals in the Baltic, the Caucasus, and elsewhere. Lord Acton's pessimism concerning the prospects of socialism prevailing over the "more absurd and more criminal" ideology of nationality has been vindicated.

One factor clearly behind the appeal of nationalism in the East is the objective weakness and instability of the Soviet Union. As the collapse of the British and French empires demonstrated after World War Two, nationalism feeds on weakness at the centre. Since the mid-eighties, the Soviet system has been in the throes of a deep internal crisis whose end, as this is written, is not in sight. Its leaders have responded to the crisis with sweeping domestic reforms and dramatic changes in Soviet international policies and defence program. Nationalism, it is important to note, was not primarily responsible for the overthrow of the Soviet satellite governments in Eastern Europe in 1989; rather, the satellites were cut loose by Mikhail Gorbachev when, as part of a wider strategy of seeking accommodation with the West and reducing costly commitments, he repudiated the Brezhnev doctrine of intervention: without Soviet power behind them, the satellite regimes collapsed at the first push from popular anti-Communist forces.

Gorbachev's stunning *volte-face* in Eastern Europe gave fresh stimulus to separatist and autonomist movements in most of the fifteen republics of the U.S.S.R. The cynicism over the economy and the palpable failure of *perestroika*, the program of economic reform, to halt the decline in Soviet living standards make right-wing nationalist and anti-Semitic movements, such as *Pamyat*, more attractive. With nationalism linked to an intractable social crisis, as in the U.S.S.R., Soviet commentators have drawn historical parallels with the situation in Germany in the late 1920s, just prior to the rise of Hitler, and have noted that

> . . . nationalism becomes dangerous in a poverty-stricken country. Tired of meat, housing and clothes shortages, disappointed with empty parliamentary talk, yearning for personal safety in the streets and in the ethnic regions, the citizens of any country may finally lend an attentive ear to those playing on their national feelings, urging them to defend their nation's and their country's honour, and promising them an immediate relief if, say, the "aliens" are driven out, to begin with. (Kremenyuk, 1990, p. 23)

Less obviously, perhaps, nationalism in what was the Eastern bloc is also a reaction by some against the alternative: that is, a reaction against a decadent capitalist West and its vision of the future. Not all Russians wish to live and work like Germans or North Americans. Nor are all East Europeans likely to support indefinitely the difficult and often painful transition from state socialism to market economies. Neo-conservative economic blueprints and constitutional reforms have little to offer by way of explanation or consolation to those who have suffered under the Soviet satellites; nationalism, the ideology of self-pity and resentment, does. If radical economic restructuring fails in Eastern Europe and the transition from state socialism to capitalism does not occur, then the prospects for democracy in a region where it has few historical roots are likely to be poor. Already the agenda has shifted in some states from building democratic institutions and market economies to national variants on "Let Bulgaria be Bulgarian" and the settling of scores with ethnic minorities.

Anti-Semitism, one of nationalism's uglier offshoots, has resurfaced throughout Eastern Europe and the Soviet Union: it is anti-Communist and populist, it feeds on economic insecurity and political cynicism, and it blames the Jews as the enemy behind the region's troubles. Unlike Western Liberal values, anti-Semitism has deep historical roots in the region, and there is a great demand for scapegoats where things have gone wrong for so long. Traditional nationalism, religion, and anti-Semitism are a potent mixture, albeit not one that is likely to underwrite a program of market economics and liberal democracy.

I do not want to exaggerate the difficulties or the prospects for failure. I hope that in Hungary, Czechoslovakia, and Poland the exist-ing democratic movements and their leaders will resist these forces and these states will become increasingly integrated into the greater European community. More likely, they will come under Germany's hegemony. However, such a transition will be problematic and pain-ful for the most advanced of the post-Communist states, and it seems plausible that right-wing authoritarian nationalist regimes could emerge in some parts of Eastern Europe, even in the Soviet Union, after a lengthy and deeply frustrating period of experimenting with Western economic and political models. In this case, much of the East would be fragmented politically, autarkic in economics, and probably too backward to be integrated into the dynamic economies of the European Community: it would remain a backwater in the European political economy. In any event, there is a good chance that it will be traditional nationalism, and not liberal democracy, that succeeds communism in some of the East European states.

Nationalism, it can be argued, has always had a powerful appeal to those groups and classes who feel uprooted and unsettled by the forces of industrial and economic change, and who want some sort of spiritual compensation. Generalizations are risky, but it can be argued that nationalism succeeds when it is able to act as a surrogate for spiritual faith, as a psychic balm for a wound suffered by a society. Nationalistic identities, like those of religion, can be a powerful bond that can hold a society together in opposition to an external threat and contain the destructive instincts and mutual hostilities that threaten civilization with disintegration. As Freud wrote:

> It is clearly not easy for men to give up the satisfaction of this inclination to aggression. They do not feel comfortable without it. The advantage which a comparatively small cultural group offers of allowing this instinct an outlet in the form of hostility against intruders is not to be despised. It is always possible to bind together a considerable number of people in love, so long as there are other people left over to receive the manifestations of their aggressive-ness. (Freud, 1982, p. 51)

Freud said that civilization must use its utmost efforts to limit man's aggressive instincts "and to hold the manifestations of them in check by psychical reaction-formations" (Freud, 1982, p. 49). The creation of communities based on nationality characteristics is one way of displacing this instinctive aggressiveness, turning it away from the national group toward "the intruders."

Nationalism took root in nineteenth-century Europe because it offered a new vision of life to those who were facing a traumatic adjustment to the forces of modernization: far from being progressive, nationalism can be seen as a romantic reaction against modernity and the alien ideas of rationality and progress that accompany it. Perhaps there is a parallel here with the upheavals of our own day. Like all great revolutions, the 1989 European upheaval has had many unanticipated consequences. Communism has collapsed across Europe and Soviet power has retreated everywhere. The German problem is again on the great power agenda. The post-war alliances have lost much of their *raison d'être*. The forty-year Cold War and its ideological blocs are passing, and with them has gone the unifying (and psychologically reassuring) factor of a common external threat. Do we still have enemies? Do we need allies? Is there a purpose in having military forces? We seem to be in unfamiliar territory with neither a map nor a compass.

Notwithstanding the movement toward a world economy that sets the pace for even the largest national economies, and despite the undeniable need for supranational institutions and international regimes to cope with global problems beyond the jurisdiction of any nation-state, there is, as I have indicated, much evidence to suggest that we are already in a new era of aggressive nationalism. There is a sharp discontinuity between the trend toward economic unification and the growth of the centrifugal forces of nationalism. Indeed, it may be argued that rapid economic change and the appearance of a multitude of world environmental problems are, paradoxically, helping to create the psychological setting of fear and uncertainty in which nationalism has often thrived and nationalist movements have acquired power. If this is so, then the central ideological conflict in the post-Cold War period will be something already very familiar to Canadians: on one hand, the forces pushing for global economic and technological integration supported by multilateral institutions and rules; on the other, those forces who see themselves at the mercy of the market dynamic and want – often with good cause – to use the nation-state to protect themselves.

To sum up, it is foolish to ignore the powerful psychological or spiritual allure of nationalist ideas. In the final analysis, nationalism may be called an ersatz religion, a surrogate for divine faith that performs equivalent roles: nationalism is one of those secular ideologies that we worship and kill each other over. Nationalist ideology has it that all are equal within the nation just as all are equal before God. Therefore, all class privileges or ethnic distinctions must be dissolved, along with individual identity, in a great communal feeling. Rousseau's advice to the Poles about building national sentiment and institutions emphasized the use of rituals, ceremonies, and spectacles to make love of one's nation the dominant passion. "You must invent games, festivals and solemnities so peculiar to this particular court that they will be encountered in no other." Nothing, he said, should be exclusively for the rich and powerful. "Have many open-air spectacles, where the various ranks of society will be carefully distinguished but where the whole people will participate equally, as among the ancients" (Rousseau, 1772, pp. 171–72). In strikingly similar language, Stendahl, in his *Vie de Napoleon*, says of revolutionary France in 1794: "we had no sort of religion at all; our deep and inner feelings were corresponded in this one idea: *being useful to our country.* . . . For us who know no other social world, there were festivals, numerous and touching ceremonies, which came along to nourish the sentiment which dominated everything in our hearts. It was our only religion" (Minogue, 1967, pp. 49–50). In an important sense, nationalism continues to play this same role: providing the symbols and rituals that give individuals an identity, an explanation for their confusion, and the promise of redemption through political action for the "multitudes who seek a universal cure for many special evils, and a common restorative applicable to many different conditions" (Acton, 1907, p. 133).

Freud said that civilization is perpetually threatened with distintegration by man's strong inclination to aggression, and that the instinctual passions can only be controlled by inducing people to form identities and relationships that restrict the sexual and aggressive instincts and channel aggressiveness into hostility toward intruders. In this respect, Freud remarked sardonically, the Jewish people had rendered "most useful services to the civilizations of the countries that have been their hosts" (Freud, 1982, p. 51). From this standpoint, nationalism constitutes a most powerful mechanism used by society for binding us together in fear of outsiders and the "aliens" within. There is nothing new in this. The ancient Greeks used purification rituals to rid their communities of the *Pharmakos* – the scapegoat, the impure member of society – as a prerequisite to a new beginning. The victim to be driven out is first brought into close contact with the community, then purged or killed as an outcast by those who are pure. As with modern nationalism, the aggression excited by fear is concentrated on a loathsome outsider; everyone is relieved by the communal feelings of fury and hostility, as well as by the certainty of being on the side of justice (Burkert, 1985, pp. 82–84).

A Cloak for Self-Interest

Nationalism can also be likened to a veil or a cloak that conceals the self-interest and ambitions of particular groups. These groups use the abstract ideas of the nation and the national interest to acquire power for themselves and to fashion a "national economy" controlled by nationals (often by the state) in order to redistribute wealth from foreign to local interests. In reality, however, the redistribution is usually from society as a whole to special interest groups who enjoy political advantages.

Economic nationalism is a form of fraud committed with a flag. It is what provoked Dr. Johnson's famous outburst about patriotism being the "last refuge of a scoundrel." Of course, other ideologies also conceal the ambitions of the strong – "free trade" has been used by powerful states or corporate interests to mask an ambition to acquire access to protected markets or resources – but economic nationalists are less willing than others to admit that their policies represent the interests of particular groups or that protectionism redistributes wealth from society as a whole to these same groups. Nationalism appeals because it alleges society and state to be a unitary whole; what government does is in behalf of the national interest. But this is an illusion.

Modern democratic societies are divided along many lines, and what government does is usually decided or strongly influenced by the tugging and pushing that goes on among the most powerful interests within a society. Nationalism is simply one view of which classes or groups in society ought to determine what the state does, and for whose benefit. And whether economic nationalists acknowledge it or not – some of them appear to believe they really do speak for an indivisible nation-state – their policies are no more neutral, and certainly they are no more progressive, than those of, say, free-trade liberalism (Gilpin, 1987, pp. 32–34, 187). English-Canadian left-nationalists strongly supported the Trudeau government's National Energy Program of the early 1980s, despite the fact that its central objective was to redistribute surplus profits from the oil-producing provinces and the petroleum industry to consumers and Canadian capitalists interested in gaining entry to the oil and gas sector (Pratt, 1982). Representatives of Canadian labour and critics of the free trade deal with the United States have expressed fears that low-wage Mexican workers could gain jobs at the expense of their better-paid Canadian counterparts if Mexico enters a North American free trade area. And some prominent English-Canadian left-nationalist intellectuals endorsed a "tactical alliance" with those business and political interests who supported the Liberal Party's flag-waving protectionism in the 1988 federal electoral campaign. These are reactionary policy positions as well as evidence of real confusion.

The nationalist view of economic life is an extension of the cultural and political ideas set out earlier in this chapter. Economic nationalism evolved from a critique of the English free-trade doctrines of such economists as Adam Smith, David Ricardo, and James and John

Stuart Mill, and for inspiration it harkened back to the economic beliefs and practices of the older European system of mercantalism that Smith had attacked. In mercantilism, a system oriented to power politics and war, the economy was subordinated to the power potential and the goals of the state. The mercantilist state was autarkic, expansionist, and militaristic. Exports and imports were rigidly controlled. Stocks of precious metals were accumulated. Shipping and the fisheries were fostered as a source of naval power, and (in England) the population was required to eat fish twice a week – it was known as "political lent" – in order to support a merchant marine. The real purpose of the economy in mercantilism was to generate military power as well as wealth, to unify the national state and to prepare it for war.

Nationalism is a rejection of all that is universal or cosmopolitan in favour of what is peculiar and particular about the nation. Nationalism denies the possibility of an international society based on mutual obligations and responsibilities. It denies the claim that "commerce cures destructive prejudices" and unites nations in a common interest in peace (Montesquieu, 1989, p. 338), and it portrays humankind as perpetually divided by the unique traits of nationalities – language, race, historical tradition, and so forth.

Economic nationalism begins from the assumption that an interdependent and integrated world economy is neither feasible nor desirable – the nation-state must control the economy. The German nationalist, Friedrich List, wrote in his influential 1841 study, *The National System of Political Economy*:

Between each individual and entire humanity . . . stands THE NATION, with its special language and literature, with its peculiar origin and history, with its special manners and customs, laws and institutions, with the claims of all these for existence, independence, perfection, and continuance for the future, and with its separate territory; a society which . . . is still opposed to other societies of a similar kind in their national liberty, and consequently can only under the existing conditions of the world maintain self-existence and independence by its own power and resources. (List, 1985, pp. 174–75)

List rejected the "cosmopolitical economy" approach of Adam Smith, with its false premise that the individual's well-being is dependent on the well-being of humanity. On the contrary, said List, only where the interest of the private individual has been subordinated to the unity of the nation, and where successive generations of a nation have striven for one common objective, can the productive powers of an economy be developed. These productive powers reside in the nation, not in individual self-interest or international commerce.

International trade was far less important in reality, List argued, than how the nation developed internally and whether, in particular, it had its own manufacturing sector. The key to a state's international status lay in its capacity to industrialize, using the state's powers to protect its young industries from foreign competition. List was obsessed by Germany's backwardness and fragmentation in the face of England's hegemony and wanted a unified, industrial Germany to hold sway from the Rhine to the Vistula and from the Balkans to the Baltic. Germany should acquire Denmark, the Netherlands, Belgium, and Switzerland, then lead a European bloc to check British power. There was little about economics in this grandiose scheme. Like all nationalists, List was primarily concerned with power – the power of the national state, that is – and he viewed all international economic activity as a zero-sum rivalry, part of the perpetual struggle for power. Relative gain is what matters to the nationalist, not mutual gain: what is the good of free trade if it enriches my adversary and allows him to become stronger than me?

The appeals of economic nationalism should not be underestimated. The logic of the modern welfare state has been to retain national control over much of the economy, to steer and manage it, and to intervene in order to protect the basic framework worked out between capital and organized labour in most Western states after the war. It should be noted that nationalists are not the only ones who support the welfare state or who wish to preserve its basic elements. While not all supporters of the welfare state are nationalists, virtually all nationalists defend the welfare state. Nationalists support the welfare state as a component of their demand that the national government be responsible for the elimination of economic distress. Under strong political pressures from organized labour and other groups to preserve hard-won gains in times of crisis, national governments are encouraged to shift the burden of unemployment and economic adjustment to other states (Gilpin, 1987, pp. 60–61). The preservation of the national welfare state in the face of an interdependent world economy is a central theme of contemporary economic nationalism, so much so that it can be called the first of its two principal goals.

The second is the forestalling of economic decline in the face of foreign competition. In the United States, for over a decade, the economy has lost ground and the national government, because of domestic politics, is unwilling to confront or incapable of addressing the country's own economic ills. Hence, the foreign devil can be used to deflect blame and to keep the nation mobilized behind the government. Here we can revert to Freud's argument about the need of societies for an outlet in the form of hostility to outsiders. Is it merely coincidence that at the moment when Americans began to realize that Soviet communism no longer represented a major threat to their security, they started to hear warnings about the need to "contain" Japan's economic expansionism? ("Containment" was, of course, the policy adopted by the Truman administration in dealing with Stalin's U.S.S.R. in 1947.) Outside pressure was required to reform Japan's industrial and financial system, for "the Japanese political system, like Japan's constellation of economic forces, cannot save Japan from its excesses." Allowing American consumers unlimited access to cheaper and better Japanese products would be wrong, as wrong as child labour:

> Inconveniently, offering consumers the best price is not the only thing involved in building a good society. Permitting children to work in garment factories, for instance, would lower the price of shirts and help the American consumer, but it is against the broader national interest. In the case of Japan's expansion, the harm comes from the erosion of numerous elements of American strength, especially those being left to erode because of a sense that the United States is so deep in debt that it can't afford to do many of the things a leading power should do – explore space, improve its schools, maintain its military bases in Japan so that Japan doesn't build its own army, and so on. (Fallows, 1989, p. 53)

In other words, if America has a $50 billion trade deficit with Japan it is *Japan's* problem. Obviously, there is still a market for protectionism, and not only in the United States. But all arguments for economic nationalism as a strategy begin to have a ring of futility about them once we ask what is happening to the world economy. While it is crucial not to exaggerate the process, what liberals call economic interdependence and Marxists call the transnationalization of capital is now so far developed that national control of capitalism's central structures – international production, finance and credit, knowledge and technology – does not exist even in the leading capitalist states (Cooper, 1968; Strange, 1988; Gill and Law, 1988). This loss of national control to an interdependent international economy has been experienced by capitalist states as powerful as the United States, and it is also in evidence in Gorbachev's U.S.S.R. No state can successfully insulate itself from world economic forces.

What does this loss of control mean? Peter Drucker, the dean of American management studies, argued in the mid-eighties that economic dynamics have decisively shifted from the national to the world economy, that the latter is now "in control," superseding the macroeconomic axiom, as he calls it, of the nation-state. From now on, he said, "any country – but also any business, especially a large one – that wants to prosper will have to accept that it is the world economy that leads and that domestic economic policies will succeed only if they strengthen, or at least do not impair, the country's international competitive position" (Drucker, 1986, p. 791). While there is a good deal of truth in this, Drucker exaggerates the eclipse of the national state and (as do many American commentators) assumes that the American state – which, incidentally, does not typically act as though it has ceded "control" – is a paradigm for all states. Fortunately, it is not.

States that are in a strong surplus position with respect to their balance of payments and budgets, as the U.S. was after World War Two and as Japan and Germany are today, are also in a position actively to shape world economic and political trends. Indeed, given the pressures they are under to lead, they must do so. And within the limits imposed by an interdependent global economy, there is still room for individual nation-states to manoeuvre and experiment with alternative mixes of public policy. To argue against a strategy of outright protectionism, then, is not to fall into the trap of economism (i.e., assuming all political acts are determined by economic forces). On the other hand, neither is it to deny that our economic decisions and policy choices are shaped and altered by those of other states, as theirs are by our own; this condition of mutual need or reciprocal dependence is, in the long run, far superior to the prospect of a return to economic conditions that would resemble the *sauve qui peut* world of the 1930s.

CONCLUSION

Nationalism is a way of looking at the world that emphasizes only its divisibility and fragmentation, and none of its true unity and interdependence. It is a delusion but a very potent and dangerous one. As an ideological image, it fractures the world into an artificial system of homogeneous nation-states, each based on attributes such as language, race, and culture, and, in effect, declares illegitimate all multinational states, hegemonial orders, federal systems, and other institutions that are used to mitigate disorder in the real world of politics. The principle is basically one of fission, of splitting, and part of its appeal is that the agenda is open-ended. It can never be satisfied or exhausted; there are always new nations to be invented and old states to be broken up. By some accounts, there are between 4,000 and 5,000 so-called nationalities in the world that could claim the right to form their own state, and since there are only about 200 states that presently claim sovereignty over the world's habitable territory, it would clearly be premature to expect this idea's early demise. Its "logic," if we can call it that, is a world of hundreds of micro-states: more borders, more passports, more weapons, and more war. The breakup of a large old state or empire, such as India, increases the numbers of borders and frontiers to be defended, and also increases the number of potential disputes and military interactions. Post-war decolonization, which greatly increased the number of sovereign states, many of them bitterly hostile to the West, was followed by many wars in the Third World and by regional arms races. A rise in the number of states is, other things being equal, likely to promote an increase in levels of militarization (Gill and Law, 1988, p. 109). This is simply another way of saying that nationalism causes war. For a world becoming more integrated and interdependent by the day in every sphere *but* politics, this vision of perpetual fragmentation, this script for an infinite number of distinct nation-states, is absurd. Surely the plight of the peoples of so many Third World countries, especially in Africa and the Middle East where formal independence was won as recently as the 1950s or 1960s, should make us hesitate before we embark on a new round of national self-determination at the expense of existing states. In truth, the world requires far *fewer* sovereign political units.

Nevertheless, it seems that the resurgence of nationalism has only begun. The ending of the Cold War and the dissolution of the two great blocs has signalled to nationalists everywhere that their moment of power has arrived, and we are now confronted with the real possibility that great powers such as the Soviet Union may break up because of the pressure from nationalities claiming sovereignty. It may be doubted whether this, if it occurs, will usher in a more just or peaceful world: the disintegration of great powers has seldom been a quiet affair. "A great power does not die in its bed" (Wight, 1986, p. 48). As for justice, today's nationalists claim to be the oppressed, but as Napoleon remarked, among those who dislike oppression are many who like to oppress. In Eastern Europe, the Balkans, and the republics of the Soviet Union, the forces of right-wing nationalism will be fed by anti-communism, economic troubles, and the need for scapegoats. As I have attempted to argue, nationalism continues, unfortunately, to offer a tempting yet false "universal cure for many special evils."

Nor are the Western democracies, unexpectedly released from their forty-year struggle with Soviet communism and facing dramatic shifts in the global balance of power, likely to be spared further nationalist excesses. Notwithstanding the renewed push for political unification in the European Community – a very welcome develop-ment – nationalist tensions seem likely to intensify within the Japan/ NATO bloc now that the common threat has disappeared. These tensions will be over economic issues, especially trade and industrial strategies, but they will be exacerbated by conflicts over the future of the U.S.-led alliances. And there is, moreover, the problem of finding an ideological substitute for anti-communism, something that can bind Western society together and redirect our aggressive instincts. The Third World is a very plausible target.

The Cold War has played a central role since the early 1980s in keeping neo-conservative forces in power (and leftist forces out of power) in the West, and its demise – together with NATO and its massive coalition-wide security infrastructure – is certain to reshape the domestic political balance in countries such as the United States, Britain, Canada, France, Germany, and Italy. Can the political right retain power without its antithesis, communism, alive and well to frighten the voters? To this writer it seems all too probable that the fear of communism will give way to class-inspired fears of the low-wage have-not nations of the Third World. Right-wing racial and nationalistic attacks on Third World immigrants and goods, common enough during the 1980s, may be the leading motif of the politics of the post-Cold War era, particularly if economic conditions deteriorate in the industrialized states. Nationalist ideology is made to order for those who argue that white Western societies are in danger of being overrun by the illegal immigrants and cheap goods of the Third World, and that the "have" powers should use their superior resources and military power to keep the "have-nots" in check.

All of this is reason enough to worry about the resurgence of nationalism, and it should give ample cause for progressive Canadians to reconsider any commitment they have to nationalist causes and principles. Without giving up their love of country or their civic patriotism, Canadians should abandon the nationalist ideologues with their violent discourses, whether on behalf of the Canadian, Québécois, Mohawk, or some other "nation." Nationalism is part of the shame of this bloodiest of centuries, but it need not be part of the burden we pass on to the next. Aside from its legacy of destructiveness and its delusive emphasis on language as the first criterion of a political community, nationalism is simply inappropriate in an age of global economic and ecological interdependence. We need fewer sovereign states, not more; we need larger political units, not smaller ones; and we need far more internationalism, far less nationalism.

REFERENCES

Acton, Baron (1907). "Nationality" (1862), in *History of Freedom and Other Essays*. London: Macmillan.

Anderson, Benedict (1983). *Imagined Communities: Reflections on the Origin and Spread of Nationalism*. London: Verso.

Brenda, Julien (1969). *The Treason of the Intellectuals*. New York: Norton.

Berlin, Isaiah (1981). *Against the Current: Essays in the History of Ideas*. Oxford: Oxford University Press.

Burkert, Walter (1985). *Greek Religion*. Cambridge Mass.: Harvard University Press.

Camus, Albert (1974). "Letters to a German Friend" (1942–44), in *Resistance, Rebellion, and Death*. New York: Vintage Books.

Clausewitz, Carl von (1976). *On War* (1832). Edited and translated by P. Paret and M. Howard. Princeton, N.J.: Princeton University Press.

Cooper, Richard N. (1968). *The Economics of Interdependence: Economic Policy in the Atlantic Community*. New York: Columbia University Press.

Dietz, Mary G. (1989). "Patriotism," in Terrance Ball, James Farr, and Russell L. Hanson, eds., *Political Innovation and Conceptual Change*. Cambridge: Cambridge University Press.

Drucker, Peter (1986). "The Changes in World Economy," *Foreign Affairs* (Spring).

Fallows, James (1989). "Containing Japan," *The Atlantic Monthly* (May).

Freud, Sigmund (1982). *Civilization and Its Discontents* (1930). Revised and edited by James Strachey. New York: The Hogarth Press and the Institute of Psycho-Analysis.

Gerth, H.H., and C. Wright Mills, eds. (1958). *From Max Weber: Essays in Sociology*. New York: Oxford University Press.

Gill, Stephen, and David Law (1988). *The Global Political Economy*. Baltimore: Johns Hopkins University Press.

Gilpin, Robert (1987). *The Political Economy of International Relations*. Princeton, N.J.: Princeton University Press.

Hroch, Miroslav (1985). *Social Preconditions of National Revival in Europe*. Cambridge: Cambridge University Press.

Kedourie, Elie (1985). *Nationalism*. Second edition. London: Hutchinson.

Kremenyuk, Victor (1990). "A historical parallel," *New Times*, Moscow (April 17–23).

List, Friedrich (1885). *The National System of Political Economy* (1841). Translated by S.S. Lloyd. London: Longmans, Green and Co.

Meinecke, Friedrich (1970). *Cosmopolitanism and the National State*. Princeton, N.J.: Princeton University Press.

Mill, John Stuart (1962). *Considerations on Representative Government*. Chicago: Henry Regnery Co.

Minogue, K.R. (1967). *Nationalism*. London: B.T. Batsford Ltd.

Montesquieu, Charles de Secondat (1989). *The Spirit of the Laws* (1748). Translated and edited by Anne M. Kohler *et al.* Cambridge: Cambridge University Press.

Pratt, Larry (1982). "Energy: The Roots of National Policy," *Studies in Political Economy*, No. 7 (Winter).

Ranke, Leopold von (1981). *The Secret of World History: Selected Writings on the*

156

Art and Science of History. Edited by Roger Wines. New York: Fordham University Press.

Rousseau, J.J. (1953). *Considerations on the Government of Poland and on Its Proposed Reformation* (1772), in Frederick Watkins, ed., *Rousseau: Political Writings*. New York: Nelson.

Strange, Susan (1988). *States and Markets: An Introduction to International Political Economy*. London: Pinter Publishers.

Trudeau, Pierre Elliott (1968). *Federalism and the French Canadians*. Toronto: Macmillan of Canada.

Wight, Martin (1986). *Power Politics*. Second edition. London: Penguin.

9   In Search of a Foreign Policy

Introduction

Lester Pearson once described foreign policy as "domestic policy with its hat on." The description is apt, given the current malaise plaguing Canadian foreign policy under the Mulroney government. The country's foreign policy has been adrift in recent years as the world around us is changing in revolutionary ways. The past year has seen the stable and often comforting Cold War assumptions that governed much of Canada's post-war foreign policy crumble along with the Berlin Wall. While the future remains largely undefined, Canadian policy-makers have been slow to set any course. Instead, they seem to have retrenched into ever closer alignment with old verities even as these lose their credibility. At a time when Eastern Europe and the Soviet Union are undergoing revolutionary transformations, when the world moves quickly and definitely toward a multipolar structure, when the indifference and hostility of the capitalist powers sink the Third World, especially Africa, into greater depths of debt and poverty, and when the health of the planet is itself in jeopardy, Canadians appear too preoccupied with national and continental matters to respond effectively.

The early years of the Mulroney government gave mixed signals about the direction foreign policy would follow. The Prime Minister left no illusions about his attitude toward the United States. Campaigning on the promise that "good relations, super relations . . . would be the cornerstone of our foreign policy," he set out on a course of close alignment with the Americans, and subsequently secured the free trade agreement. The government indicated its preference to seek

security and prosperity through close bilateral linkages on the premise that the United States would remain the leading economic and
political force in the world.

In opposition to this dominant trend there were also indications of
an alternative option that was less narrow and potentially more progressive. The Mulroney government sought and secured wider recognition and representation in multilateral associations. During the
past five years it increased its international status and responsibility in
la Francophonie, the Commonwealth, and the Group of Seven. It
obtained a temporary (through 1990) seat on the UN Security Council
and, most recently, joined the Organization of American States (OAS).
Its success in moving to the upper echelons of international institutions is a clear indication of the respect and influence Canada is able to
carry in international circles. These developments lend support to the
view that Canada has moved to the perimeter of the core of the
capitalist world economy (Resnick, 1989). Canada now has an opportunity to abandon the policies of a dependent power, to reject both
continentalism and isolationism, and to resist the temptations of protectionism. Instead, in a spirit of constructive internationalism we can
help to build a new international order that is not only stable but more
peaceful and just. The Mulroney government's interest in maintaining
and furthering its multilateral links displays a willingness to continue
the policies of internationalism evident in previous governments. Too
often, however, the commitment to multilateralism has faded once
the status of membership has been achieved.

The number, variety, and significance of Canada's international
connections provide rich opportunities for enhancing Canadian
influence over international events. Yet opportunities are useless if
they are not grasped and utilized. Not only has Canada acquired
membership in the most exclusive of international clubs, the international system is now more open to change than at any time since the
end of World War Two. There is now considerable room for creative
foreign policy leaders to help construct a new international order. To
date, both the government and the three major political parties have
been reticent in devising policies that respond to this challenge. Political vision remains dominated by old orthodoxies. Foreign policy for
both the right and left in Canada is still defined with respect to the
United States. Our politicians' visions appear limited to either closer
contact or isolationism, while the rest of the globe is moving toward
ever greater interdependence.

Now is the time for innovative policies. A new international order
will be created whether Canada chooses to participate or not. It is
better that we participate actively and not leave that task to others. If

the new order is to be one of greater peace and justice, it will require more progressive policies than we have seen in recent years. It will also require widespread domestic support.

THE CHANGING GLOBAL TERRAIN

A glance around the globe today reveals that international politics have reached a critical juncture. The confines of the Cold War no longer define relations between states. The superpowers have lost much of their ability to control other states. The Soviet empire has collapsed. The American empire is waning. New power centres are emerging in Europe and the Pacific. Despite strong forces of national resistance, the world capitalist economy is less amenable to the control of core states and requires collective management. Each day brings additional confirmation that the physical environment is deteriorating rapidly and perhaps irrevocably. As national (if not always individual per capita) wealth increases in the leading capitalist economies, many Third World countries are experiencing deteriorating economic conditions. The convergence of these developments, while not all recent in origin, suggests a fundamental transformation of the pattern of international politics. Each development raises important and difficult choices for Canadians.

The opening of the Berlin Wall in November, 1989, marked the end of the Cold War. Whether viewed as an intense military competition between two hostile blocs or a more fundamental ideological conflict between competing social and economic systems that dates back to 1917, this Manichean period of international politics has come to a close. The popular revolutions that swept across Hungary, Poland, East Germany, and Czechoslovakia, and the more violent struggle in Romania, accomplished what NATO never could, the largely peaceful liberation of the peoples of Eastern Europe. While the results were a vindication of the influence of liberal democracy, the West did not "win" the Cold War. We were mere spectators. The victory belongs to the people of Eastern Europe, with the influential assistance of Mikhail Gorbachev. For it was Gorbachev who decided to dismantle the Soviet empire and it was the people of Eastern Europe who had the courage to seize the moment with such far-reaching results. The contribution of governments in the West was clearly limited. Almost uniformly sceptical of Gorbachev's vision of reform, these governments were taken by surprise when the vision became reality throughout most of Eastern Europe.

Canada, like many other states, had been greatly influenced by the ups and downs of tensions across the Iron Curtain. Former Prime Minister Trudeau once lamented that all of Canada's foreign policy had been determined by the military arrangements devised to cope with the Cold War. Canada's assessment of the post-war situation in the late 1940s, the growing pressure from the United States for closer military ties, the fear of another war in Europe, and the need to maintain some institutional links with European states led the government to pursue actively the establishment of the North Atlantic Treaty Organization. It soon became, alongside the United Nations, one of the cornerstones of Canada's post-war policy of active internationalism. Although it did not dictate foreign policy, as claimed by Trudeau, NATO was instrumental in furthering many other foreign policy objectives, as Trudeau himself was to discover in the mid-1970s and again in the early 1980s when he launched his peace initiative. The Canadian commitment to NATO wavered as the alliance became more and more preoccupied with military solutions and nuclear-based strategies, but it was nonetheless maintained by successive governments who viewed it as a means for stabilizing power relations in Europe, deflecting and influencing the security concerns of the United States, retaining an institutional link with Western Europe, and later establishing a basis for Canadian participation in arms control deliberations with the Soviet Union and the Warsaw Pact.

In the wake of the revolutions in Eastern Europe, NATO and the Warsaw Pact are destined to fade away. The Pact is already in disarray as Soviet forces are withdrawn from Hungary and Czechoslovakia and the two German states become one. At its 1990 summit, the Soviet Union was able to prevent the complete collapse of the Pact by agreeing that its military structure be dismantled and that it shift its attention to political co-operation with NATO. The Soviet government had little choice, given pressures from Hungary and Czechoslovakia and the changes in East Germany. Pact members had lost whatever concern they had had of a NATO attack. As the Czech foreign minister, Jiri Dienstein, put it, "the only problem with NATO is that we don't belong to it." Now it is NATO leaders who are struggling to redefine their alliance and keep it afloat.

With fundamental political change under way in the East, NATO has lost its primary *raison d'être*. Designed initially to shore up the politically unstable post-war regimes in Western Europe and subsequently redesigned as an integrated military force to meet the potential challenge from Soviet-led military forces, NATO is now an alliance without an enemy. As Eastern European governments move toward democracy, an alliance that would place Canadians alongside Turkish forces against the Poles and the Czechs makes no sense. While the Soviet Union will inevitably remain a great military power armed with nuclear weapons, its direct threat to Western Europe is vanishing as rapidly as its empire. Even Western military leaders have acknowledged that the Soviet military threat no longer applies. Combined with these new political realities, there are economic, demographic, and political pressures for substantial reductions in military expenditures. These are already evident throughout the alliance, including Canada and the United States. Despite protests from some quarters, these pressures will likely lead to the removal of Canadian and American forces from Europe. The U.S. Army has already drawn up contingency plans to remove all its forces from Europe by the year 2000.

In response to this rapidly changing situation, NATO leaders are advocating that the alliance turn its attention to other matters. In a speech in Berlin in December, 1989, American Secretary of State James Baker advocated that NATO address other concerns, such as verifying arms control accords, dealing with regional conflicts, and fighting drug wars. The search for new enemies is likely to be a difficult and ultimately futile task. NATO is not well suited for intervening in regional conflicts in the Third World, such as the Persian Gulf, where the interests of member governments are often in conflict and where members such as Canada often prefer UN involvement. Nor are NATO members likely to agree on a collective effort to eliminate drug merchants, especially if the American invasion of Panama is an example of how this is to be done. Others are attempting to resurrect the Canadian article, Article 2 of the North Atlantic Treaty, that calls for co-operation in non-military matters. While potentially a more useful objective, past failures to use the article, the success of other institutions, such as the Organization for Economic Co-operation and Development (OECD) in the economic realm, and the fact that NATO has for more than three decades presented itself almost exclusively as an anti-Soviet military alliance all make it unlikely that NATO will be able to embark on this new course. Its short-term role would appear largely limited to finalizing arms control agreements and providing a temporary security structure until new ones have been created. In the longer term it must yield to a new security regime that will encompass all of Europe, including the Soviet Union.

Whatever the process and pace of change in Europe, it is evident that Europeans are assuming a greater degree of control. Clearly the superpowers, and especially the Soviet Union, have been instrumental in bringing about these dramatic events. Yet on issues as important as the unification of Germany and the economic and political integration of the European Community (EC), the superpowers have been forced to react to German and European proposals. The 1989 Bush-Gorbachev summit at Malta could in no way replicate the settlement at Yalta more than forty years earlier because the power of European states has grown so significantly. As the influence of the superpowers wanes, there is an emerging power vacuum in Europe that Germany seems destined to fill. The emergence of German power has generated concerns in both East and West and in turn creates a certain instability.

The societies and governments of Eastern Europe and the Soviet Union also face enormous difficulties as they try to cope with implementation of free markets and capitalist economies. Individuals throughout Eastern Europe, having achieved a measure of political liberation, face the threat of economic deprivation as social support systems are dismantled and the market pushes others into unemployment and poverty. These conditions may very well be compounded if the West insists on the usual austerity measures of the International Monetary Fund (IMF) as a prerequisite for economic aid. There is also the real possibility that long-suppressed nationalist antagonisms will develop into violent clashes, as have already occurred in the Soviet Union and Romania. The success of the revolutions in the East, let alone the peace of the continent itself, is by no means a certainty. For this and other reasons, some Europeans wish to see the Americans remain actively involved on the continent even as American power to control events dimishes.

The growing influence of Europeans over the future of the continent will be furthered by the full economic integration of the European Community proposed for 1992. "Europe 1992," while still not freed from national obstacles that may delay full integration, nevertheless will mark a further evolution in the growth of European power on the continent and, potentially, beyond it. The further integration of the EC and its possible expansion to incorporate the newly formed democracies of Eastern Europe will increase its already considerable influence among the world's capitalist powers. Alongside that of Japan, the Community's economic power confirms that unilateral American policies will no longer dictate global economic affairs. The threat of a Fortress Europe that is both economically unified and isolated would clearly exacerbate the already creeping regionalism that has infected the world capitalist economy. A further intensification of Japan's pursuit of regional economic supremacy in the Pacific would only push this trend further. The growing regionalization of these capitalist powers without the cohesive bonds of the Cold War will likely generate new forms of political conflict in the 1990s. This emerging political order will have significant if as yet unpredictable ramifications for global economic relations. For countries such as Canada the lines are less clearly drawn and the options as well as the potential pitfalls are increasing. The end of the Cold War in Europe is not "the end of history"; it is the beginning of a new phase.

While Europe may be the source of the most significant changes in international politics, it is not the only development that Canadians must confront. As Europeans bask in the light of peaceful democratic liberation, the peoples of the Third World continue to struggle under the darkness of debt, underdevelopment, and oppression. The liberation of polities and economies has not yet spread to the Third World. From Southeast Asia to Central America to Southern Africa the struggle continues for peace, democracy, and economic justice. If Europe is hopeful, the Third World remains bleak. On the economic front, the South continues to fund the economic prosperity of the North. As interest rates soared in the late 1970s, Third World borrowers caught with floating interest rates found their debt-servicing costs escalating as the global economy moved into a prolonged recession. Under lower, more reasonable interest rates, the aggregate payments of debtor nations would have paid off most loans. But debt levels remain high and interest rates are on the rise again. Third World borrowers will once again feel the pain more directly and more severely than most Canadian consumers could imagine. As a result of the uncontrollable burden of debt, the people of these countries have been forced to accept a drop in income between 10 and 40 per cent over the past five years. In an absurd case of punishing the poor, for the past five years the net transfer of funds has flowed from the South to the North, reaching nearly $50 billion per year. More than $1 billion of this money comes annually to Canada. Through debt servicing, capital flight, and other transfers the Third World provides financial support for the growth of the First.

As capital flows from the poor to the rich, Third World producers find First world markets closed to many of their exports. Restrictions on trade in textiles, clothing, and other products have additionally punished low-wage producers in Third World countries. The agricultural subsidy war between the United States and the EC has further disadvantaged the South. Agricultural exporters in the Third World have lost substantial revenue. Food-importing countries have enjoyed the short-term advantage of lower prices, but this benefit will last only as long as the subsidy war. In the meantime, many of these countries have abandoned the production of local products and the opportunity to further agricultural self-reliance.

The last sustained effort to provide relief to the Third World that emerged out of the UN's Special Session on Africa failed, in no small part, because Western nations were unwilling to meet their end of the bargain. Despite worsening inequities, North-South negotiations have ceased. Instead, Third World governments have had to rely exclusively on the IMF, the World Bank, and the General Agreement on Tariffs and Trade (GATT) in their efforts to establish a more just international economic order. While these governments have accepted the necessity of working with these institutions, they lack the bargaining leverage to influence decisions. As a result, Third World demands have become increasingly marginalized in negotiations on international economic reforms. As Eastern Europeans look for assistance for their own ailing economies, the leaders of the Third World may find it even more difficult to get a hearing.

Many in the Third World have also missed the liberating tendencies brought on by the end of the Cold War. Violence rages undiminished in the Middle East, Central America, and Southern Africa and threatens to erupt again in South and Southeast Asia. As the Cold War ends in Europe, it needs to be acknowledged that this was a global conflict and that the victims were not only in Europe but in many parts of the Third World. While the Cold War brought militarization and repression to Europe and North America, it brought violence, death, and poverty to the peoples of Central America, Southeast Asia, and Eastern Africa. In these and other places wars continue, motivated by an ugly mixture of ideology and long-standing internal divisions and fought with the second-hand weapons of the leading cold warriors.

There are, however, some positive signs here. The dawning of a new era in East-West relations has led to Soviet and American co-operation in responding to some regional conflicts. Their common position on halting arms sales to Iraq following its invasion of Kuwait is a significant and positive change. In the Soviet government, unilateral support for national liberation movements has given way to an interest in resolving conflicts through the UN. The United States seems less willing to renounce armed intervention, as evidenced by its move into Panama. Yet the Bush administration's willingness to allow a UN-supervised observer mission to operate in Central America and aspects of its diplomacy during the Iraqi crisis are perhaps indicative of a new approach to regional conflicts.

The economic and political crisis confronting the Third World has coincided with an environmental crisis of global proportions. It is premature to speak of the "greening of international politics," but environmental concerns have forced their way onto the agenda of inter-state relations. Ozone depletion, global warming, and the destruction of rain forests have become matters of public debate in many corners of the globe. Growing public concern about the social and economic consequences of continued environmental abuse has forced governments to respond to this challenge. The report of the World Commission on Environment and Development (1987) called for policies of sustainable development and has influenced policy debates throughout the international system. Public opinion polls in Canada and other industrialized countries now indicate that the public sees the environment as the major problem facing governments. The renewed interest in environmental protection has spawned numerous international conferences and conventions. Despite this, rhetoric so far has outpaced national and international action.

In addition to the far-reaching changes that Gorbachev unleashed in the Soviet Union and Eastern Europe, he has also taken a fresh approach to the United Nations. Unlike his predecessors, Gorbachev now looks upon the UN as a useful instrument for the establishment and maintenance of international peace and security. The Soviet Union has supported a UN role in Afghanistan, Angola, and Kuwait. It has paid past debts to the organization. This new faith in multilateralism on the part of the Soviet leadership comes at the end of a decade in which the United States adopted a critical tone toward the UN. The Bush administration seems eager to restore American credibility by repaying its outstanding debts. However, the U.S. congress is still influenced by the hostile views of the Reagan administration. As one author recently noted, "Multilateralism has not yet fully recovered from this period of aloofness and hostility" (Weiss, 1990, p. 8).

All these developments are indicative of a world in change. It is a change more widespread and substantial than any during the past forty years. The Cold War touched most aspects of international politics. There were few innocent bystanders as the superpowers painted every issue with their Cold War brushes. It is unlikely that such simplifications will recur. Instead, global politics are uncertain, and old verities no longer apply. Governments in Canada and around the world now confront the challenge of change.

THE NEO-CONSERVATIVE PATH

In the face of these sweeping changes one looks in vain for a vision of the future course of Canadian foreign policy. With some notable exceptions the Mulroney government's response has been limited. The government's attempts to secure greater international representation, its role in the Commonwealth on the South African issue, and its efforts in response to the famine in Ethiopia indicate a persistent strain of internationalism in Canadian foreign policy. Yet there are more systematic signs of a reorientation in Canadian foreign policy toward the neo-conservatism that has guided much of domestic politics since 1984. By "neo-conservatism" in foreign policy, I mean a policy rooted in narrow self-interest, motivated primarily by economic considerations; one that relies slavishly on the market to control both economic and political outcomes.

This neo-conservative path has led to a relative decline in government expenditures on foreign policy. Recent budgets designed to reduce the deficit have taken a heavy toll on the foreign policy departments of CIDA, External Affairs, and Defence. Between the 1984-85 and 1989-90 fiscal years Ottawa's spending under the "Official Development Assistance" category grew slightly, from $2.1 to $2.4 billion. After adjustment for inflation, however, spending declined in real terms; it also fell as a share of GNP (Wilson, 1990). The Department of External Affairs is reducing its staff "as part of a $70-million budget cut over the next four years" (*Globe and Mail*, 29 June 1990). Even in the defence sector, where spending has been increased at an annual rate of 5.2 per cent since 1984–85, there has been little growth in real terms (Dosman, 1988). The integration of Trade and Commerce officials with the diplomats in the Pearson Building (initiated by the Trudeau government in 1982) has led to the domination by the former over the latter. The result has been a limited view of the economic costs and benefits that will result from political change and a concomitant desire to protect Canada's export dependence on the United States.

As Gorbachev and Reagan neared the completion of the Intermediate Nuclear Forces Treaty in 1987, the Canadian government released its long-awaited White Paper on Defence (Department of National Defence, 1987). In a style more reminiscent of the 1950s than the rapidly improving East-West relations of the 1980s, the paper adopted a strikingly hawkish tone. Three years and a new world later the government is finally setting its Cold War assumptions aside. The visit of Mulroney to Moscow in the fall of 1989 suggested belated interest in and support for the political and economic reforms that Gorbachev had launched. Indeed, private Canadian firms, such as the property development company Olympia and York, and even American branch plants such as McDonald's, which opened the first McDonald's restaurant in the Soviet Union, have been taking greater initiatives.

On arms control the government has been unwilling to move in advance of its fellow alliance members in discussions with the Soviet Union. This is inexcusable with respect to Arctic security matters, where the Mulroney government has adopted a consistently negative tone to various Soviet proposals launched by Gorbachev in his Murmansk speech of October, 1987. Despite the direct and long-term benefits that a security regime in the Arctic would present for Canadians, the government appears content to wait until the issue has been addressed by the Americans or in NATO councils. Only after a lengthy delay did Ottawa indicate a willingness to discuss, but not negotiate, security concerns in the Arctic with the Soviets. For the present, the government has remained committed to keeping forces in Europe and to continued participation in NORAD. Thus, in many areas the 1987 White Paper would still seem to hold. Yet, ironically, the specific force and equipment proposals of the White Paper have been totally vitiated by the 1989 and 1990 budgets. Thus when one considers the lack of any clear budgetary direction for Canada's future defence roles, a persisting commitment to maintain forces in Europe, continued demands for Canadian peacekeeping forces, and renewed demands for a larger and more effective maritime capability, the only reasonable conclusion is that Canadian defence policy is in disarray.

The government's expressed interest in a substantial reform of NATO and the institutionalization of the Conference on Security and Co-operation in Europe indicates that it is catching up to the changes in Europe. Ottawa supported changes to NATO's nuclear strategy away from "flexible response and early use of nuclear weapons" to one where the weapons would be used "as a last resort." A great deal remains to be done, including the denuclearization of Central Europe, the removal of Canadian forces from Europe, and the dismantling of the Cold War's North American alliance, NORAD. Once these problems are resolved the Canadian government will be able to concentrate on a new defence agenda in the areas of enhanced maritime capabilities and improved mobile forces for multinational peacekeeping contributions.

Canada's Europe policy may be faulted for its late start, but in Central America the problem has been one of contradictory messages. The government's decision to participate in the OAS was viewed as an indication of the growing importance of Central America in Canadian foreign policy. Yet, given this and past governments' performance in the region, it remains uncertain whether this new institutional link grows out of bilateral interests with the Americans or reflects a more constructive multilateral approach to the region. Historically, Canada has participated in multilateral institutions to further Canadian involvement in international politics beyond the North Atlantic. For example, Reid (1989, p. 252) argued that Canada's participation in the Commonwealth in the 1950s "helped Canada break out of the confines of Canadian isolationism, North American isolationism, North Atlantic isolationism. . . . It helped us to face these crucial problems: colonialism and its aftermath, racial discrimination, cultural imperialism, the misery of half of the people of the world." Viewed from this vantage point the OAS could act to liberate Canadian policy in Latin America. It would also, however, force Canadians to confront the Americans in what remains their primary sphere of influence.

Unfortunately, the Canadian reaction to the American invasion of Panama suggests that concerns about Canada's bilateral links may be more important than more progressive policies for the region. Despite Mulroney's previous expressed opposition to third-party intervention in the region ("whoever the third party may be, and regardless of its legitimate interests in the area"), he was quick to support the American invasion of Panama, a violation of international principles on armed intervention. Abandoning an opportunity to reinforce an important legal principle of special significance to Latin American governments, the Canadian government used its place both at the UN Security Council and at the OAS to defend the American action. Coming as it did immediately after Canada joined the OAS, the decision marked a continuing reluctance to challenge American actions in the region. Despite the passing of the Cold War and the supposed freedom from American economic pressure on Canadian foreign policy that the free trade agreement provides, Ottawa is still reticent in opposing Washington directly – even when, as was the case in Panama, important principles were at stake and the overwhelming majority of the international community condemned the invasion. However wrongheaded, the government's response to the invasion of Panama should not lead to the total rejection of the OAS. The potential remains for Canada to use the organization in the future to increase our involvement in the region and to devise creative policies.

The increasingly desperate plight of people in the Third World also raises important and difficult policy choices for Canadians, and especially those on the left. The Mulroney government has lost interest in expanding Canadian assistance to the impoverished sectors of the world because of the chronic deficit in the federal budget. Despite Conservative promises to increase Canada's aid-to-GNP ratio, the ratio fell to 0.43 per cent of GNP in 1989, a figure lower than when the government took office in 1984 and less than half that which other leading middle powers such as Norway, Netherlands, Denmark, and Sweden have been giving in recent years (*Economist*, 30 June 1990, p. 99). Furthermore, Canada increasingly supports the austerity measures often applied against Third World borrowers through "structural adjustment plans." According to the president of the Canadian International Development Agency, Marcel Masse, "CIDA has taken the leap of faith and plunged into the uncharted seas of structural adjustment. . . . (it) figures among the priorities for Canadian development assistance." Canada's first significant participation, in setting up such a program for Guyana, was rewarded by angry demonstrators outside the Canadian High Commission in Georgetown, the country's capital.

Ottawa has granted some debt relief for Third World states. One recent example was the cancellation of some $182 million in official debt owed by the Caribbean Commonwealth states. The real costs to Canadians for such debt relief is slight. Many of these loans were offered years ago at very low interest rates and with lengthy repayment schemes. They also account for only a small portion of Third

World indebtedness to Canadian interests, which amounts to more than $20 billion, the chartered banks holding most of it. Viewed in this light, the fanfare surrounding this write-off generates cynicism, not respect. And Ottawa continues to stay in line with other Group of Seven members in rejecting broader debt-forgiveness schemes. More importantly, the government invests considerable resources in protecting its position in the American market under the free trade agreement, but it ignores Third World demands for free trade opportunities. For example, Canada continues to protect its domestic textile sector and opposes the dismantling of the restrictive Multi-Fibre Agreement.

A more progressive policy can be seen in the government's response to the problems faced by international institutions. In appointing Stephen Lewis, a high-profile New Democrat, as ambassador to the UN, Mulroney symbolically gave special emphasis to Canada's UN role. Canada subsequently undertook a successful diplomatic effort to secure a seat on the UN Security Council. External Affairs Minister Joe Clark has taken a constructive approach to Commonwealth action against apartheid in South Africa. Canada stepped in as Britain abandoned its leadership position.

Unfortunately these creative policies have not been sustained – either in the Security Council or in the Commonwealth. Canada has been reluctant, for example, to endorse additional sanctions against South Africa, which would require real domestic costs. Such policies might also offend important allies and put a strain on Ottawa's participation in great power summits (Nossal, 1988). Ottawa's decision to commit naval forces to the Persian Gulf in advance of a Security Council mandate to enforce its sanctions of Iraq also indicates a greater interest in winning the approval of the Americans than in strengthening the capabilities of the UN. The government is willing to move only when its direct interests are not adversely affected and when it poses little risk of offending our great power allies.

If multilateralism in the international system is to thrive, the UN must remain a viable entity. With the support of the Soviet Union the UN could begin to play a more effective role in reconciling regional conflicts and furthering the acceptance of international law. There is a need to restore active U.S. support for the UN and to strengthen the institution's capacity in regional conflicts. The willingness of the U.S. to allow the UN to establish an observation force in Central America is a significant shift in American policy. Similar action in response to the Iraqi crisis in conjunction with the Soviet Union would have added greatly to the UN's stature.

The future international system will not be freed from violent conflict. The Cold War was too often and too easily injected into many regional conflicts, but the roots of such conflicts are more often in competing nationalisms, religious differences, and domestic inequities. These persist. As a result, there will still be a need for the sort of peacekeeping activities in which Canada has so actively participated. If the Americans and the Soviets can learn to co-operate effectively in the UN and if the institution acquires a greater capacity to initiate peacekeeping measures, there will likely be an even greater demand for such forces in the future. The end of the Cold War may very well increase the range of potential participants, but Canada will have to retain the necessary military capabilities to fulfil this important international responsibility. The Canadian armed forces should emphasize mobility; therefore, additional military transport capabilities will be required. We cannot shy away from these responsibilities into a pacifist isolationism. Defence spending will have to be maintained at a level that allows this country to participate in multilateral efforts to prevent or to end violent conflicts. In the longer term this will be the most important peace dividend.

POLICIES FOR THE FUTURE

Recent Canadian foreign policy has demonstrated uncertainty in political direction mixed with a strong dose of neo-conservative economics. The world will not wait for Canada to chart its future course. Creative policies to contribute to a new international order must come soon. There is good reason to start with Europe, but we cannot stop there.

In response to the revolutionary developments in Eastern Europe, NATO leaders must dismantle the old alliance structures and create a new basis for the common security of all of Europe, including the Soviet Union. It is no longer necessary or desirable that NATO present a threat, military or otherwise, to the Soviet Union. The time has come for policies of reassurance and integration, not threat and division. The initial steps to change NATO's nuclear strategy have been undertaken and must now be matched with both nuclear and conventional force reductions. While ex-British Prime Minister Thatcher and others may find it difficult to abandon a beloved offspring, NATO's strategy for first use of nuclear weapons makes no sense given the changed complexion of the "enemy." It is imperative that NATO work to eliminate all short-range nuclear weapons, thereby adding another range of weapons to those already banned in the Intermediate Nuclear Forces (INF) treaty. It will also be necessary to reduce conventional forces. Now that Gorbachev has accepted continued German membership in NATO, all foreign forces, including Canadian forces, should be withdrawn from Germany. For Canada, this means removing forces first sent in 1951. Each of these measures will send important messages to Moscow and the leaders of Eastern Europe that the West supports their foreign policy changes. The measures will reassure Gorbachev and his military leaders that further change can proceed in a non-threatening environment.

NATO planners will not find these steps easy, given their past dependence on nuclear weapons and on foreign forces in Germany. NATO has been an important institutional link between Canada and Europe for forty years and Canadian forces in Europe have helped to solidify that link. While NATO will likely survive in the short term, and with it Canadian participation, Canadians should push to have the alliance move quickly on arms reduction, including the eventual withdrawal of Canadian forces. NATO may appear to be a suspect institution to negotiate arms reductions, but it is likely that only an alliance-wide commitment to reduce Western military forces in Europe will allow Europeans – in the East as well as the West – to live securely with the unification of Germany.

The ideological orthodoxies of the Cold War presented NATO as an alliance that required massive conventional and nuclear arms to ward off a potential Soviet attack on Western Europe. Yet at the time of its inception the alliance was designed to stabilize the European balance of power to prevent the outbreak of another war. The initial commitment was for political stability in the face of economic and political uncertainty clouding the future of war-torn European nations. Not incidental to the whole process was the desire for a mechanism that would allow German rearmament under multinational constraints.

The need remains for a mechanism to enable the German people to reunify in a manner that does not threaten either friends or foes. There seem to be two available mechanisms, the European Community and the Conference on Security Co-operation in Europe (CSCE). The CSCE was launched during the first wave of détente in the 1970s to negotiate a political settlement of the Cold War. It has since operated as a negotiating forum addressing issues such as human rights and confidence-building measures between East and West. Its membership includes all of the states of Europe, alliance members and neutrals alike, plus the United States and Canada. The thirty-five-member Conference operates without a permanent secretariat, and agreements require unanimous consent. For some this makes it an inappropriate security system. Yet it is the only European chamber that includes Canada and the United States and all European states. From a Canadian perspective the CSCE is the preferred choice for a future European security regime because it would allow this country an opportunity to participate actively in the process. As Canadian troops are returned from Europe and NATO exits from centre stage, it is important that

Canadians not neglect the transatlantic connections that NATO secured. There are in Europe many potential supporters among the secondary powers for a more progressive foreign policy. If and when Canada chooses to pursue a progressive policy, it can work with these European allies.

For all these reasons, it is important for Canadian policy-makers to strengthen the CSCE and to divert an ever-increasing number of tasks from NATO to the CSCE. Support for Canadian involvement in such a project has come from a number of sources, including both the Soviet and West German foreign ministers. Soviet Foreign Minister Shevardnadze has, for example, called "for the United States and Canada to continue to be highly involved partners in the pan-European process" (Shevardnadze, 1990).

Developments in Europe present substantial difficulties for Canada. Canadians have relied on their NATO connections with Europe to offset the imbalance of relations with the United States. As European integration deepens and expands to encompass the states of Eastern Europe, Canada will find it more difficult to maintain European links. Active participation in the CSCE will help. Additionally, we will have to foster new linkages, if not with the EC, then with European middle powers over issues of common interest, including Arctic co-operation and relations with the developing world. As a member of the Group of Seven, the Commonwealth, and la Francophonie, Canada is potentially well placed to maintain a window on the European continent. It would be a fatal error to assume that Fortress Europe is inevitable and that Canada must resort to a Fortress North America in response.

We are already much more locked in our own continent than we have been for some time. Pushed by the economic priorities of the Mulroney government into a North American economic accord that has in turn encouraged others, such as Pacific nations, to look for regional schemes, we have tended to neglect our interests in the European balance. The belated visit of Mulroney to Moscow is symptomatic of the general disregard that European affairs have suffered under the current government. In particular, Canada must expand new independent links with the Soviet Union. Yet this is not happening. Instead, policy-makers in Ottawa refrain from making initiatives in advance of our allies. As mentioned earlier, this practice has led to neglect of our security concerns in the Arctic. Costly expenditures on maritime defence could be postponed indefinitely if such a security regime were established.

An important event will be the next renewal of the NORAD treaty, due for 1991. This presents a good opportunity to abandon the continental air defence scheme devised during the height of Cold War fears, to replace it with more passive air surveillance, and to bring to the North American continent the principle of "open skies" that the government has recently vaunted. The pressing need is to take advantage of these opportunities while they exist, to entrench a new security regime that enhances Canadian and global security, furthers Canadian flexibility, and reduces the need for costly military expenditures. Canadians also have a strong interest in expanding arms reductions to include air-launched cruise missiles and sea-based nuclear weapons.

The Third World presents an equally demanding and equally important challenge. Here, too, Canadians are presented with an opportunity to devise internationalist policies that will respond in a more progressive way to globalization of the international economy. Third World states are increasingly demanding full integration into the international economy. They have become active participants in the Uruguay Round of the GATT negotiations to liberalize trade. They are expanding their own trade options with bilateral and regional trading schemes such as that between Argentina and Brazil, and Mexico is seeking a free trade arrangement with the United States. Yet these countries often come to these negotiations with distinct disadvantages.

An active internationalist foreign policy demands that all Canadians, not solely the government, respond creatively. Canadians on the left have been supportive of increased aid expenditures, but they have tended to turn protectionist when faced with opening Canadian markets to Third World exporters. If we are to contribute to a more just international order, we cannot be selective traders and reject requests from Third World states for access to our markets. The future growth of the international economy will depend on the expansion and integration of their producers and markets. Such integration is ultimately in Canada's self-interest because the alternative is regional trade blocs that threaten our exports. The most important example is agriculture. The export-subsidy war between the U.S. and EC has led to the collapse of international cereal prices and turned prairie farmers into welfare recipients. Canada is a member of the Cairns group of agricultural exporting countries – many in the Third World – lobbying to liberalize agricultural trade in the Uruguay Round.

It is not sufficient to claim that low wages "exploit" Third World workers. As Pratt (1990, p. 161) has written, "The mere fact that wage levels in a Third World country are much below those in a developed country is not a legitimate reason to ban imports from that country. To block their imports because their wages are lower than wages in developed countries is to deny them the opportunity to utilize what is often their main comparative advantage, their low wages." This issue takes on immediate significance as Third World states press for a more just trading order in the Uruguay Round and as Mexico begins to negotiate a free trade regime with the United States.

The domestic costs of more open trading policies will require generous programs of retraining for displaced Canadian workers and reinvestment in more competitive industries. But retraining and reinvestment, not greater protection, are the public policies to stress. The long-term costs of failing to do so will leave us with inefficient domestic producers and limited alternatives to our export dependence on the United States.

Canada should actively participate in the Mexico-U.S. free trade negotiations. It would be both morally wrong and economically short-sighted to try to exclude Mexico from the North American market. To fight a rearguard action to protect our privileged access to the American market is foolish. Canada should seek wider participation in international markets and not narrowly confine itself to the United States, but we should do so on terms that are more just than those applied in the past. Canada has always sought multilateral forums as a way of diluting American pressure. If GATT stalls, a North American trade agreement, including Mexico, may be the next best option.

Similar guidelines should influence our role in the World Bank and the International Monetary Fund. Many Third World governments have had to accept the structural adjustment measures proposed by these international lending institutions. Often this has been done at great domestic political risk. Such adjustments adversely affect politically powerful interest groups, and to implement them governments often resort to political oppression. Structural adjustment also creates serious social problems for many Third World citizens living at the margin of subsistence. However legitimate structural adjustment to balance government accounts or to end inefficient state subsidies may be, there are equally strong competing claims to preserve basic social services and political freedom. Structural adjustment needs a human face, and countries such as Canada should ensure that compensatory measures are put in place. As Third World governments tackle their economic problems under the strictures of the IMF and the World Bank, additional aid from industrialized economies can alleviate the attendant social and political costs.

There are likely to be new demands on Canadian aid as the states of Eastern Europe recover from decades of economic mismanagement. While it is of obvious importance to help these emerging democracies cope with the social cost of transition to capitalist economies, it should not be at the expense of lower aid to much poorer Third World countries. Government aid is probably less vital in Eastern Europe than in the Third World, because the private sector is likely, at least in the initial stages, to find Eastern Europe more attractive. This can already be seen in the rush of private investors to Eastern Europe and the Soviet Union. Canadian investors are participating in various funding schemes – including a Central European Development Fund with existing capital of about $100 million.

The problems for the Eastern Europeans of restoring their economies to health will be exacerbated if, in the enthusiasm to throw off communism, they lurch to the other ideological extreme and accept uncritically the ideology of free markets and a limited role for the state. Some Eastern European governments, such as Poland, have accepted IMF-style austerity measures without adequate evaluation of the attendant costs. Poland's Solidarity government inherited in 1989 a very sick economy – hyperinflation, crippling foreign debt arising from past investments in heavy industry operating at low productivity, an absurdly overvalued domestic currency (the zloty) and consequent rampant illegal currency exchange, and a large government deficit due to subsidies for state firms producing a wide range of goods. Solidarity accepted IMF-style austerity measures: making the zloty convertible and allowing easy imports, cutting subsidies drastically, controlling wage increases, freeing markets, and privatizing state firms. They have enjoyed success: inflation has been controlled. But the costs, for example a 30 per cent decline in industrial output during the first half of 1990, have been unexpectedly high.

The Canadian government could show some leadership with the IMF and the World Bank instead of giving unconditional support to structural adjustment programs. Canada should insist that such programs be accompanied by far more comprehensive programs to compensate the losers (for example, unemployment insurance and labour retraining are woefully inadequate in Eastern Europe) and could pressure other Group of Seven members to move quickly with new investment into those countries that accept austerity measures. Without such compensatory programs, the rapid transition to market economies will likely wreak social and political havoc without real economic benefit. Failure of this economic transformation would not only hurt the people of Eastern Europe; it would discredit their liberal democratic governments, provide fertile grievances for authoritarian nationalists to exploit, and, potentially, reverse the peaceful evolution of East-West conflict.

Finally, it is of considerable importance that Canada attempt to reestablish a constructive North-South dialogue. Initially, given the indifference of other capitalist powers, this could start in the Commonwealth or la Francophonie. Later, of course, it must expand to encompass the Group of Seven if real reform is to occur. There are reasons, however, not to wait. Most important is the desperate plight of Third World societies. Equally important is the recognition that the primary source of future international conflict is likely to be the economic disparities that divide the rich from the poor. Even apart from moral considerations, self-interest demands policies of reform. Moreover, given the diffusion of power in the system and the lack of direction among the leading capitalist powers in bodies such as the GATT, Canada's location at the periphery of this core group provides good opportunities for coalitions of middle powers (Wood, 1990; Ostry, 1990).

Just as the government must wrestle with the rapid political changes in Europe and the intractable economic problems of the Third World, so, too, must it confront its environmental responsibility. As in so many areas, Canada has not shied away from active involvement in international environmental policy-making. But as in so many other areas, Canadian performance has not matched its apparent activity. Participating in international meetings will not be an adequate response to the environmental crisis confronting the planet. The 1988 Toronto Conference on the Changing Atmosphere recommended a 20 per cent reduction in global carbon dioxide limits by the year 2005, yet levels continue to rise and subsidies for environmentally damaging activities continue unabated. A Canadian who worked on the Brundtland Commission, Jim MacNeill, observed, "When you compare \$40 to \$50 billion a year (in subsidies) in North America to promote fossil fuels, and hence to promote acid rain and global warming, with the decreasing amounts spent on efficiency and alternatives to fossil fuels, it is simply no contest. Acid rain and global warming win hands down" (Bush, 1990, p. 7). Delaying remedial actions only intensifies the dangers that already exist.

This is one area in which the most effective immediate response must involve domestic reforms. Canada prides itself on being among the world's moral leaders. Yet in the environmental area our actions have not been exemplary. Canadians are the highest per capita consumers of energy in the world. We produce more solid waste and recycle less than virtually any other country. Directly and indirectly, through its demand for goods and services, the average Canadian family produces (if that is the proper term) more than 2,000 litres of waste water per day, and we are among the top five per capita producers of carbon dioxide. As much as we decry the ravages of the rain forests of the Amazon, as host to 10 per cent of the world's forests and 16 per cent of the world's fresh water, we have a responsibility to preserve our own natural habitat. Canada has been actively involved in recent international conferences to curtail production of ecologically damaging compounds. At a fifty-five nation conference in London to strengthen the 1987 Montreal Protocol on Ozone Depletion, Environment Minister Robert de Cotret committed Canada to halt the production of ozone-destroying chemicals by the year 2000. He further stated that, if international agreement were forthcoming, Canada would be prepared to advance the ban to 1997. Yet Ottawa's Green Plan to deal with environmental problems at home was repeatedly delayed because of the opposition of some cabinet ministers. When finally published in December, 1990, it contained few specific programs. It is absolutely necessary for Canada to develop benign alternatives to existing harmful products and to become an exemplar for other states. A major opportunity is coming at the World Conference on Environment and Development to be held in Brazil in 1992.

RESHAPING THE DOMESTIC CONSENSUS

The problems confronting Canadian foreign policy cannot simply be blamed on a lack of government leadership. There also appears to be an eroding public consensus in support of more progressive foreign policies. Canada's post-war internationalism was strongly endorsed by the overwhelming majority of Canadians. Much of this resulted from the coalescing effects of the Cold War. Canadians were convinced of the need to respond to the Soviet threat through active participation in international alliances. In turn, as the Cold War wanes and as new issues crowd onto the international agenda, the consensus is slipping. Both reformists and cold warriors have in the past supported aid to Third World regimes, but the anti-Communist rationale for such policies has faded, and so, too, has support for such policies. As the pressing threats of the day shift from military security to economics and environmental management, the costs involved in foreign policy initiatives will increase. Canadians will no longer be able to take a free moral ride.

Reformist international policies, especially those designed to alleviate global poverty and restore a greater measure of health to our planet, will generate domestic costs. These costs have prompted domestic debate in which social democrats have not always been generous. For example, if the Third World is to be allowed an opportunity to participate effectively in the global economy, it must not be singled out for trade restrictions. Yet social democrats in Canada and elsewhere do just that. They push for restrictive trade measures against Third World products even as they speak the language of a liberal international trading order.

These tendencies are perhaps indicative of a change in Canadian values, which, according to pollster Allan Gregg, are no longer defined by a willingness "to be more generous, more tolerant, more peaceful" (Newman, 1990). As neo-conservative values of self-interest take hold at both the state and societal levels, the prospects for a more progressive Canadian foreign policy look bleak. Equally disturbing are the results of a Decima poll conducted in the summer of 1989, which indicated that 38 per cent of Canadians would support or strongly support "Canada and the United States adopting common and identical policy on all matters relating to defence and foreign policy" (*Maclean's*, 1989). This startling result is a clear indication of the depressing depths to which our continentalist preoccupations have brought us. It is clear from these findings that the initial battle for a reformed international order will have to take place in Canada. We must re-establish the basis for an internationalist foreign policy, one that rejects continentalism and isolationism, that abandons our preoccupation with the Americans, accepts the inevitable economic and environmental interdependencies, and sets aside nationalist and protectionist options. Effective leadership can help in this respect, but so can extensive grassroots action. Important in this respect will be church groups and others who have maintained an activist internationalist posture across a broad range of political and economic issues. Finally, Canada's unions must work to find domestic policy alternatives that do not rely on protectionism against Third World competitors.

CONCLUSION

One commentator has noted that certain governments (of which Canada was one):

> were content to meet from time to time in the Like-Minded Group [a group of middle-power states led by the Netherlands and Norway that since the mid-1970s had been meeting for consultations on the New International Economic Order proposals vaunted by the Third World in 1973-74]. They welcomed the reputation thereby acquired that they were amongst the more internationalist of the industrialized countries. But their other alliances and associations, be it NATO, the EC, or the Summit Seven, and their special bilateral relationships with other states were far more important to them than these nebulous and loose links with the other like-minded countries. (Lovbraek, 1990, p. 45)

Successive Canadian governments have taken great pride in being admitted to international clubs. The country's international associations are among the most extensive of any state. But associations alone do not make a foreign policy. Clinging to the coattails of international power does not, however, leave one's hands free for more creative tasks. In opting for access to privileged clubs Canada may be undermining its own longer-term opportunity to make a contribution to the future international order. Unless the government chooses to use these associations more creatively than it has to date and unless it is willing to alter its own policies in ways that will better serve the international community, this opportunity will be squandered.

As the world searches for new political alignments to replace the arthritic structures of the Cold War, Canada has the advantage of a state that has grappled with limits to sovereignty imposed by its own federal polity. It has a potentially creative role in multilateral organizations, all of which entail some limits to national sovereignty in the interest of international goals. The ending of the Cold War, the demise of the Soviet empire, and the multilateralization of the West all suggest much greater success for independent Canadian initiatives in the field of security and economic policy. John Holmes once quoted a fellow civil servant as concluding in the late 1940s that "Pax Americana was better than no pax at all." Fortunately, now there are other choices. Canadians must shake their current lethargy, cast aside the selfish policies of recent years, and respond with a great deal more vision than we have witnessed lately.

As Stephen Lewis (1990, p. 13) rightly stated, "Canada has a remarkable legitimacy and force in this world, should we choose to exercise it."

REFERENCES

Bush, K. (1990). "Facing up to Climate Change," *Peace and Security*, 52, p. 7.

Department of National Defence (1987). *Challenge and Commitment: A Defence Policy for Canada*. Ottawa: Supply and Services.

Dosman, E. (1988). "The Department of National Defence," in K.A. Graham, ed., *How Ottawa Spends*. Ottawa: Carleton University Press.

Economist (1990). "Economic and Financial Indicators" (30 June).

The Globe and Mail (1990). "External Affairs Department cuts 250 jobs" (29 June).

Lewis, S. (1990). "Canada as Peacemaker," *Ploughshares Monitor* (March), pp. 13–16.

Lovbraek, A. (1990). "International Reform and the Like-Minded Countries in the North-South Dialogue 1975-1985," in C. Pratt, ed., *Middle Power Internationalism*. Montreal: McGill-Queen's University Press.

Maclean's (1989). "Portrait of Two Nations" (3 July).

Newman, P. (1990). "A frightening threat to Canadian values," *Maclean's* (26 March).

Nossal, K.R. (1988). "Out of Steam? Mulroney and Sanctions," *International Perspectives*, XVII, 6, pp. 13–15.

Ostry, S. (1990). "Changing Multilateral Institutions: A Role for Canada," speech delivered at Conference on Canada and International Economic Regimes, University of British Columbia.

Pratt, C. (1990). "Has Middle Power Internationalism a Future?" in Pratt, ed., *Middle Power Internationalism*.

Reid, E. (1989). *Radical Mandarin*. Toronto: University of Toronto Press.

Resnick, P. (1989). "From Semiperiphery to Perimeter of the Core: Canada's Place in the Capitalist World Economy," *Review*, XII, 2, pp. 263–97.

Shevardnadze, E. (1990). Testimony before the Standing Committee on External Affairs and International Trade. No. 37. Ottawa: House of Commons.

Weiss, T. (1990). "Leading the Horse to Water," *Peace and Security*, 5, 1, pp. 8–9.

Wilson, M. (1990). *The Budget*, Ottawa: Department of Finance.

Wood, B. (1990). "Towards North-South Middle Power Coalitions," in Pratt, ed., *Middle Power Internationalism*. 69–107.

World Commission on Environment and Development (1987). *Our Common Future*. G.H. Brundtland, chairperson. Oxford: Oxford University Press.

PIERRE FORTIN

IO

Credibility, Controls, or Consensus: Is Full Employment without Inflation Out of Reach in Canada?

MACROECONOMIC POLICY IS THE ART OF ACHIEVING FULL EMPLOYMENT with low inflation. By that measure Canada's performance in the last quarter-century has been a failure. From 1966 to 1974 we had low unemployment and rising inflation; then, from 1975 to 1983, we had high unemployment and high inflation; and finally, from 1984 to the present, we have had high unemployment and low inflation. The obvious questions are: why have we failed, and can we do better in the future?

I start with the observation that there are currently three workable approaches to the containment of inflation in modern economies: *credible* monetary restraint, wage and price *controls*, and income policy based on social *consensus* – the three c's.

In outline, I shall make the following case. I first argue that pure monetary restraint (whether credible or not) is inconsistent with full employment and should be rejected outright. Second, I point out that Canadian-style wage and price controls did reduce inflation effectively and without employment loss in the years 1975 to 1978. Nevertheless, wage and price controls encroach upon basic freedoms and threaten economic efficiency; they should only be used in an emergency. Third, I conclude that the only acceptable means of attacking inflation is a softer form of incomes policy, based on social consensus instead of legislated norms, such as can be found in the few industrial countries that have been and still are macroeconomically successful. The development of national consensus-based institutions able to pursue this third way is the foremost economic challenge confronting Canadians of all political persuasions, and social democrats in particular. In addition, these institutions would have to be consistent with Canada's history and social traditions. Obviously, present institutional arrangements and public policy are very far from this ideal.

THE ASTRONOMICAL COST OF MONETARY RESTRAINT

Over the period 1966 to 1981 Canada suffered a string of inflationary shocks – on the prices of food, energy, and imported goods, and indirectly due to higher indirect taxes. Short of accepting ever-accelerating inflation – a politically and economically unthinkable option – the government had to act to reduce inflation. The preferred instrument has been, and still is, monetary restraint exercised by the Bank of Canada.

Restrictive monetary policy basically operates through setting higher interest rates, which in turn implies a higher value for the Canadian dollar relative to other currencies. This cools off demand for interest-sensitive goods (such as consumer durables, housing, and business investment) and for exchange-rate-sensitive exports. Sales, production, and employment fall, and the resulting increase in unemployment then exerts negative pressure on wages and prices. The policy is essentially based on the existence of an inverse relationship between unemployment and inflation. This is nothing other than the celebrated "Phillips curve" of elementary economics textbooks. Restrictive monetary policy reduces inflation by raising unemployment.

The unfortunate problem with the Canadian Phillips curve is that it is pretty flat: large increases in unemployment reduce inflation by only small amounts. Standard estimates indicate that to reduce the annual inflation rate by 1 per cent (from, say, 6 to 5 per cent) requires an increase of two percentage points for at least one year in the national unemployment rate (Fortin, 1989). Since each "point-year" of unemployment is in turn normally associated with a 2 per cent decline in annual gross national product, it follows that each one-point reduction in the inflation rate costs at least 4 per cent of annual GNP, about $26 billion in 1990 dollars. The phrase "at least" is not innocuous. Through reduced investment and deteriorating human capital, high unemployment also reduces *future* national income, and the unpriced *human* cost of unemployment has not been calculated. The estimate of 4 per cent of annual GNP is thus likely to underestimate substantially the true total cost of a one-point reduction in the rate of inflation.

Whatever the precise trade-off between unemployment and inflation, the inescapable conclusion from the simple arithmetic is that the cost of fighting inflation this way is staggering. The benefit from reduced inflation is obviously not worth such a high price. Nevertheless, attacking inflation by raising the unemployment rate is exactly the kind of game the Bank of Canada has played in the past, and has been playing since inflation began to accelerate again in 1987.

Over the years the Bank of Canada has developed three lines of defence for its contractionary monetary policy. First, it claims that the cost in lost potential GNP due to inflation is very high. Some economists who support the Bank's policy estimate one percentage point of inflation to cost 2 per cent of annual GNP (Howitt, 1990).

Second, the Bank emphasizes that, while the unemployment cost of inflation reduction is only temporary ("short-term pain"), the benefit from lower inflation lasts forever ("long-term gain"). For example, adding up 2 per cent of GNP for each year into the indefinite future can, depending on the discount rate used, turn up a figure as high as 100 per cent of current GNP as the present value⋆ of the benefit of permanently reducing inflation by 1 per cent.

Third, the Bank argues that an unyielding stance against inflation on its part will eventually, through enhancing the "credibility" of its policy, lead wage and price setters to *anticipate* lower inflation and adopt a non-inflationary behaviour without having to be convinced to do so by the ordeal of higher unemployment rates, business failures, and the like. As a result, smaller and smaller doses of unemployment will be required to reduce inflation by a given amount.

All three arguments are, to say the least, very controversial. First, critics point out that the obsession of central bankers with inflation leads them to overestimate seriously its negative effect on the level of GNP. Second, many argue that, as the unemployment rate is increased to cool down inflation, the critical level of unemployment below which inflation begins to accelerate (sometimes called the NAIRU, for "non-accelerating inflation rate of unemployment") does not remain constant but tracks the actual unemployment rate upward. This important phenomenon ("unemployment hysteresis") was first observed in Europe after the recession of the early 1980s, but it now looks as if it applies to Canada as well. In the 1960s inflation used to accelerate when unemployment fell below 4 per cent, but it now appears to do so when unemployment falls below 8 per cent. Canadian unemployment has exceeded 8 per cent for most of the past decade and has been accompanied by accelerating inflation since 1987. The implication is that events of the last two decades have

---

⋆Present value is an operation that generates a value, at the present, equivalent to a series of cash flows stretching into the future. Before being summed to yield the present value, each cash flow is discounted relative to the one previous at some predetermined discount rate, say 4 per cent. By this operation, the further into the future is a cash flow the more heavily it is discounted.

undermined the presumption that the unemployment cost of inflation reduction is only temporary.

Third, the argument that central bankers can reduce the unemployment cost of disinflation through building a reputation as "tough guys" is dubious. Even if you believe that the Bank of Canada is seriously committed to the goal of price stability, you will not adopt a non-inflationary wage or price behaviour because you know there is every chance that your neighbour will take advantage of this opportunity to get ahead of you. If he does not, then you will not miss the chance to get ahead yourself. Hence, neither of you wants to be the first to disinflate and follow the course that best promotes the common good of price stability. Thus, inflation remains just as costly to eradicate when the central bank is credible as when it is not. Whatever the central bank's policy, we have a classic prisoners' dilemma.*

I personally agree that central bankers tend to exaggerate the cost to the economy of low to moderate inflation, that an important part of the unemployment cost of disinflation is permanent damage to our social fabric, and that the credibility argument is wrong. We should reject pure monetary restraint as anti-inflation policy because the economic and human costs are much too high. We should fight inflation with other weapons.

WAGE-PRICE CONTROLS: A THREAT TO BASIC FREEDOMS AND ALLOCATIVE EFFICIENCY

Between 1975 and 1978 Canada did employ a different weapon against inflation: wage and price controls. Success in co-ordinating the mutual de-escalation of wages and prices requires that cheating be punished and fairness guaranteed. This seems to be the major reason why the Anti-Inflation Board (AIB) controls program of 1975-78 was so much more effective than the U.S. controls program of 1971-74. In their study of Canadian controls Barber and McCallum (1982, ch. 2) identified seven key ingredients of success: consistent rules stated in advance, effective wage guidelines, appropriate fiscal and monetary restraint, wage-wage equity, wage-profit equity, minimum resource misallocation, and the provision of a role for collective bargaining.

---

*"Prisoners' dilemma" serves to define a set of mathematical games. Each player, A and B, can make either a "selfish" or a "co-operative" move. The payoff to each player depends, however, on the joint decisions made by both. A does best if he is selfish and B co-operates. His second-best payoff arises when both co-operate. Third-best is that neither co-operate. A's worst outcome arises if he co-operates and B makes a selfish decision. The payoffs are symmetric for B. Whatever one player decides, the other player does better by acting selfishly. However, if they both act selfishly they are both worse off than if they co-operate.

On each ingredient the Canadian program was deemed vastly superior to its U.S. predecessor.

Canadian controls under the AIB were particularly cost-effective in wrestling down inflation. Overall, the ten empirical studies of the experiment are unanimous that controls had a very significant impact on inflation. The median estimate of these studies is that the AIB lowered inflation by five percentage points. There is no evidence of a post-AIB "bubble" effect, of wages rising dramatically after removal of controls. The only loss of national income reported stems from the relatively small administrative, compliance, and allocative costs. Under no reasonable assumptions could all these costs exceed $500 million in 1978 dollars, which amounts to one-quarter of 1 per cent of that year's GNP, or one-twentieth of 1 per cent of GNP per point of inflation reduction. Since, as I indicated earlier, the cost of disinflation through pure monetary restraint is at least 4 per cent of GNP per point of inflation, controls were at a minimum eighty times more cost-effective as an anti-inflation weapon. To reinforce this comparison, in 1990 a similar 5 per cent decline in the inflation rate would cost $130 billion under monetary contraction; less than $2 billion under controls.

Put another way, of the two anti-inflation weapons Canada has so far tried, monetary contraction is extremely costly and wage-price controls entail only a small cost. It would therefore seem logical that the country adopt controls as its standard weapon for reducing inflation. However, this sidesteps the fact that controls are a basic encroachment on the freedom of buyers and sellers to arrive at mutually agreed contracts. Also, the allocative cost of controls could rise appreciably with frequency and duration of use. For their part, social democrats face a very unpalatable choice with no alternative other than monetary restraint or wage-price controls. The astronomical economic and human costs of monetary stringency call for outright rejection of that approach. But wage controls contradict the principle of free collective bargaining, the *raison d'être* of the labour movement. And the labour movement is a traditional stronghold of support for social democracy. At the end of the day, protection of employment should be the overriding objective of macroeconomic policy and controls should in extreme circumstances be imposed, even if the labour movement objects that it would temporarily suffer. We should keep controls in our toolkit, in case inflation again rises to high levels and we have no acceptable alternative.

But, over a number of years, it is our duty to put in place a *third way*, which is able to deal with inflation without requiring higher unemployment and without violating basic freedoms and allocative efficiency. To anticipate my conclusion, Canada needs a new institutional mechanism that would develop and support an effective social consensus about the desirable rates of annual wage and price increases. Whether we can successfully put such an institutional mechanism in place remains doubtful.

IS AN INCOMES POLICY BASED ON SOCIAL CONSENSUS A MIRAGE IN CANADA?

Before advocating any particular anti-inflation strategy, it is crucial to have a clear view of the nature of the problem to be solved. To a good first approximation, we should be little concerned about inflation, the simultaneous rise in all prices, *per se*. What really matters for economic welfare is not the absolute dollar levels of quoted prices (nominal prices) but comparisons between prices (relative prices), which change when some prices increase faster than others.

For example, I should not care whether my pay raise is 2, 5, or 8 per cent, but whether it is smaller or larger than that of my neighbour, or whether it keeps up with the rise in the average price of what I buy (change in the consumer price index). If price inflation is 8 per cent and I get a 10 per cent raise (because, say, general productivity increases), my purchasing power goes up by 2 per cent (10 minus 8). I get the same 2 per cent increase if the inflation rate is 4 per cent and my raise is 6 per cent.

Everyone would no doubt agree that the second scenario is preferable to the first. The legitimate reason to fear inflation is that a higher rate of inflation is usually associated with larger, less predictable changes in relative prices and incomes. Inflation can destroy profitability and employment in industrial sectors most exposed to foreign competition. It can be detrimental to vulnerable groups unable to index their incomes to the price level. On finer analysis, inflation is generally harmful to the efficient functioning of the economy and to long-term economic growth. For example, higher inflation usually leads to greater uncertainty about future relative prices and hence to more mistakes in investment decisions. And, if unchecked, inflation rates may accelerate without limit.

It would seem easy to develop a social consensus around the goal of reducing the overall inflation rate from 8 to 4 per cent, as in the above example. We would only have to agree collectively, and then implement our wage and price contracts accordingly. Unions would accept wage settlements of 6 instead of 10 per cent. They would *know* that price inflation would decrease from 8 to 4 per cent and that corporations would not take advantage of union moderation to increase the profit share of the economic pie. In turn, corporations would agree to price increases of 4 per cent because they would *know* that unions would now present more moderate demands. *Simple comme bonjour.*

Unfortunately, the world does not and cannot function so smoothly. The central difficulty seems to be that economic activity in modern economies is decentralized and that nominal wage and price changes do not occur harmoniously and in step but at long discrete intervals and in staggered fashion. When one particular wage is adjusted at a given point of time, all other wage contracts are fixed. Therefore, the outcome is interpreted as a change in *relative* wages. Those who get the raise like it, and all others do not, even if over time all wage contracts finally come up for renegotiation and the overall wage structure remains pretty stable over time. The consequence is an unending process of wage and price leapfrogging. It is extremely difficult to break into this inflationary leapfrogging; it has great momentum. Those who are locked into contracts at the time of any initiative to lower inflation feel cheated for not being allowed to catch up. To sum up, the central problem is the frequency and timing of wage and price decisions and contracts.

We obviously have a massive co-ordination problem. Decentralized markets are simply unable to resolve it by themselves. To succeed, we need an external government or group intervention.

This leapfrogging process explains why pure monetary contraction without additional intervention is so astronomically costly. If we could somehow suppress the co-ordination problem, then, as soon as economic agents realized that the central bank is tightening the money supply, they would all reduce their wages and prices proportionately, immediately, and in step. Instead, what we observe in the short run is that a large number of wages and prices are fixed or rising at contractually predetermined rates. The monetary shock in the short run produces reduced levels of production, changes in relative wages and prices and hence in income distribution. Higher interest rates and exchange rates reduce demand, production falls, unemployment increases, and wage and price inflation slows in a protracted painful sequence, again with persistent leapfrogging. One lesson to learn from the failure of anti-inflationary monetary policy is that any successful solution must not offend conceptions of relative equity; the impact on relative wages and on wages relative to profits must be minimized. Actually, this is a restatement of what Barber and McCallum (1982) concluded Canadian wage and price controls were able to achieve between 1975 and 1978, and hence why the AIB was so successful. The general perception of effectiveness and fairness of controls is obviously related to the fact that public opinion consistently favoured the policy in 1975-78, and favoured a return to controls in 1981-82. What we now need is a fair set of rules that could be agreed through social consensus and not be imposed through authoritarian controls.

Several authors (McCallum, 1983; Bellemare and Poulin-Simon, 1986; Milner in this volume) have documented the ability of a small group of "corporatist" countries – Austria, Japan, Norway, Sweden, and pre-1980 West Germany – to sustain social consensus and maintain low unemployment rates even during episodes of successful disinflation. These countries seem to have a unique and powerful commitment to full employment, a unique situation of mutual trust between labour and business, and unique centralized and/or synchronized labour market institutions in which the macroeconomic implications of microeconomic wage and price decisions are internalized. General wage and price trends are co-ordinated annually at the national level. They have found practical solutions to the prisoners' dilemma through social customs and institutions.

Can Canada become such a "corporatist" country and yet remain consistent with its own history and social traditions? I am not sure. At least on the surface, our tradition of extremely adversarial industrial relations seems totally inconsistent with the development and efficient functioning of consensus-based institutions. The average Canadian strike rate (defined as person-days not worked due to strikes and lockouts per thousand paid non-agricultural workers) over the last two decades has been second only to Italy's among the seven major OECD countries, higher than the rate in Britain and the United States, and far higher than that in France, West Germany, and Japan. Although the Canadian strike rate fell in the 1980s relative to the 1970s, we retained our dubious ranking as second-worst. Furthermore, Canadian governments are not committed to genuine full employment. The constitutional fiasco of the Meech Lake Accord is the most recent illustration of the fact that we lack the strong sense of *national* community shared by all the countries included in the "corporatist" list.

Apart from a few welcome exceptions, Canadian business leaders have looked to Reagan and Thatcher for models of labour relations, and the cornered labour leaders interpret any suggestion for reform as a direct threat to their established prerogatives. Few Canadian opinion leaders show any sense of alarm at the long-term deterioration of our employment performance, or realize that an entirely new approach to macroeconomic policy management is required. Least of all do those in the Bank of Canada and in the Finance ministry indicate any desire to change. Social consensus seems out of reach in Canada, except perhaps in times of perceived national emergency.

I am thus led to the pessimistic conclusion that there is currently no politically feasible policy in Canada to reduce the pain of combatting inflation. The credibility game is of doubtful usefulness. Controls *à la canadienne* seem pretty efficient, but we all hesitate to recommend authoritarianism as a permanent way of life. Social consensus is for now the antithesis of the Canadian practice of industrial relations. We do not know yet how to implement mutual de-escalation of wages and prices with minimal side effects on relative wages and prices, on real activity, and on economic freedom to bargain.

Can Canadian social democrats prove me wrong?

REFERENCES

Barber, C., and J. McCallum (1982). *Controlling Inflation*. Toronto: Canadian Institute for Economic Policy. chap. 2.

Bellemare, D., and L. Poulin-Simon (1986). *Le Défi du Plein Emploi*. Montreal: Albert Saint-Martin.

Fortin, P. (1989). "How 'Natural' is Canada's High Unemployment Rate?" *European Economic Review*, 33 (January), pp. 89-110.

Howitt, P. (1990). "Zero Inflation as a Long Term Target for Monetary Policy," in R.G. Lipsey, ed., *Zero Inflation: The Goal of Price Stability*. Toronto: C.D. Howe Institute.

McCallum, J. (1983). "Inflation and Social Consensus in the Seventies," *Economic Journal*, XCIII (December), pp. 784-805.

JOHN MCCALLUM

II · Economics and the New Democratic Party: Confessions of a One-Time NDPer

I WANT IN THIS ESSAY TO PROVIDE A SOMEWHAT PERSONAL ACCOUNT OF why, over the past fifteen years, I changed from a moderately enthusiastic supporter of the NDP to one who cannot take that party seriously. (In this essay the term "NDP" should be interpreted as "federal NDP." For me as a Quebecer this is the only visible branch of the organization.)

Let me say first that "some of my best friends are NDPers" and I greatly respect certain NDP leaders, including Ed Broadbent, Allan Blakeney, and Howard Pawley. Let me also say that I sympathize with many of the fundamental objectives of the NDP. I agree with NDPers that Canada can be a more just society and that government policies can and should help people with low incomes and other disadvantages. My quarrel is not with the ends of social democracy but with the means chosen by the NDP. In general, I will argue, NDP policies make no sense. They do little or nothing to achieve their objectives; they would, however, inflict severe damage on the economy in the unlikely event that the NDP ever had a chance to implement them. To make my case I will take seven topical areas of economic and social policy. In each area I will analyse the general drift of NDP policy and suggest alternatives that are not only more equitable but more efficient. First, however, I want to consider two more general points that provide something of a unifying theme.

First, NDP leaders often seem to think that they know more about what is good for people than the people themselves. NDP leaders want, for example, to tax people to pay for very expensive state-funded child-care centres. They oppose tax breaks or direct grants to parents for child care on the paternalistic grounds that parents will use inferior privately run centres or informal home-based care. I do not like it when government officials or politicians tell me how to live my life and raise my children, and I do not think I am alone in this feeling. The second general point is that NDP policy is dominated by special interest groups, especially unions and women's groups. To continue with the child-care example, the NDP's preferred option amounts to the extension to earlier ages of the public school system; it would create a large number of well-paid and probably unionized jobs. It is not coincidental that the NDP's preferred option is that promoted by public-sector unions. I do not think I am "anti-union," and I am certainly not "anti-woman," but I think it bad when a party's policies for the country as a whole reflect to such a degree the goals of groups promoting narrow interests.

In fact, matters are worse than I have suggested because frequently neither union leaders nor the leaders of the women's groups reflect the views of their constituents as a whole. How could it be otherwise? If the NDP got the votes of all women and all union members – or even a majority of each – then obviously we would have a permanent NDP government in Ottawa. So it is not that NDP policy is controlled by union members or women in general, but by the leaders of these groups. While I do not doubt the honesty or sincerity or good will of these leaders, it is clear that they have their own narrow interests to pursue.

With this introduction, I turn to the seven areas.

1. INFLATION, UNEMPLOYMENT, AND THE ELUSIVE "THIRD OPTION"

With a few qualifications I agree with almost everything said in Pierre Fortin's essay on this subject. I am probably less "soft" on inflation than he; I would place more emphasis on the costs to the economy of high inflation. I would also emphasize somewhat more the need for government to be consistent and clear and hence generate public credibility for its chosen anti-inflation policies. Finally, when Fortin expresses pessimism on the possibility of a "third option" for dealing with inflation in Canada, I am even more pessimistic!

As Fortin discusses, a first option for controlling inflation is to pursue tight monetary policy alone. The problem is that this often leads to high unemployment. A second option is to combine a sound monetary policy with direct controls on wages. This policy can and did work in Canada in the past, and it did result in much less unemployment than would otherwise have been required to control inflation. But controls represent a major infringement on the freedom of companies to set prices and unions to bargain collectively. They may well result in major economic distortions if applied too frequently. Hence the search for a "third option," a search that often focuses on

the consensual politics and centralized or synchronized wage bargaining to be found in Sweden, Austria, Japan, Norway, and Switzerland. This is the "Group of Five" whose enviable unemployment-
inflation performance provides the incentive for the search.

For Fortin the main reason we in Canada cannot follow the route of
these countries is that our wage and price decisions are highly decentralized. We face a massive co-ordination problem. The implication
is – although Fortin does not quite say it – that if only our governments, companies, and unions could get together and agree on a
centralized wage bargaining system, then we could enjoy the
unemployment-inflation performance of the Group of Five. In a
sense Fortin poses the problem as technical or organizational.

In my view the problem is much deeper and more intractable. A
centralized bargaining system confers enormous market power on
the bargainers. If this power is used wisely and for the "public
good" – as is, in general, the case in Sweden – then we can all be better
off. But if the power is used to further the narrow, short-term interests of the parties, then we could easily be worse off. Imagine a strike
over wages that involves not just Stelco steelworkers but *all* union
members in Canada.

Now, the well-known political economist Mancur Olson (1982)
has put forward the theory that "encompassing" interest groups are
more desirable than "narrow" interest groups representing a small
fraction of the population. Olson argues that narrow interest groups
will concentrate on redistributing income to their members and
ignore any resulting damage done to the economy as a whole because
their members, being relatively few, will not bear much of the costs of
economic inefficiencies. Encompassing interest groups will, Olson
argues, concern themselves with the efficiency consequences of their
tactics. Why? If the interest group is large enough relative to the
economy, its members will probably bear a sizable share of the "spill-
over effects" on the economy as a whole. As it applies to unions,
Olson's theory suggests that narrow craft unions will, for example,
seek to maximize wages in the short run and simultaneously to
restrict the adoption of new, more productive technology employing
different labour skills. Large industry-wide unions will temper short-
run wage demands and any opposition to new technology because
their leaders will assess the potential productivity gains and expect in
the long run to capture some of the gains for their members.

Despite Olson I am not convinced that centralized or synchronized
bargaining, which entails unions becoming more "encompassing,"
would work in Canada. Certainly Quebec's experience with centralized bargaining in the construction and public sectors has not been
encouraging.

Whatever my reservations, the NDP, as a social democratic party that claims to be vitally concerned about unemployment, should be in the vanguard of the search for a "third option." It isn't, and the reason is obvious. Both incomes policies and any third option involve some limitation on free collective bargaining. Incomes policies and "third options" may be in the interest of Canadian workers – including unionized workers – but they are not in the interest of union leaders whose *raison d'être* is collective bargaining. Union leaders have not only controlled NDP policy in this area; they have also exerted internal pressure on the NDP to censor open debate on the subject. The typical response of union leaders when asked for an anti-inflation policy is for government to control every price under the sun – except the price of labour. While NDP leaders on occasion refer to the superior unemployment-inflation performance of Scandinavian social democratic countries, they never come clean and state that a crucial ingredient of policy in these countries is to constrain decentralized collective bargaining.

2. THE DEFICIT

The past five years – until the onset of recession in mid-1990 – would have been a good time for a vigorous attack on government deficits and debt. The economy was strong, unemployment was falling, and inflation was edging gently upwards. Indeed, between 1985 and 1989, the Canadian economy grew faster than those of all other major industrial countries except Japan. Yet, for all this, only Italy has done worse than Canada in controlling government debt. Federal government net debt rose from 40 per cent of GDP in 1983-84 to 54 per cent in 1989-90 – and it is still rising (Wilson, 1990, p. 116).

Because of the loose fiscal policy in Ottawa – compounded at the provincial level by Ontario – the burden of fighting inflation fell to the Bank of Canada. As Clarence Barber discusses, the Bank's restrictive monetary policy led to high interest rates and an overvalued dollar, which crippled the manufacturing sector just as we entered into the free trade agreement with the United States. It would have been far, far better if fiscal policy had been tighter and monetary policy that much easier over the past five years.

Moreover, the future outlook for federal debt is gloomy. Even under the rosy growth and interest rate assumptions of the last budget (Wilson, 1990) – which will obviously be wrong – total program expenditures will have to remain frozen in real terms just to stabilize the debt: GDP ratio at around 45 per cent by 1997. So, unless the overall tax burden is to rise, *real per capita federal program expenditures will have to be on a declining trend until the turn of the century.*

Where did the NDP stand on all this during the previous five years? (I use the past tense because I am talking about the period 1985 to 1989. At the time of writing, in August, 1990, the economy has entered into a recession, and it has become conventional wisdom among most analysts that monetary policy should be less tight.) The NDP consistently attacked Bank of Canada policy. Fair enough, but they had no alternative to offer. They wanted lower interest rates, but they said nothing about lower interest rates leading to devaluation of our dollar and more inflation. They had no policy for inflation – no fiscal tightening to counterbalance monetary ease, and certainly no incomes policy or "third option." They talked about major new program expenditures with little or no comment about the implications for taxes or the debt. In short, their policy was at best a non-policy, at worst totally dishonest.

3. Universality

Universality is a sacred cow in NDP circles. The argument in favour is that universal programs treat all Canadians as equals; they avoid the stigma of "welfare" surrounding recipients of means-tested programs. Universality may also generate greater political consensus in support of the income redistribution entailed by social programs. Now, in certain areas, such as health care, I think a strong case can be made for universality. But, especially in the context of the budgetary situation just described, I do not see the logic of universal family allowances or, for example, essentially free university education. Taxpayers pay up to 90 per cent of the cost of universities. Sad though it may be, it is a fact that university students come overwhelmingly from relatively prosperous families. Universality here amounts to a subsidy of the rich by the poor. A policy of higher tuition fees combined with more generous scholarships and bursaries would be a progressive tax on the rich and would provide more financial aid to the children of poor families wanting to pursue an education.

In her time as education minister, Margaret Thatcher became famous for abolishing free school milk in British schools. I understand that free milk remained for poor students who were issued special cards attesting to their poverty. So the poor were issued milk and the rich went without. That is clearly an awful system; it illustrates the stigma-based case for universality.

But there is little stigma attached to declaring one's income to the taxman (or taxwoman), and that is all that would be required to phase out all of Canada's major universal programs. So why not phase out many universal programs and use a part of the revenues saved for larger tax credits to low-income families, seniors, and students? One would have to pay careful attention to the principle of "horizontal equity," but still the result of more selective programs could be more help to those who need it, a more equal distribution of income than we have today, and more revenue to be used for deficit reduction or worthy expenditure projects.

Why does the NDP automatically regard any suggestion of selective programs as heresy? The answer lies, I think, in the NDP's being captured by special interest groups with no knowledge of or interest in the art of governing. To design a better tuition/bursary/scholarship system for our universities requires some skilled public administration. Federal NDP leaders have no understanding of the art of governing; they have given themselves over to the art of advocacy. To the extent NDP leaders think about this issue, they instinctively respond to the short-term demands of interest groups representing current university students – most of whom, ironically, are from relatively wealthy families.

4. THE GOODS AND SERVICES TAX (GST)

If an attack on universality is heretical for someone on the left, consider the following: *the GST is a good tax, but there should be no exemption for food.* Certainly the GST is far better than the manufacturers' sales tax it replaces. Moreover, because of the GST tax credit for the poor, it is a progressive tax. Lower-income people will pay less tax than at present.

If social democrats want generous social programs, they will lose credibility unless they are consistent and advocate realistic tax policies to pay for them. The NDP talks vaguely of "taxing the rich" – higher corporate tax rates, higher marginal rates for the personal income tax, an end to tax loopholes. While there is potential to render the tax system more progressive, it is silly to imply that such reforms will provide enough revenue to replace the GST.

One of the principles of taxation is that governments should diversify revenue sources and avoid putting too many eggs in any one basket. For example, imposing very high marginal tax rates on personal income inevitably induces a great deal of tax evasion and inefficient tax avoidance behaviour that harms overall economic productivity. Most social democratic parties in Europe understand this principle and accept the need for *both* the income tax *and* a broadly based sales tax such as the GST. It is a good thing to introduce the GST and reduce the federal government's reliance on the personal income tax, which, as the NDP has long argued, is excessive.

Another principle of taxation is that, in general, taxes should be universal and neutral, that they apply to all economic activity and not distort peoples' decisions by exemptions. Exemptions to the GST for certain classes of goods, notably food, greatly increase the cost of administering the tax, as well as detracting from its efficiency and equity. The argument here is basically the same as the argument against universality. Why should the grocery bills of Conrad Black and Charles Bronfman be exempt from taxation? Why not tax everyone's groceries and use part of the extra revenue to enrich the GST tax credit? That way the poor would be better off, the overall tax rate (or the deficit) would be lower, the tax would be more efficient, and the administrative costs would be lower. Tell me, NDPers, where is the flaw in this argument?

5. THE MANITOBA NDP'S "STAY OPTION"

Maybe only Manitobans will recall this policy. Between 1974 and 1976 I worked in the Cabinet Planning Secretariat for the NDP government of Ed Schreyer. One of the main planks of government policy was the "stay option"; it embodied the principle that people had the right to stay in their communities despite changes in market conditions that affected the availability of jobs and level of incomes. As an economist, I am now embarrassed to admit that at the time I thought this was a super policy and failed to ask the question that should be obvious. Fine, of course people have the right or the option to stay, but at what price, at what wage, at whose expense?

Many millions of dollars were poured into small communities in the name of the stay option. Most of this was to finance government-owned or government-subsidized enterprises that produced enormous financial losses. Economists, of which I was one, carried out social cost-benefit analyses, and with appropriate assumptions we were usually able to show triumphantly that the social benefits outweighed the social costs. Cost-benefit analysis is a set of techniques designed to assess the total social effects of a public policy. We made the convenient assumption that those employed in subsidized enterprises would otherwise be unemployed; they were not being diverted from producing other goods and services. Their wages represented a financial cost, but not a real social cost (i.e., we used a zero "shadow price" for labour). Even with such dubious assumptions, however, it was often difficult to show a positive net social benefit and sometimes, as in the infamous case of Saunders Aircraft, it was impossible.

In some cases I think, even now, there probably was a positive net social benefit. In other cases that failed, notably in northern native communities, the social problems were extremely severe, and it seems proper to devote considerable resources even though the success rate will be very low. In many other cases, however, it is obvious with hindsight that a great deal of money was wasted. If the money actually spent had simply been paid out in cash to the intended beneficiaries, they would have become quite rich – and might well have exercised their option *not* to stay. But of course they were never given that option.

The Atlantic fishery provides a modern example of the "stay option" on a grand scale. Here is a case where I think it would be a good idea to follow the Swedish example. Sweden and Canada spend about the same share of GDP on labour market policies. In relation to Canada, however, Sweden is very stingy when it comes to transfer payments (such as unemployment insurance) and very generous on retraining and mobility assistance. It seems to me we in Canada should move in this direction. It is not at all clear that the government is doing people a favour when it funds a long-term dependence on transfer payments or welfare – as is the case in most of the Atlantic fishery. Yet "small-l" liberals and *a fortiori* NDPers reacted with horror and indignation when this view was set forth by Claude Forget in his report on unemployment insurance (Commission of Inquiry on Unemployment Insurance, 1986). Forget may have been too imprecise in designing an alternative; that does not deny the validity of his critique of the status quo.

6. Free Trade

In my opinion the signing of the Canada-U.S. free trade agreement (FTA) was a positive development. We are shielded a little more than before from U.S. protectionism, and guaranteed access to the world's biggest market surely is a good thing to have. Most of the constraints on our domestic policy are desirable limitations on the political power of narrow interest groups. I do not see how the FTA reduces our sovereignty or independence in a significant way.

Now, of course many people disagree with this view, and maybe I will be proved wrong. As before, however, my criticism of the NDP is that its opposition to the FTA was based mainly on the knee-jerk response of special interest groups that were going to be subjected to more intense competition (e.g., unions in sectors subject to international competition and beneficiaries of marketing boards). It was not a reasoned response that presented credible alternatives. I recall, for example, a paper written by Bob White (1988), head of the Canadian Auto Workers, during the year of the free trade election. His vision of an ideal Canada, once having rejected the FTA, sounded like Albania, so detailed and direct would be government control and regulation of Canadian industry.

7. CHILD CARE

Last but not least, I comment on the NDP call for universal, government-provided child care. This proposal embodies all that I like least about the NDP. The program would be universal and free for all. Where would the money come from, and why should the taxpayer subsidize child care even for the most prosperous professional couple? The proposal implies a homogenizing of child care. We shall not, for example, be allowed to have child-care centres run for profit, only the government-run or government-approved non-profit variety. We shall be financially penalized if we resort to informal child-care arrangements involving neighbours or relatives. Here is a case of women's groups telling the mothers and fathers of Canada what is best for their children.

The NDP should accept the view that parents are the ones best able to make decisions for their children. Let the government provide tax credits to parents who need them – and let these tax credits be very generous for those in greatest need. But then let individual parents, not the government or those committed to a particular form of child care, be the judges of how best to spend that money in the interests of their children.

Maybe the foregoing has been unfair to the NDP. After all, could one not attack the Liberals on the same grounds – no alternative policies on issues of inflation, deficits, GST, and so on? Perhaps so, but the NDP lays claim to a higher morality and higher political standards than the Liberals. The NDP claims to be earnestly interested in the substance of politics, not in the rhetorical froth of politics. And so, at least to me, the NDP's deficiencies in these seven areas are that much more galling. Also, because the special interest groups that lie behind the Liberal Party are more diversified, there is often more intellectually open debate among Liberals than among NDPers, a greater willingness among Liberals to explore the complexity of public policy. As a result, Liberal policies are generally more sensible, in my opinion, than those advocated by the NDP.

What does one conclude? Some readers will disagree with everything I have said. But for those who agree with at least part of the argument, a natural question to ask is how one might improve the economic policies of the NDP. Unfortunately, some problems have no solution, and I think this is just such a problem. The very nature of the NDP is to be a coalition of a small number of special interest groups. So long as it remains true to its nature, it functions like a "zero-sum game." What one interest group yields is taken up by another special interest group. There is no sense within the NDP of policy for the country as a whole, independent of special interest groups allied to the party.

REFERENCES

Commission of Inquiry on Unemployment Insurance (1986). *Report*. C.E. Forget, chair. Ottawa: Supply and Services.

Olson, M. (1982). *The Rise and Decline of Nations: Economic Growth, Stagflation, and Social Rigidities*. New Haven: Yale University Press.

White, R. (1988). "Social Democracy and the Limits of Sovereignty in an Open Economy," paper presented at "The Economics of Social Democracy," a conference sponsored by the Douglas-Coldwell Foundation and the Department of Economics, McGill University.

Wilson, M.H. (1990). *The Budget*. Ottawa: Department of Finance.

CLARENCE BARBER

_____

12   Can We Avoid a Serious
            Depression in the
            Near Future?

IN A COUNTRY AS DIVERSE AS CANADA WE STILL HAVE SOME WAY TO GO
before achieving a social democratic consensus on important economic issues. In this essay I am going to tackle the question of economic stability.

Most economists feel instinctively that the depression of the 1930s
is something we can safely forget. But if the stock market can lose a
quarter of its value in one day, as it did on "Black Monday" in
October, 1987, it seems to me we should not be so confident about
economic stability. Such events raise anew the question, can we avoid
another Great Depression?

One might answer "yes," because of major social and economic
changes since the 1920s. What are these changes? In 1929, roughly
one-third of our labour force was still employed in agriculture. (I was
among that one-third, incidentally.) Canada's economy was more
heavily dependent then than now on the production and export of
resource-based products. In the early 1930s all of these resource
industries experienced sharp declines in prices, and the real incomes
of those working in them fell sharply. In agriculture real income per
person employed fell about 60 per cent between 1929 and 1933.
Today farm employment is only 4 per cent of total Canadian employment, and other resource industries have declined a good deal in
relative importance, too.

At that time, also, the government sector in almost all countries was
much smaller. In Canada, expenditures at the federal level were about
5 per cent of GNP in the late 1920s, and the expenditures for all levels
of government were only about 15 per cent of GNP. Analogous figures
in 1988 were 22 per cent and 47 per cent. In addition, today's structure of taxes and expenditures provides more of an automatic check

on any decline in aggregate demand. In any future depression, government fiscal policy would presumably be more supportive than it was in the 1930s. Although local and provincial governments increased their public works spending at the beginning of the 1930s depression, many governments increased tax rates in the face of declining revenues. In Canada, the federal sales tax was raised from 1 per cent to 4 per cent in 1931, and to 8 per cent in 1936. Personal and corporate income tax rates were increased as well. As a result total government revenue, which had been only 16 per cent of GNP in 1929, reached 24 per cent in 1936. These increases acted as a huge brake on economic recovery. It required the large public expenditures of World War Two finally to pull the North American economy out of protracted depression. In the absence of a war there is no telling how long the U.S. and Canadian economies would have remained in a severely depressed state.

In the monetary field, there have been striking changes as well. In 1929 most developed countries were on the gold standard, committed to maintaining fixed exchange rates for their respective currencies per unit of gold and, hence, fixed exchange rates relative to each other. This required a country to give first priority in monetary policy to preserving the value of its currency in foreign exchange markets. This might, for example, mean raising domestic interest rates, regardless of domestic unemployment, if that was required to sustain demand for the currency at the fixed rate. Only after Britain abandoned the gold standard in September, 1931, was there a widespread international shift to easier monetary policy. Canada lacked a central bank until 1935 and had little in the way of an active monetary policy throughout the depression.

The North American monetary system has been strengthened also by widespread insurance of bank deposits. The runs on banks and bank failures forced the complete closure of the U.S. system in 1933 and drastically cut the supply of credit. Such disruptions in the domestic money supply have little chance of recurring. This gain in domestic stability has been offset, however, by enormous bank loans to Third World countries.

Today's world economy is much more open than in 1929. The Treaty of Versailles, terminating World War One, created many new smaller countries in Europe, each with a high tariff wall and restrictive immigration policy. Trade is much freer today. For the major industrial countries comprising the Organization for Economic Cooperation and Development (OECD) the ratio of exports to gross domestic product has increased from 13 per cent in 1960 to 21 per cent in 1985. However, there is a down side to this. As the economies of all countries have become more open, each has become more dependent on external markets and less able to control its own macroeconomic destiny. Fiscal policy has become a weaker tool and, given the volatility of exchange rates, even monetary policy has become a less dependable tool for many countries. Under the Canada-U.S. free trade agreement, economic models have predicted that the ratio of Canadian exports to GNP will rise from its present level of 30 per cent to over 50 per cent – a still further erosion of Canadian fiscal autonomy.

What, then, can be said about the likelihood of a major depression today? In *The General Theory* Keynes argued that "there has been a chronic tendency throughout human history for the propensity to save to be stronger than the inducement to invest. The weakness of the inducement to invest has been at all times the key to the economic problem" (Keynes, 1936, pp. 347-48). This is still true today. Indeed, had governments around the world not been willing to tolerate large increases in their deficits over the past decade, the world now would be in the midst of a severe depression. As evidence of this, consider the following. Over the four years, 1983 to 1986, International Monetary Fund (IMF) data show the average central government deficit for all industrial countries was just over 5 per cent of GNP. Data for the world as a whole are similar. Consider the world as a closed economy. In these circumstances the aggregate government-sector deficit must mean that the private sector is running a surplus of savings in excess of capital spending of 5 per cent, an amount equal to government deficits. OECD countries in 1988 were generating a surplus of private savings over capital spending of $500 billion (U.S. dollars).

Some economists argue that government deficits have crowded out private capital spending, but I believe the exact reverse is true. The large private-sector surpluses around the world have "crowded in" government-sector deficits. Attempting to reduce government deficits without at the same time stimulating a corresponding decline in private-sector surpluses is a recipe for economic disaster. Yet that seems to be the dominant approach taken in our financial press.

As an alternative, consider the case of Sweden. In 1982, the Swedish Social Democrats returned to power after an absence of six years. They faced economic problems not unlike those faced by the Conservatives upon their election to office in Canada in 1984 – large deficits in the government budget and in the current account, and widespread public opposition to any increase in government spending as a share of GNP. Should Canada, as Pierre Fortin has suggested elsewhere in this volume, have followed Sweden's policy of using a depreciation of the exchange rate to revive her economy and restore a more normal level of growth and capital spending? There is much to be said in support of this proposal – notwithstanding the current difficulties of the Swedish economy. At the time of writing (September, 1990)

Swedish wages are rising at an annual rate of 10 per cent. This in turn has induced inflation at a comparable rate and a small deficit in the current account. These are, however, the problems of success. Sweden has consistently lowered its unemployment rate during the 1980s until it now stands at 1.8 per cent – compared to 8.4 per cent in Canada. By some combination of income policies and fiscal and monetary restraint, Sweden will, I hope, succeed in lowering its inflation rate without seriously increasing unemployment. Even if new anti-inflation policies triple the domestic unemployment rate – and the government is trying to minimize increases in unemployment – Sweden would still have an unemployment level below all seven major OECD countries except Japan.

In 1982, Sweden faced a government deficit of 6.3 per cent of GNP, a current account deficit of 3.5 per cent, and a level of government spending equal to nearly two-thirds of total output. For the preceding decade growth in real output had averaged only 1.7 per cent annually, and most of Sweden's employment growth had been in the public sector. Because 38 per cent of Sweden's exports in the early 1970s were capital goods, she suffered severely from the sharp decline in international capital spending that followed the first OPEC oil price rise.

Immediately upon their election, the Social Democrats launched a major macroeconomic initiative in which a 20 per cent depreciation of the krona was a key element. The initiative also included policies of fiscal restraint and relative monetary ease, combined with financial deregulation and a program of industrial restructuring. The results of this initiative were impressive. By 1987 the government sector was showing a surplus of 4 per cent of GNP. The current account was back in surplus by 1984, although it returned to a deficit in 1988. The ratio of public debt to GNP, which exceeded two-thirds in 1985, has declined significantly and the government budget is still (in spring, 1990) in surplus.

Economists often dismiss currency depreciation to stimulate the economy as a "beggar-thy-neighbour" policy. However, if the policy is successful in reviving the domestic economy and restoring a higher level of capital spending, it will help rather than hurt other countries. Export growth will be followed within a year or two by higher imports – as was the case for Sweden. Economists also reject depreciation on the grounds that the stimulus usually proves temporary since it leads to offsetting increases in wages and prices. However, Sweden's centralized wage bargaining and other measures (a temporary tax on dividends, a once-and-for-all tax on wealth, and some temporary price controls) illustrate that the trade-off between unemployment and wage increases can be far more favourable than has been the Canadian experience.

Would such a policy have worked in Canada? The opportunity certainly was there. By pursuit of easier monetary policy the government could have resisted the rise of one-fifth in the value of the Canadian dollar since 1986 (from U.S. $0.72 in 1986 to U.S. $0.87 in 1990). Such a policy would have improved Canada's current account position and would also have kept down interest charges on the federal debt, thus reducing the overall deficit. As it is, Canada's tight monetary policy has led to current account deficits. The 1989 current account deficit in Canada was larger – relative to GNP – than in the United States.

Paradoxical as it may seem, one reason for the success of Sweden's depreciation was the low savings rate. The private-sector balance of savings over capital spending, which averaged 4 per cent of GNP for the years 1983 to 1985, became negative to the tune of 3.5 per cent of GNP by 1987. The strength in consumer spending made the government budgetary surplus possible. Sweden's household savings rate was -2.6 per cent of disposable income in 1987, and over the period 1980 through 1987 averaged only 1.2 per cent. This contrasts with a Canadian rate over this period of 14.3 per cent. Not until 1988 did Canadian private-sector saving and capital spending come near to balancing. When consumer spending is strong, the government can raise taxes and reduce spending without fear of an economic depression. When savings rates are high, as they have been in Canada, this may not be possible.

Canada ran a huge private-sector surplus through most of the 1980s. For the private sector, total savings from 1982 through 1988 exceeded private capital spending by some $145 billion. This was balanced by a total deficit in the government sector of $183 billion and a net deficit on current account of $38 billion. It was the failure of the private sector to balance its position that was primarily responsible for the large government deficits Canada experienced throughout most of the 1980s. A policy of depreciating the Canadian dollar – or even delaying its appreciation – could have revived private capital spending much sooner and thus avoided the need for continued government deficits to support the economy. Such a policy could also have avoided the deterioration of our balance of payments. To achieve this result would have required a much easier monetary policy, a tougher fiscal policy, and perhaps some resort to an incomes policy to keep inflation under control.

One of the major characteristics of the Great Depression was a large and sustained fall in capital spending. This decline was especially evident in Canada and the United States. The primary cause of this fall, I have argued elsewhere (Barber, 1978), was the decline in the rate of U.S. population growth and household formation, a decline that started in the U.S. in the mid-1920s. Once the depression was under way, there was no strong underlying growth in household formation to stimulate a revival in capital spending. Given the philosophy of that era, governments undertook little discretionary economic stimulation. The small size of governments, the nature of taxation, and the absence of social security mechanisms meant that there was little automatic support.

Does the current economic situation resemble in anyway that which existed in 1929? Population growth in developed countries displays some parallels. After the baby boom following World War Two, birth rates fell sharply in almost all developed countries. (Quebec is one of the most dramatic examples of this decline.) Industrial countries now have birth rates either at or below replacement level. As a result, the age cohorts now moving into the labour force and forming households are smaller. On the other hand, there is an immense number of people in Third World countries eager to emigrate to the developed world. Indeed, developed countries often find it difficult to keep them out! On the basis of our current fertility levels Canada will face a declining population in about twenty years – unless immigration rates rise above their average level since World War Two. This is hardly a scenario that will stimulate strong capital spending.

The world's current economic malaise, manifested in high unemployment rates and government deficits, is not unrelated to this demographic analysis. During the twenty-five years from 1948 to 1973, world economic output grew in real terms (adjusted for inflation) at an annual rate of about 5 per cent, and real capital spending in the OECD group of developed countries grew fairly steadily at a rate of 6 per cent a year. But since 1975 the world growth rate of output has fallen to about 2.5 per cent and there has been almost no growth in the level of capital spending.

Here we have the basic problem facing capitalist economies. The volume of savings is a function of the *level* of income; the volume of capital spending is a function of the *rate of growth* of income. When growth rates of income fall sharply, for whatever reasons, capital spending falls below the level of savings; unemployment rates and government deficits rise. This problem will undoubtedly worsen as population in developed countries – apart from immigration – approaches a stationary or declining level. The problem is exacerbated by economic policies that foster high savings rates (such as tax deferral through RRSPs) and maintain high real rates of interest.

Perhaps the first step toward avoiding another major depression is a recognition of the underlying character of the problem we face.

REFERENCES

Barber, C. (1978). "On the Origins of the Great Depression," *Southern Economic Journal* (January), pp. 432–56.

Keynes, J.M. (1936). *The General Theory of Employment, Interest and Money.* London: Macmillan & Co.

Contributors

Clarence Barber is professor emeritus, University of Manitoba, and Adjunct Professor, Department of Economics, University of Victoria. He taught at the University of Manitoba from 1949 to 1983. His major interests are macroeconomic theory, international economics, and monetary theory. From 1966 to1970 he was Commissioner on Farm Machinery, in 1972 Commissioner on Welfare (for the province of Manitoba), and from 1982 to 1985 he was a member of the Royal Commission on the Economic Union and Development Prospects for Canada. His publications include *Inventories and the Business Cycle* (1958), *The Theory of Fiscal Policy as Applied to a Province* (1966), and, with John McCallum, *Controlling Inflation: Learning from Experience in Canada, Europe and Japan* (1982).

Gregory Baum is presently professor of religious studies at McGill University. He holds a doctorate in theology from Fribourg University in Switzerland and has engaged in sociological studies at the New School for Social Research in New York City. For decades his special interest has been the interaction of church and society. His books provide an evaluation of recent Roman Catholic social teaching: *The Priority of Labour* (1981), *Ethics and Economics*, with Duncan Cameron (1984), *Compassion and Solidarity* (1988), and *Theology and Society* (1989).

Allan Blakeney was born in Nova Scotia, graduated in law from Dalhousie University, and attended Oxford as a Rhodes Scholar. He worked in the public service of Saskatchewan and practised law before being elected to the Saskatchewan legislature in 1960. He was a member of the legislature for 28 years, serving in many cabinet positions, as Leader of the Opposition, and as Premier from 1971 to 1982. He was a member of the cabinet that in 1962 introduced Canada's first universal medicare program and was Premier when major Crown corporations dealing in oil, uranium, and potash were established. Since 1988 he has been teaching at York University and the University of Saskatchewan.

Robert Cairns obtained his Ph.D. in economics from the Massachusetts Institute of Technology in 1978. He then joined the Department of Economics and the Centre for the Study of Regulated Industries at McGill University. He has been there since, and in 1986 he also became an associate member of the Centre de Recherche et Développement en Économique at the Université de Montréal. His interests are industrial organization and regulation, non-renewable resource economics, and public policy.

Pierre Fortin is professor of economics and head of the Centre de recherche sur les politiques économiques at the Université du Québec à Montréal. In the last fifteen years he has authored over seventy books and articles, mainly in the areas of macroeconomic policy, wage and employment dynamics, public finance, and economic demography. Professor Fortin has been associate editor of the *Canadian Journal of Economics*, president of the Société canadienne de science économique, member of the Economic Council of Canada, principal economic adviser to the Premier of Quebec, and member of the Economic Advisory Panel of the Minister of Finance of Canada. He is currently editor of *L'actualité économique*.

Tom Keating is an associate professor of political science at the University of Alberta, where he teaches Canadian foreign policy and international politics. He has previously published articles on Canadian foreign and defence policy, and is co-author (with Larry Pratt) of *Canada, NATO and the Bomb* (1988). He is currenty preparing a manuscript on Canada's involvement in international organizations.

John McCallum is a macroeconomist whose research interests have included theoretical, applied, and policy issues. In the early 1980s he wrote a monograph on Quebec and Ontario economic history, as well as two studies of macroeconomic policy for the Canadian Institute of Economic Policy (co-authored with Clarence Barber). Since that time, most of his work has been published in academic journals. He has been Chair of the Department of Economics at McGill University since 1987. Before that he was a professor at Université du Québec à Montréal, Simon Fraser University, and the University of

Manitoba, and was a research economist with the Cabinet Planning Secretariat of the NDP government in Manitoba.

Lynn McDonald is the former Member of Parliament for Toronto Broadview-Greenwood and environment critic for the NDP caucus. She is a sociologist and author of *The Party that Changed Canada: the New Democratic Party Then and Now* (1987). Currently she is active in the Campaign for Nuclear Phaseout, which is based at Energy Probe, where she was a member of the founding board. She was recently elected chairperson of the Public Social Responsibility Unit of the Anglican Church of Canada, where she has also served as chairperson of the Environment Working Group.

Henry Milner is author of *Sweden: Social Democracy in Practice*, published in 1989 by Oxford, as well as of four books and numerous articles on Quebec politics and society. Born in West Germany in 1946, he grew up in Montreal and received his B.A. from McGill and M.A. and Ph.D. from Carleton. He is a founder of the Montreal Citizens' Movement and was international secretary on the executive of the Parti Québécois from 1980 to 1985. He is professor in the Department of Economics and Political Science at Vanier College in Montreal.

Larry Pratt teaches in the Department of Political Science at the University of Alberta. He is a graduate of Carleton University, the University of Toronto, and the London School of Economics. He is the author of a number of books, including (with John Richards) *Prairie Capitalism* and (with Tom Keating) *Canada, NATO and the Bomb*.

John Richards served as a member of the Saskatchewan legislature during the first term of the Blakeney government. For the first two years of his term he was legislative secretary to the Minister of Health. In mid-term he crossed the floor and sat as an "independent socialist" in the opposition. He has since mellowed and rejoined the NDP. With Larry Pratt he co-authored *Prairie Capitalism* (1979). He has subsequently written on natural resource economics, labour relations, and social democratic politics. He received his first degree from the University of Saskatchewan; he received higher degrees in economics from Cambridge University and from Washington University in St. Louis, Missouri. He currently teaches in the Faculty of Business Administration at Simon Fraser University.